When We Were
Almost Young

Remembering Hydra
through War and Bohemians

Compiled & edited by Helle V. Goldman

Tipota Press

This book is an anthology of memoirs. The contributions reflect the authors' recollections of experiences that occurred many years ago and are subject to the vagaries of memory and subjectivity. Each contributor is responsible for the accuracy of his or her contribution to this volume.

Daniel Martin Klein's contribution is reprinted with permission of the author and Penguin Books USA.

Cover photograph of Hydra by James Burke, 1960. Used with permission of Getty Images.

Tipota Press
Tromsø, Norway

For the people of Hydra,
who shared their island with strangers.

Contents

Foreword

> It is a diverse and tantalising collection of human
> beings sprawled about these rocks and ledges on
> a hot cliff far from their native lands, insurgents
> all who have rebelled against the station in which
> it pleased God to place them. What devious
> roads brought them to this small island, what
> decisions and indecisions, what driftings, what
> moments of desperation and hope? And what are
> they looking for?
>
> Charmian Clift[1]

Betwixt and between the Argolic Gulf to the west and the Saronic
Gulf to the east lies Hydra's spindling outline. The island is about
twenty kilometres long and is a good day's sail through the Aegean Sea, or three to four hours by old-fashioned ferry, from Piraeus.

Named after long-extinct freshwater springs, the rugged island
rises steeply out of the soft blue sea. Evidence of farming and
herding stretches back to the third millennium BCE. Hydra was a
Venetian possession in the 13th through 16th centuries and was
then subsumed in the Ottoman Empire. Prosperity came in the
17th and 18th centuries, when Hydra became a commercial maritime powerhouse. In the early 19th century Hydra's money, ships
and sea captains were decisive in winning Greece its independence from the Turks. After this glorious heyday, the island entered
into a decline. Men went off to risk their lives on sponge-fishing
expeditions to other parts of Greece or the waters off North Afri-

---

[1] *Peel Me a Lotus*, Collins, Sydney, 1969, p. 24. (First published by Hutchinson, London,
1959.)

ca, but the island's economic downslide was inexorable. By the middle of the 20th century the population that had once numbered perhaps as many as twenty-five thousand had dwindled to a tenth of that. The ruins of houses were as numerous as occupied dwellings. Ransacking for timbers and tiles during the Second World War had hastened their deterioration.

Just before the war, Henry Miller, accompanied by the Greek poets George Seferis and George Katsimbalis, visited the quiet, car-less island. Among the cluster of Greek artists living there were painter Nikos Hadjikyriakos-Ghikas and artists associated with the School of Fine Art, which had been established in the Tombazis mansion by another painter, Perikles Vyzantios, in 1936. Miller's enraptured description of Hydra – a "promised land" that was aesthetically "perfect", a rock that caused him to lose "all sense of earthly direction"[2] – was published in 1941, bringing the island to the attention of the international literati.

The world war and Greece's civil war over, a handful of creative expatriates settled on Hydra in the mid-1950s. There was the Australian writing duo, George Johnston and Charmian Clift, along with Lily Mack, the larger-than-life Russian whose father had painted miniatures for the Shah of Persia, and her husband Christian Heidsieck, a ceramicist from the well-known champagne family. These couples were the first foreigners to buy homes on Hydra.

Boy on a Dolphin, starring Sophia Loren and Alan Ladd, was filmed on the island, to be followed by *Phaedra*, in which Jules Dassin directed Melina Mercouri and Anthony Perkins. These and other motion pictures exposed Hydra to the world.[3] More expatriates came to live on the island, including the brash young Norwegian novelist Axel Jensen, Jensen's girlfriend Marianne Ihlen and a young Canadian poet named Leonard Cohen. Ihlen later became known as Cohen's enigmatic muse. (The title of this volume, *When We Were Almost Young*, borrows a line from one of the songs she inspired.) The writer Patrick Leigh Fermor and the

---

[2] *The Colossus of Maroussi*, Henry Miller, New Directions Books, New York, 2010, pp. 60-61. (First published by Colt Press, San Francisco, 1941.)

[3] See the filmography/bibliography at the end of this anthology.

painter John Craxton stayed at Hadjikyriakos-Ghikas' house for a time, writing and painting.

Around this nucleus, the foreign colony grew over the next decades, while celebrities like Henry Fonda, Audrey Hepburn, John Lennon and Jackie Onassis, as well as royals like Princess Diana, flitted to the island for a day or two.

This anthology of memoirs offers various perspectives on those bohemian decades in which so much was written, painted, carved, sung, imagined, lost and loved. The emphasis is on the community of foreigners who settled on Hydra for periods of a few years or several decades. Whether they came to Hydra at the urging of friends already there or they stumbled upon it almost by accident – whatever "devious roads" delivered them to this island and whatever they were looking to find or elude – the recollections the contributors to this book have held dear all this time share many elements in common. Striking figures like the English painter Anthony Kingsmill and his beautiful, razor-witted American wife Christina, and Jimmy, the Greek peddler of dead people's clothing, make frequent appearances, as does the Katsikas family, who had a shop and café that everyone patronised and who were known for their kindness.

Other leitmotifs include meeting friends at the port – the town's centre – and the laborious accomplishment of daily chores. (People were prone to grousing about the effort demanded in preparing a meal, for example, but they were well aware that it was precisely the primitiveness of Hydra that made the island what it was and kept them there.) Some of the same anecdotes crop up, briefly alluded to in one contribution but recounted in full in another, and sometimes conflicting in smaller or larger details (for example, stories told by me and my sister, Johanne). Such is memory, personality and point of view.

The volume has no ambitions of representing the complete social fabric of Hydra. Most of the recollections within these covers constitute glimpses into the expatriate experience in a particular time and place, offered by people who were, rather like the island itself, betwixt and between two realms, partly of both and partly of neither.

The foreigners who lived on Hydra were transformed by it, as

Hydra was transformed by them, sometimes in ways they would not have wished for. Hydra has become a place of parasol-shaded beach beds and imported sand instead of uncomfortable (and incomparably beautiful) beach shingle. Chic restaurants and bars serve cocktails and international cuisine instead of the peasant Greek fare, washed down by sturdy tumblers of retsina replenished from large wooden barrels, that the people who animate the pages of this collection enjoyed in the early years – even if they sometimes also enjoyed complaining about it. Cheek by jowl with the fishermen's cottages that some foreigners (and island natives) keep in a condition not far from their original simplicity are the luxurious holiday homes maintained by other foreigners as well as Athenians. In the harbour, gleaming yachts throbbing with power overshadow the battered little caïques, each bearing a carefully painted saint's name.

Yet much remains virtually unchanged. Because the entire town of Hydra is classified as a national historical landmark, the external appearance of buildings is strictly regulated. With these rules enforced, the port of Hydra will never become the strip of glass- and neon-fronted nightclubs that blight other Greek islands. Hydra's topography is another saving grace, precluding proper roads, except for stretches along the coast, which island residents – Greek and expatriate – have fought to keep unpaved, inhospitable to any traffic apart from human and animal feet.

I am grateful to those who have opened up the treasure chests they carry in their hearts of memories of Hydra, sifting through them and bravely holding them up to the light in the memoirs that make up this volume. With a few notable exceptions, the authors of the pieces presented here are not professional writers, which makes their efforts all the more precious. I hope they have found the experience of reflecting on their early years on Hydra, and putting these deeply personal recollections onto paper, a rewarding one if also sometimes gut-wrenching. I am particularly beholden to contributors Alison Leslie Gold, Johanne Rosenthal, Brian Sidaway, Valerie Lloyd Sidaway and David Fagan for guidance, editorial assistance and errands run on Hydra and in Hermione, as well as to Kevin McGrath, who conceived this project and carried it through its first phase with me.

Other people whose moral and editorial support helped propel this book from idea to press are Marianne Ihlen, Tordis Hveem, Ivar Stokkeland, Jennifer Kelland and Aris Tsikontouris (at the publishing house Arteon). Another champion of the book is Barbara Lapcek, who has known Hydra intimately for fifty years. As small children, my sister Johanne and I picked almonds from her trees together with our mother. Her daughter Tayu was our playmate. Circumstances got in the way of Barbara contributing her own memoir to this volume, but her note of apology perfectly encapsulates the zeitgeist of this anthology:

> My ashes eventually will be part of its soil, as I am already mixed with its rock. Whatever I might write, however well, it would echo all the rest of us who fell in love with the isle. A different time of no water, no electricity, no separation – the foreigners and the kind, vital Greeks. The Marigoulas, the Katsikas, the Dragoumis, the Voulgaris, the Ghikas, the Lambessis and especially the unknown old man who smiles as he passes, giving you the perfumed flower he plucks from behind his ear.

Helle V. Goldman
Tromsø, Norway
March, 2018

Hydra in War and Peace

Stamatis Vlachodimitris

The poverty that existed on many islands during the interwar period made fishermen travel far away to the north coasts of Africa for sponge-fishing. One of them was my first father, Christos. He left his last breath on that unfriendly foreign shore.[1]

During the late 19th century there were two methods of sponge-fishing in the Greek islands. The easiest way was scanning the sea bottom for sponges in shallow waters with the aid of a *gyala*, a glass-bottomed metal cylinder. The sponges were brought up with a spear at the end of long poles fitted together. If the sponges were too deep to be collected this way, skin divers went down for them. They were helped by the *skandalopetra*, a rounded stone weighing about fifteen kilograms, which was tied to the boat by a rope. The diver held the *skandalopetra* and jumped overboard. He plummeted to the sea floor, cut off the sponges and jerked the rope to signal that he was ready to be pulled up with the catch. This ancient method was still practiced in my own time.[2]

In the 1880s the hard-hat diving suit – the *skafandro* – was widely adopted by Greek sponge-divers, while some boats continued to use the old methods when working in shallower waters. The *skafandro* increased the scale of the industry considerably but at the cost of many lives. Expeditions set out from Hydra, Aegina,

---

[1] Editor's note: Aris Tsikontouris (at Arteon), David Fagan and Brian Sidaway are thanked for their great help in securing this contribution for the anthology.

[2] Editor's note: readers interested in the technology, economics and culture of sponge-fishing are referred to this informative article: "Kalymnian Sponge Diving," H.R. Bernard, *Human Biology*, vol. 39, no. 2, May 1967, pp. 103-130. See also *The Sponge Divers*, C. Clift & G. Johnston, Collins, London, 1956.

Symi, Kalymnos and Hermione to the southern and eastern edges of the Mediterranean and were away for as long as half a year.

Before sunrise, the boats set out to look for sponges. Wearing *skafandro* and fed air pumped through a hose from the ship, a diver could walk on the sea floor for much longer than skin divers and could descend even deeper. The divers went down one at a time, their depth and time on the bottom watched at the surface. The harvested sponges were transferred to the storage ship. They were attached by hooks to long ropes, like bunches of figs, and later the men trod on the sponges on deck to squeeze out their milky spawn. The sponges were then stretched, dried and packed into sacks.

At nightfall the men ate their one meal of the day, which the cook made from his store of macaroni, beans, lentils, tomato paste, oil and small amounts of preserved meat. There was also hard-tack, which grew weevily with time. The tough bread was broken against a hard surface and the pieces soaked in water until they could be chewed.

The skippers closely observed each other's harvests. The catch of each diver and each fishing boat was stored separately inside the hold of the storage ship. Individual divers collected different quantities and qualities of sponge and one boat might have better divers than another. This was the root of much misery. Envy and anxiety about the captains' loans made people vicious. Money bewitched them. The victims were the divers.

The divers were paid by the captain in advance, putting him into considerable debt. If the expedition was not successful, the captain would not be able to pay back his loans. The skipper and the dive-watcher were in cahoots and used dirty tricks to make the divers go deeper and longer. If a diver was at forty fathoms, the dive-watcher signalled that he was only at thirty fathoms. Using his hour-glass, the dive-watcher kept the time, counting off three minutes when in fact five minutes had passed. All too often, decompression sickness, paralysis or death were the result.

Many of the divers were young and inexperienced and were easily manipulated into going deeper and deeper. These fresh recruits wanted money for their sisters' dowries or had ambitions of starting a shop or buying a small fishing boat. They saw the brave, hardened sponge-divers returning to islands like Hydra at the end of a season, flush with money that they spent lavishly at tavernas. It was exhausting and dangerous work but the pay-off was big.

Returning from Africa, a company might have ten to fifteen percent casualties. Besides decompression sickness, there were also mechanical failures, like leaks in the air hoses and the suits, and the air pumped to the divers was contaminated with oil particles that coated the men's lungs. At home, if the crew talked about mishaps they wouldn't be recruited for the next expedition. These were small communities, and the divers depended on the captain's goodwill. There is a saying: just as a woman forgets her labour pains, a seaman forgets the rough sea, the saltiness and the fatigue.

∾

One of the worst tortures was the drinking water. It always became warm and wormy in the tanks. The men were constantly getting sick from the bad water. Some even died from it.

On my father Christos' last expedition, he was among a group of men who were assigned to bring the water casks to land to refill them with fresh water. These barrels weighed fifty kilograms. The men rowed hard for three miles from the mother ship toward land. The sea was too rough to safely reach the shore with the boat, so the men hopped into the water with their barrels. My father had gone about thirty metres toward shore when the other men lost sight of him. They heard him cry "*Oh!*" and searched for him but could not find him. The waves had swallowed him up as if a hand had reached up from the bottom and dragged him down.

Night was coming and it was time to return to the mother ship. The next morning, they went back to look for my father. Someone spotted him on the beach. No one will ever know if he died of a gas embolism, which can happen hours after coming up too quickly from a dive, or if he simply drowned. A few words from the Gospel were said over his body and he was buried in the sands of North Africa. The next day they forgot about it. The incident was recorded in the ship's journal and a letter reporting the loss of

Christos Ladas was dispatched to the Port Authority in Piraeus. The Port Authority sent a letter of condolence to his widow, my mother Kyriaki, in Hermione, a town on the Peloponnese.

My mother was working in a vineyard when she received the news. She was nineteen years old and pregnant with my brother Charis. She already had Adrianos, who was a year old. Two years passed and God sent to her life George, a good fisherman. He was a poor, handsome man with black hair. As he made repairs to the nets on his boat, his singing could be heard all across the small port of Mandrakia. Kyriaki's father, Andreas, met George frequently at the local tavern and knew that he was a widower. Soon George met Kyriaki and fell in love with her. In two months they were married and in 1935 I was born.

~

My two older brothers, Adrianos and Charis, loved me, but our poverty forced them leave home early to make their way in the world. I stayed with my mother in Hermione. From time to time my brothers sent us money, which supplemented my father's income. When I was five years old a new disaster struck my family. My father developed an illness in his eyes and in a few months he went blind. One year later, when I was six years old, the Second World War broke out.

The German Occupation was a time of great hardship in Greece, except for the black marketeers, who profited from the misery of others. Those who were canny enough to predict the Occupation had stored up foods like beans, grains and oil, which they exchanged for the family heirlooms that their hungry countrymen offered up. Trade was solely the exchange of goods; money was virtually worthless.

After establishing themselves in Athens and Piraeus, the Germans turned their attention to the islands of the Argo-Saronic Gulf. Hydra lay across the water from Hermione, within sight of it on a clear day. Age-old historical and familial ties bound the two communities together. I had relatives there and as a young man I would settle there to make my living as a fisherman and to find a wife. On Hydra, the German officer in charge was cruel and blood-thirsty. He had the whole island under his boot-heel. The island was often visited by German ships, and in the harbour a black German boat fifteen metres in length connected Hydra with Hermione and Spetses.

Of all the islands of the Argo-Saronic Gulf, Hydra was the most unfortunate. The island was isolated and had little livestock and wild game. In their small, slow-moving boats, the inhabitants struggled to reach Hermione, and even Leonidio and Monemvasia, to trade their belongings for bread. The Hydriots' homes were full of precious things collected by their ancestors, proud seamen and sponge-divers who had the sea running in their veins and who had sailed to every corner of the world. The island's mansions were appointed with opulent furnishings and expensive clothing brought from abroad in those glorious years. Even an ordinary sailor brought home the most precious things he could find in the distant lands he visited.

Many Hydriots were sailing the ocean when the war started. Quite a few died on ships that were torpedoed in the Atlantic. Among all the Greek islands, Hydra had more women wearing black than any other. Facing starvation, these widows begged the black marketeers to come to their homes and take whatever they wanted in exchange for food for their children. A beautiful silk scarf from Alexandria might buy one *oka* of oil. Those who had something to sell, survived. Those who did not, suffered. (The black marketeers later made a fortune selling the fine furniture and other treasures they had acquired.) Great numbers of children and adults died with bellies swollen from malnutrition. Gradually, Hydra's houses were emptied out. Next, people removed the tiles and beams from the roofs, windows and doors to give to the black marketeers, who took them to the Peloponnese to exchange for other goods. This explains the fallen-down state of many of the abandoned houses on Hydra in the postwar period. In this way the people of Hydra made it through the war.

Throughout their time on the island, the Germans killed, arrested, abducted and blackmailed. If they heard that someone had hidden gold, they would capture that person on the charge of being in the Resistance and they would beat him and threaten to send him to a concentration camp. Who would refuse to give up his gold?

Men in the Resistance movement would come covertly by sea, to monitor German activities. One night, with the help of three Hydriots, they disabled a German guard and made off with four guns. They got away on a boat to Hermione and then to the village of Didyma, about ten miles away, where the rebels were headquartered. One of the young Hydriots who assisted in this operation was Michalis Danampasis. The identity of the other two remains uncertain.

The Germans were enraged by the theft. They gathered the locals at the port and took six children, detaining them inside their headquarters. The days went by and the parents were frantic with worry. The mayor of the island went secretly to Didyma to explain that the guns had to be returned to save the children. The next day the Germans received their stolen weapons and released the children. But the Germans were still determined to discover the identity of the men who had made them look like fools. Someone betrayed Michalis and so the Germans surrounded the Danampasi house one night and arrested their son. At headquarters he was tortured to reveal the names of his associates, but Michalis kept his mouth shut. He was taken to Athens and subjected to further torture. He died there, without betraying anyone.

~

When I was ten years old, Greece was liberated from the Germans. The Americans sent food and clothing. An English soldier gave me a big square of something and told me to eat it. I didn't know what it was and was reluctant to try it. I had never seen chocolate before.

That summer – 1945 – my brother Adrianos came to visit. He came off the ferry carrying two suitcases. In the small one was a gramophone. In five days I had learned all the songs on the records he'd brought. I had a good voice and music filled me with joy. Many years later Adrianos revealed to me that he had been a famous rebel during the German Occupation.

Two years later, when I was about to start sixth grade, my

mother made me quit school and sent me to work for a fisherman named Master Kostas. It was almost impossible for me to stay awake during the night fishing. I sometimes fell asleep on the ropes. At home I cleaned and cooked and tried to keep things as nice as I could. My mother was debilitated by poverty and I was ashamed at the state of our home. We didn't even have a proper table and chairs to sit at while we ate. Later, when I was a little older and had made some money, I bought a table and chairs and told my mother to put a table-cloth on it so we could eat together in a civilised way, like other people.

My mother had two older brothers, Mitsos and Stamos. Neither of them had lifted a finger to help my mother since she became a widow with children at a young age. But when I was thirteen, my uncle Mitsos came: he wanted to take me to work on his boat. I was afraid to go all the way to Lavrion, at the southern tip of the Attic Peninsula, with people I hardly knew. I would be away from home for many months, sleeping rough. But my mother told me that my uncle would take care of me. And we needed the income. She was always after me to find work and bring back money.

I wasn't strong enough for the hard work of rowing the boat and I was never given enough to eat. The hunger and fatigue were constant. Mitsos beat me when a fish that I was untangling from the net flopped back into the sea. He hit me for other misdemeanors too. With the few coins I had squirrelled away, I saved up enough to buy a shiny harmonica and taught myself to play. The music was a comfort. Even though we caught a lot of fish, when Mitsos took me back to my mother, he told her that I hadn't done well and he gave her only a little money. It was enough to buy food and some cheap clothes. I bought toothpaste and a brush to clean my teeth but my mother threw them away, saying that such things were only for women.

Next, my mother sent me off to work on the boat of my other uncle, Stamos. When we fished at night, if I started to doze off at the oars, Stamos' son Thodoros would smack me in the face with a sponge soaked with seawater. When the moon was full we didn't fish but stayed in port at Lavrion. If my uncle and my cousin went ashore to eat at a taverna, I had to stay on the boat to guard the money, which my uncle kept in rolls inside a bag in a padlocked chest. He was saving for his daughter's dowry. One night when I was alone on the boat, playing my harmonica, some soldiers and other passersby stopped to praise me and sing along. When the soldiers saw that I had only a crust of bread to eat they felt sorry for me and brought me a helping of the beans they'd had for dinner. When uncle Stamos came back, the young soldiers scolded him for not giving me more to eat. That earned me a beating after they left.

Ashore at Lavrion and Sounion, it was my task to peddle the fish we caught from door to door. One woman always bought fish from me, paying more than the asking price. I hid the extra money for myself. Kyria Sophia was a woman of thirty-five or forty. She made me feel welcome and gave me generous lunches of eggs and sausages and other meats, which I ate hurriedly. I had to get back to the business of selling fish and bring the money back to my uncle. He and his son kept close tabs on me.

One day when I was in the town square, where I'd sold two of the five fish I carried on a string, I heard the most wonderful music. A young man was playing the accordian, an instrument I'd never seen before. Happy couples were dancing. I was enthralled. Two hours passed. Suddenly I was struck down by a blow from behind: Thodoros had found me. As I went on my way to sell the rest of the fish, my mind reverberated with accordian music. In my head I prayed to the Virgin: "Let me have the gift of playing the accordian and I will make the whole world dance!"

When I got back to the boat I was given a thrashing on account of the time I'd wasted in the square, but I was consoled by the secret knowledge that one day I would play music. I promised myself that I would save for a fishing boat of my own. I would have an assistant on the boat who would also be my friend. I would have a decent home and an accordian. The hunger and beatings would not go on forever.

One day when I visited Kyria Sophia with my fish, she said she would buy all of them. Then she hugged and kissed me. "Don't be afraid," she said, "I'll teach you everything. Stop trembling." I was stricken by shame. Should I run out the door or stay? The fish had not been paid for yet. Next door to the kitchen was the bedroom. We sat on the bed. I put myself in her hands.

I kept visiting her. She made me food and we slept together and enjoyed one another's company. She told me she loved me.

Stamos cut back on my rations so he could put away more money in the locked chest. One day, driven by hunger, I took more bread than had been allotted to me. Thodoros went for me. It was the last straw. I grabbed a lit lamp and smashed it into Thodoros' head. Blood ran. I ran as fast as I could to the Port Authority, Thodoros on my heels. The Harbour Master believed my story of months of deprivation and harsh treatment and when my uncle was summoned he was ordered to pay a stiff fine. He also had to agree to return me to my mother in Hermione within ten days.

I went on to work on other fishing boats, but the captains all cheated and underpaid me. Without anyone strong standing behind me, I was easy to take advantage of.

My fortune changed in the spring of 1949, when a kind old man named Ioannis Kokonis gave me the chance to go sponge-fishing off Halkidiki, in northern Greece. His son Georgios was going too. We fished with spear-tipped poles and collected a lot of sponges. Georgios and I became inseparable.

At the end of the season, when we were in Piraeus to sell the sponges, I bought a mattress to take home. I'd always slept on straw. That was about to end. In Hermione, I sat at Ioannis' table while he tallied up the expenses and earnings of the expedition. After months of hard work, I was expecting to walk away with almost nothing again. At last Ioannis counted out my earnings: two thousand and two hundred drachmas, a fantastic sum, for me. I couldn't believe so much money was mine. I gave two hundred to my mother and the rest I gave to a boat-builder named Ioannis Kotaras as down payment on a new little boat. I paid the balance I owed him after my next sponge-fishing season in Halkidiki. When the boat was completed in October, my friends helped me carry it to the sea. They threw me in the water too, for good measure.

~

I had to get away from my mother, who had such a difficult nature, and I wanted to take music lessons from the customs officer who worked on Hydra. I had a cousin, Marina, who was married on Hydra so I went to visit her. She had a pleasant husband, Lefteris, and four children. They were pretty hard up and didn't have an extra room for me, but Marina found lodgings for me owned by a woman named Kyria Vasso. Not knowing the squalor I was used to at home, she apologised for the simple state of the rooms. She fixed the place up beautifully, with a table and sofa and chairs and sheets on the bed and crockery in the kitchen. I was stunned and told my hostess and Marina, "Now I know it's true what they say in Hermione, that the housewives of Hydra are so tidy." Kyria Vasso had given me the rooms as a favour to her friend Marina and did not want to take my money. But I insisted.

I fished with Lefteris. I was good at it and had a knack for finding good fishing grounds. Some of the other fishermen admired me and some were envious and said that I drugged my bait.

I was a man now and people talked about finding a bride for me. But I was already falling for Lenia Vasso. The girl had an unusual beauty and was pure and well groomed. She was also out of my league. We kept our feelings secret except for a few confidants. I rebuffed efforts to match me up with other potential brides. I had my heart set on Lenia.

My childhood prayer had been answered and I had become an accomplished musician. I played the accordian at tavernas and special occasions. At a wedding once an old man got up and tucked a hundred dollar bill in my shirt. "Play 'Komparsita'!" he demanded. I agreed to play the song but gave him back the money. "Go back to America!" I said.

Lenia's father had been living in America for sixteen years. She had been two years old when he left and now, when he sent word that he was about to return, she was eighteen. I was worried that he would come back a rich man and would never consider a son-in-law with such a sorry background as mine. He wasn't happy when he heard the rumours about Lenia and me. There were many obstacles standing in our way – her father, my serious health problems and other things – but Lenia stood by me and became my wife.

~

In the summer of 1961, the American director Jules Dassin arrived on Hydra with his future wife, the Greek singer and actress Melina Mercouri, to shoot the film *Phaedra*. Hydra was suddenly swarming with movie stars, extras, journalists and photographers and had become world famous for its beauty.

To capitalise on this, I had installed seats in my fishing boat. By now it had an engine too. In those days, even an old engine was a big deal. It was a giant step up from rowing. To make my boat stand out from the others, I re-named her *Mermaid* and had Ioannis Rappas, a fisherman talented with a brush, paint a mermaid on each side of the boat. The painted mermaids attracted attention. (Rappas, who was getting old, quit fishing around that time. His paintings became popular after his death and are in great demand.) Of the three boats that took visitors around, one was bigger than mine and one was small, like my own. The *Mermaid* became the most popular. I worked day and night ferrying tourists to and from beaches around the island.

One day, a handsome Italian man came to me with his beautiful wife and their three beautiful young children, along with an interpreter. They wanted to hire me for a three-hour boat excursion. When we were about a mile away from the harbour, out in deep waters, the man signalled me to bring the boat to a stop. Moving like lightning, he grabbed the children and tossed them, shrieking, into the water. I was horrified and shouted at him, "*What are you doing, sir?*"

But the children were laughing. When I saw that they swam like frogs, we all had a laugh. It was a lovely day, with a breeze on the water. The Italians love the sea, especially in Greece. The wife looked stunning in her swimsuit. When we were heading back to the port, the gentleman informed me that they were planning to stay on Hydra for another fifteen days. He would need the boat every day and would send his interpreter two hours in advance when it was required. I agreed to put myself and the *Mermaid* at his disposal.

When we tied up in the harbour, Melina Mercouri, Anthony Perkins and other people were there to welcome the Italian family back from their outing. I asked the Hydriots around me, "What's all the fuss? Who is this man?"

It turned out that my new client was the Italian film star Raf Vallone, who was playing Perkins' father and Melina's husband in *Phaedra*. Vallone's wife was the actress Elena Varzi.

Throughout the shooting on *Phaedra* I was kept busy and made plenty of money. My boat was even in some shots of the film.

Stormie Seas:
Sam Barclay's Letters to Marianne Ihlen

Helle V. Goldman

Is not short paine well borne, that brings long ease,
And layes the soul to sleepe in quiet grave?
Sleepe after toyle, port after stormie seas,
Ease after warre, death after life does greatly please
                                        Edmund Spenser

Sam Barclay was an intriguing figure at the margins of Hydra's expatriate scene during the Fiftes and Sixties. A "handsome man, slim and tall with light hair and a body bronzed by the sun,"[1] he had ambitions of painting but made his living chartering his schooner, the *Stormie Seas*. In 1958 he befriended Marianne Ihlen, the young Norwegian woman who would become known around the world as Leonard Cohen's muse. During Marianne's visits to Norway, Sam wrote to her from Greece. Excerpts from those letters are reproduced here.[2]

Sam Barclay was born in 1920 in Norfolk, where he was raised.

---

[1] *So Long, Marianne*, Kari Hesthamar, ECW Press, Toronto, 2014, p. 73. This is the source of much of the information about Marianne's life and her relationship with Sam presented here.

[2] The letters are printed here with the kind permission of Marianne Ihlen's estate. Over dinner at her home in Oslo, just weeks before her death in the summer of 2016, Marianne and I talked about publishing excerpts from these letters as her way of contributing to this volume.

At nineteen, at the start of the Second World War, he joined the Royal Navy, later volunteering for the Levant Schooner Flotilla.[3] Operating from bases on the Turkish coast, the Flotilla's caïques were small but heavily armed, with crews of half a dozen men. They typically worked under cover of darkness, transporting commandos, rescuing Greek Resistance fighters and generally being a nuisance to the Germans.

The world war over (and Greece's civil war beginning), Sam bought the old trading ketch, *Bessie*, and for a few years he and his partner Charles Landery carried dates, salted sardines, sesame, oak, mechanical parts and other cargo between Mediterranean ports. As trade fell off, Sam sold the *Bessie* and had the *Stormie Seas* built, drawing her name from a 16th century poem.[4] The ship was designed to be comfortable and practical and was a mostly successful marriage of the Greek *trechantiri* – a kind of caïque – with the traditional Norwegian *redningskøyte*. Her deck and hatches were made of teak salvaged from a wartime shipwreck off the North African coast. Sam's plan was to roam around the Aegean on the schooner, painting, while his new partner John Leatham – a wartime colleague – intended to write.

To land the contract the Greek shipbuilders had understated the estimated costs and the money ran out before the boat was completed. Strapped for funds, Sam and John were forced to accept an offer by MI6, the British intelligence organisation. At Malta, the *Stormie Seas* was fitted out with two masts, a powerful engine that took up the entire hold and dummy fuel tanks and other secret nooks for concealing men, radio gear and other equipment.

---

[3] Information about Sam Barclay, particularly his role in wartime and post-war covert operations, is drawn from these two books: *Albania in the Twentieth Century, a History, Vol. III: Albania as Dictatorship and Democracy, 1945-99*, Owen Pearson, I.B. Tauris, London, 2006, pp. 374-376; *The Albanian Operation of the CIA and MI6, 1949-1953: Conversations with Participants in a Venture Betrayed*, Nicholas Bethell et al., MacFarland & Co., Jefferson, North Carolina, 2016, pp. 26-33; as well as this magazine article: "Sam Barclay: At War and Peace," Nic Compton, *Classic Boat*, vol. 78, December 1994, pp. 52-57.

[4] The relevant stanza of Edmund Spenser's "The Faerie Queen" appears above. The writer Joseph Conrad used the last two lines as an epigraph in his nautical novel *The Rover* (1923). The same lines were later inscribed on Conrad's gravestone.

They were then flown to England, where Sam married Eileen Hay. He'd met the blue-eyed, dark-haired Eileen at Perama, the suburb of Piraeus where the *Stormie Seas* had been constructed. She was the daughter of a Shell Company engineer stationed in Greece. Eileen had been born in Shanghai and had lived in China, Egypt, the West Indies and South America. She played guitar and sang, and she christened the *Stormie Seas*.

In the autumn of 1949 Sam and John transported small groups of trained anti-Communist exiles to the Albanian coast. Sometimes Eileen went along, doing the cooking. The company of their dog Lean-to rounded out the impression of innocent family outings in the Adriatic. Little did they know that the Albanian authorities were informed of each landing by MI6 officer Kim Philby, who was revealed to be a double agent about fifteen years later. Sam and John had no idea then that about half the men they left on the Albanian shore were immediately imprisoned or executed. Sam and John were paid fifty pounds a month and at the end of the assigment were rewarded with a bonus of five hundred pounds.

This was not the end of Sam's involvement with MI6: Sam and John agreed to shower Albanian settlements with anti-Communist leaflets. Some twenty miles off the Albanian shore, John and Sam waited for London to signal when the wind was blowing in the right direction and for instructions about how long to make the fuses. They would fill a balloon with hydrogen gas, created with carbide tablets, and attach a length of wick and about a pound of pamphlets bearing the message, "*Do not despair – we are on our way!*" The fuse was lit and the balloon released in the hope that it would float over to Albania and drop its payload of propaganda onto the target village in the mountains when the fuse burned through. In the reality of uncooperative upper atmospheric conditions, rough conditions at sea level and mechanical hitches, "It was pretty impossible […] The whole operation was a bit of a joke," Sam later recalled.[5]

Eileen came along on some of these balloon-launching capers until she became pregnant, when she went to stay with her par-

---

[5] Compton, p. 57.

ents in Pireaus. James was born in 1950 and soon after Sam and Eileen ran the *Stormie Seas* as a charter boat. Through the Fifties, wealthy holiday-makers and celebrities like Elia Kazan and John Steinbeck chartered the *Stormie Seas* from early April to the end of October. During the winters, the ship laid up in a harbour while Sam and Eileen advertised for the coming season and made repairs. Sam painted when he could.

~

At the time Sam and Marianne Ihlen met she was paired with the volatile Norwegian writer, Axel Jensen, whom she would soon marry. The couple had driven to Greece from Norway during the winter of 1957, winding up almost by accident on Hydra on a cold rainy day in January 1958. Knowing no one at first, Marianne and Axel were taken under the wings of Australian writers Charmian and George Johnston and the handful of other foreigners who lived on the island. They also befriended Sam and Eileen Barclay, who stopped in on Hydra with clients. (Sam kept writing on his old printed letterhead – "Yacht 'Stormie Seas', Hydra, Greece" – long after the *Stormie Seas*' home port had shifted to the island of Spetsai, about 12 miles west of Hydra.) Axel was a sailor at heart himself; the two men had that in common.

In the spring of 1958, it seemed to Marianne that her relationship with the mercurial and unfaithful Axel was over. At a low point, Marianne wandered around Athens, wondering what to do. Return to Norway? Find work in Greece? She sank into a chair at a café and lost herself in thought when she heard car brakes jamming.

> "Marianne! Thank God you're here! You're my guardian angel!"
> The voice belonged to Eileen [...] Plumping down into a chair at Marianne's table in her wide-brimmed straw hat, Eileen chattered about her fantastic new lover. She implored Marianne to get her out of a jam by taking her place as cook and

hostess on the yacht so Eileen could avoid joining her husband on the next trip […]

For Marianne, homeless and abandoned, the offer was like a gift from the gods.

At 8:30 the following morning she shows up at the harbour in Piraeus. Sam is standing on the deck of his schooner, and Marianne hears a boy's thin voice asking, "Isn't Mama coming?" Sam answers, "No, your mother isn't coming, but Marianne will take care of us."[6]

Marianne worked on the *Stormie Seas* for six weeks, looking after James, who was about six, and cooking for the crew – herself, Sam and a young Greek sailor – and the customers. Sam and Marianne found solace in one another and enjoyed a brief affair as they sailed among Greek islands and along the Turkish coast.

Marianne reconciled with Axel and they were married in Athens in October 1958. In their little house on Hydra, purchased for about 2,500 dollars in the part of town known as Kala Pigadia – the Good Wells – Axel concentrated on writing his book. In the spring of 1959, they both worked on the *Stormie Seas* alongside Sam, the affair between Sam and Marianne unmentioned. Marianne and Axel's only child, Axel Joachim, was conceived on board in April. Sam would become the boy's godfather.

Axel and Marianne returned to Norway late in 1959 to visit her father, who was dying of tuberculosis. At the same time, Axel's book, *Line*, was published by the Norwegian publisher Cappelen and there were publicity events to attend. (The book was made into a film in 1961.) Marianne was about seven months pregnant when her father died. Meanwhile, Sam looked after the house on Hydra and reported by post to Marianne on the progress of repairs.

In January, Marianne gave birth to Axel Joachim. The baby boy's father returned to Greece a week later. Marianne took her little son to Greece to join Axel a few months later. On Hydra, Marianne discovered that Axel had become involved with an

[6] *So Long, Marianne*, p. 73.

American painter named Patricia Amlin. Axel left Marianne and the baby to join his lover, but shortly afterward Patricia was badly injured in a car accident on the mainland. Axel was incapacitated by sorrow and shock, so Marianne stepped in and helped tend to her shattered rival in the hospital in Athens. Patricia was sent to the US for further medical care when she could be safely moved.

As Marianne's relationship with Axel fell apart, she found herself drawn to a new arrival on the island, a young Canadian poet and writer. Leonard Cohen and Marianne fell in love on Hydra during the autumn of 1960.

Later that year Leonard and Marianne drove together to Oslo, where Leonard met Marianne's mother. Leonard travelled onward to Canada while Marianne stayed in Norway with her mother. At a crossroads again, Marianne was beset by self-doubts and anxiously awaited confirmation from Leonard that they would be together. She wondered whether she should return to Hydra or take up an ordinary life in Oslo or even try to patch up her marriage to Axel for the sake of their child. She wrote to Sam of her worries. Sam replied, offering counsel and sympathy and keeping her apprised about Hydra goings-on.

After spending the Christmas of 1960 in England, Sam visited Marianne in Oslo. Sam was well aware that Marianne was in love with Leonard but that Leonard had made no promises to her and that the future of their brief relationsip was uncertain. Sam had probably loved Marianne ever since their affair on the *Stormie Seas* in the spring of 1958. In Oslo, he asked if she would marry him when her divorce from Axel was finalised. She turned him down.

Marianne in Oslo, waiting for word from Leonard, and Sam in Greece, carrying on with his chartering business, they continued to write to one another. Excerpts of Sam's half of their correspondence follow.

The earliest letter was written in the autumn of 1959 and the latest in October 1961. During these two years, Marianne and Axel had a baby and split up and Marianne fell in love with Leonard Cohen. There are no letters from Sam among Marianne's papers post-dating her departure (with her little boy) late in the autumn of 1961 to Montreal, to be with Leonard. Marianne and Leonard's relationship would last the better part of a decade, much of it spent on Hydra, where Marianne would inspire Leonard to write the songs "Bird on a Wire" and "So Long, Marianne," among others. When she lay dying, in Oslo, in the summer of 2016, Leonard wrote to her: "I'm just a little behind you, close enough to take your hand [...] I've never forgotten your love and your beauty." She died two days later. He followed a little over three months later.

Sam's letters were written during two periods when Marianne was in Norway: first, the autumn and winter of 1959-60 and, second, the first ten months of 1961. Sam wrote from Hydra, from Spetsai (also known as Spetses), from Piraeus (the mainland seaport where he had major repairs done to the boat) and from other parts of Greece as he sailed with friends and charter clients. A few letters were written during Sam's railway journey from Copenhagen to Greece in 1961. Some letters were composed over the course of several days; one seems to have been written over a fortnight. Quick line drawings of ships, harbour scenes, animals and flowers embellish some of the pages. Just a few of these illustrations have been reproduced here.

Presented chronologically,[7] Sam's letters to Marianne describe the minutiae of daily life, the rhythms of his ship and the sea and the seasons, his dealings with Greeks, his encounters with other expatriates and his attachment to his son James, whom he missed terribly when the boy went to stay with Eileen in England. Sam was more circumspect in expressing his love for the woman to whom he was writing. He knew his strong feelings were not returned and, it seems, he did not want to force her to cut herself off from him. The love he felt for Marianne comes through all the more poignantly.

Space constraints make it impossible to reproduce the entire contents of all of Sam's letters that Marianne kept. However, even the fragments presented below offer a vivid picture of life in Greece more than fifty years ago, especially of island life and

---

[7] Undated letters were dated as accurately as possible with the aid of clues in the letters and a timeline of events drawn from *So Long, Marianne*.

the life of an expatriate sailor. Sam Barclay was an idiosyncratic and inconsistent speller, and a sensitive observor. Of Hydra, Sam wrote, "No one ever leaves Hydra happier than when they arrived and yet they always want to go back."

Like all good observers, Sam stood a bit apart. He looked in from the outside, sailing in and sailing away again. "One has nothing to tie onto," he revealed to Marianne in one letter.

~

Autumn 1959. Marianne and Axel have returned to Norway to see her sick father and to launch Axel's book, *Line*. Marianne is pregnant with the child conceived with Axel on the *Stormie Seas*. The baby is due in January.

> Dear Marianne,
>
> Thank you for your two letters one of which came ages ago + which I never answered […]
>
> I am glad you are both well, that Axel has begun his new book, and that you are "enormous." I do hope all goes well in January and don't forget that you promised that I could be a godfather […]
>
> I am writing this in an hotel room in Athens, early morning. Grey light of dawn, sound of rolling barrells, only cold water in the taps, most frustrating. I have come up from Hydra to see the printers about our new pamphlet for "Stormie Seas" which is going to be coloured + much better than the last – if they ever print it. They are being terribly slow. I have brought James up too for a check up with the Doctor. He is extremely well but, as you wrote in your letter, they all have to be checked for T.B.[8] […]
>
> Your house in Hydra is in good order […] I have not had the workmen up to your house to

[8] Sam's son James spent much time with the Johnston family and George Johnston had recently been diagnosed with tuberculosis.

give an estimate yet but will do so as soon as we get back again. I was up there the other day and it struck me that, with a little cement, it would be quite an easy thing to double the catchment of water for the cistern[9] which would double your water supply [...] It rained hard in Hydra about a week ago which filled everyone's cisterns so Mastera Mitso has been carrying sand instead of water with his donkeys every since [...]

By all accounts "Lina" must have been a great success. Are they translating it into English? And if so when? I long to read the rest of it. Now you have a car! What prosperity! Is Axel still the President of the Society for the Prevention of Atomic Warfare and are you still his secretary or, now that he is writing again, is that all finished? [...]

Lots of love to you both.

Will write again soon.

Sam

*

4 December 1959. While Marianne and Axel are still in Oslo, Sam is looking after their house on Hydra, overseeing repairs, which he illustrates.

Dear Marianne,

I am writing this from your little house on the hill. It is a lovely day, warm + sunny. It rained last night.

Fransisco has just been up to give an estimate for the work to be done.

---

[9] On the virtually waterless island of Hydra, homes were traditionally constructed with cavernous lower chambers that stored rainwater run-off from the roofs and terraces. Since the implementation of a regular water supply from the mainland, many cisterns on Hydra have been converted to other uses.

DOWNSTAIRS ROOM "LISTS"[10]

ON CEILING	130. ΔX[11]
DOOR FRAME	320.
WINDOW AND FRAME	200.
GLASS × 4	38.
KITCHEN WINDOW AND FRAME	200.
GLASS × 6	38.
TOP FLOOR ROOM WINDOWS AND FRAMES (3)	600.
GLASS × 16	162.
TRANSPORT ETC:	<u>22.</u>
	1,710

For the door frame he will have to renew the compleet thing encluding the facing outside which he will do properly with a cornice at the top. The windows will be compleetly renewed, glass, frame and the inner-surround.

The outer surround and facings are pretty rotten and it would be a great economy to renew

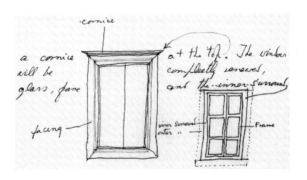

these NOW if you have the ready cash. It would

---

[10] *List* is the Norwegian word for moulding or skirting boards.

[11] Drachma.

cost another 1,410 ΔX. to do the five windows.

There is one other small expense not encluded here, that of the builder to putty up the walls after the carpenter. This, without rewhitewashing would come to about 150 ΔX for the door or 250 ΔX for door and windows togeather […]

Francisco will be using all the old clasps and hinges from the old windows. They are nice and in keeping. He can get new type iron hinges etc if you want at about 17 ΔX per window. The old windows and the glass I will keep in case you want them later. He is putting new hinges on the door as the old ones are worn out […]

I am sorry Oslo is so sad with cold and fog. Hydra has been lovely. I have not worn a jersey for some days now. There is not much wind today + it is quite warm. Anyway, I am glad you are in Oslo really because it will be better to have the baby there.

I am sorry about your father being back in hospital again. I hope so much that he will get better this time too.

George Johnstone is back in Hydra for a month over Christmas. He is looking better already[12] […] He has just finished another book.[13] Charmian's "Walk to Paradise Gardens" has been accepted in America and her "Peel Me a Lotus" (about Hydra) has just come out in England where it has had very good reviews.[14] So they are fairly pleased with themselves.

James has been to Athens to be X rayed and is perfectly clear. He will probably go home to Eng-

---

[12] George Johnston stayed in Athens to undergo treatment for tuberculosis while his wife Charmian and their three children remained on Hydra. Their house was not far from Marianne and Axel's.

[13] *Closer to the Sun*, Collins, London, 1960.

[14] *Walk to the Paradise Gardens*, Hutchinson, London, 1960; *Peel Me a Lotus*, Hutchinson, London, 1959.

land to school sometime during the summer. This is sad but I see no alternative as I cannot be here all the time he is at school, especially spring and autumn. Although the Johnstones say they love having him it is not entirely satisfactory. There is no entirely satisfactory solution for that matter.

What is Axel's new book that he has started? Is it Miracle Man or another one on the lines of the last one? [...]

Eileen is still in London and, I gather, going to stay there. She is naturally very anxious to see James. She will have to wait now till the summer as he is well settled in amongst his friends and it would be too unsettling to send him home for Christmas [...]

I miss you both so much.

Love Sam!

P.S. James is most excited about the sweater and so am I about mine![15]

*

8 February 1960, Hydra. Sam has just heard about the birth of Marianne's son, Axel Joachim, on 21 January.

Dear Axel + Marianne,

Well done! I have not seen George today but everybody in Hydra, Georgo from the post office, Niko Katsika, Fidel and all the old wives have been telling me that George has had a tellegram saying that Marianne has had a son and that you are calling it Axel Jr. I hope that his coming was without a hitch and that he is stout and strong. I am not forgetting that, in a weak moment, you said that I could be his godfather!

---

[15] Marianne had given Sam and James Norwegian cable-knit sweaters in undyed wool, made by her mother.

We are now living in your house, James and I. I think it is now probably the most weather-proof house in Hydra. The windows let in no air or rain and when the water leaks in through the door it leaks straight out again […]

The work took about 5 days in all and there was CHAOS! Shavings, cement, sand, whitewash and men everywhere. However they did not do much dammage to the rest of the house + now I have scrubbed it from top to toe + it is very nice to live in. We have all the cushions from the ship […]

The weather has been lovely, almost like summer, until about a week ago. Now it is very cold. Everyone, encluding James + me, have had coughs + colds. James was in bed for 2 days […]

Stormie Seas lies deserted in the harbor, stripped, with the engine out of her. Mitso is married and living ashore. He is rather dignified and pays small boys to do all the dirty jobs now. He won't be seen carrying water or laundry any more.

David[16] is still waiting for money. George has had another book accepted (the one about Hydra).[17] Charmian has one coming out any day now (Walk to Paradise Gardens).[18] Fidel is still waiting for money to get off the island. Magda still living with Theodoros who, I think, is a little bit nuts […] James has many friends now at the "Down" school, mostly among the shepherds and "Hill" people who, he says, are wilder and better fighters than the sons of the rich people. We seem to have quite a few charters for next year, beginning on April 6th.

---

[16] English designer David Goschen.

[17] *Closer to the Sun.*

[18] *Walk to the Paradise Gardens.*

When do you think that you will be returning.

Much love to you, all three and to Per + Elsa Berrit[19] when you see them.

Sam

*

27 March 1960. Marianne is in Oslo with the baby, staying with her mother. Axel left Oslo a week after the birth and has returned to Hydra on his own.

Got your letter today, posted on the 25th. Very quick.

I know that Axel had had a smash in a hired motor […] Apparently it was a very near thing. It is a wonder that he has not killed himself by now, and indeed he will do so if he goes on driving […] Apparently the Petersens, a Norwegian painter and his wife, who have a little boy of about 2 years old, are splitting up […] I am sorry about this. It happens to almost everyone who goes to Hydra, everyone but the Johnstones that is and it never quite happens to them. No one ever leaves Hydra happier than when they arrived and yet they always want to go back. Do you think, if you went back there, Marianne, that you would be happier in any way? […]

The charterers came on board at noon today […] There are four grown ups and two small boys of ten, all Americans. The small boys have been rowing round the Stormie Seas in the dinghy on a flat calm sea under a full moon.

I am glad to be away again […] Did I tell you that Mitso left? He came up to Passalimani thinking that I would take him back again but I cannot risk that kind of thing when I am chartering. He

---

[19] Marianne's friends Per and Else Berit had lived for a while in Athens.

would leave again next time we went to Hydra. Still, I am sorry to lose him and I liked Georgo too […]

I had a letter from Eileen today. She and James are going to Paris for Easter, I think to stay with the Soules […]

There was a girl on board who came up with us from Hydra. She stayed and helped to clean the cabins, pollish brass and generally get the ship ready for chartering. She was sad to go. Girls brighten things up so. Places are so empty when they are not there.

Good night, girl. Good night little boy.

And love,

Sam

*

January 1961. Sam is in Copenhagen, en route to Greece after visiting Marianne in Oslo. This fragment of a letter begins partway through a recollection of a dream and includes a sketch of the *Stormie Seas*.

[…] However there was a boat not far away from me and together we reached the ladder and I managed to climb on board. I remember thinking that it was a lot of pannic for nothing as she had not really dragged her anchor. Then, as I let the mainsail down with a rush, I saw that the foot of the mainmast was about six inches clear of the deck and that the whole mast was swinging, somehow caught up in the rigging of the foremast.

I shouted to everyone to stand clear and, as the mainsail came tumbling down, the mainmast came crashing with it very nearly missing me […]

I am getting rather good at remembering my dreams. It is a question of wanting to I think.

Copenhagen is fairly cold but there is no snow

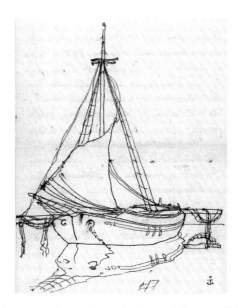

and not much ice. I wonder how Athens will be.
    My best regards to your mother and Niels[20] [...]
Rather special love to you and the Eskimeaux.[21]
    Sam

*

Early 1961. Sam is writing to Marianne as he travels by ferry from Hydra to the island of Spetsai, completing the letter in Spetsai, on the *Stormie Seas*. He has recently returned to Greece from northern Europe. Sam mentions the letter and parcels with which Marianne had entrusted him in Oslo to deliver to Axel on Hydra. Sam also refers to the old family pocket-watch he had pinned to her blouse in Oslo, when he proposed to her.

    Well, Marianne!
        Here I am at sea again, on my way at Spetsai [...] I left Axel your letter, the two parcels, and a

---

[20] Marianne's brother.

[21] Sam's nickname, spelled variously, for his godson Axel Joachim.

letter from myself saying simply that I was sorry to miss him, that I had seen you and Per + Elsa Beret, and that you were, on the whole, well.

I hope you are.

Saronis[22] is drumming along. The sea is grey, the sky is grey and there are rain drops splattering against the window frames. There is only one other person besides myself in the first-class lounge. I suspect that he too has a second-class ticket!

David's house is looking nice now [...] There is enough water in the top cistern, using twelve barrells a week, to last them a whole year. And hot and cold water actually comes out of all the taps! If you light the fire in the boiler that is. I had a bath there this morning, so I know.

A small boy rode up to David's house on a donkey last night and asked for me. He said he had two mattresses for "Marianne's house", and where did I want them put? Hydra is a funny island.

"Yerakina"[23] on the radio. Vibration of the engines, Hermione looming up ahead [...]

Can't stop writing to Marianne! Never mind, she does not have to read it. Shrills of bells from the engine room, swirls of turquoise and white marbled water, engines drum up the full beat and we are away, at sea again [...]

You say in your letter you feel a lot different to when you were in Hydra. You are a lot different, Maryanne. You are a person now and will be more of a person yet. That is something I cannot put into words and if you don't know what I mean I cannot tell you.

Oh Marianne! What a silly sort of letter to

---

[22] The *Saronis* ferry served the islands of Aegina, Methana, Poros, Hydra and Spetsai from 1959 to 1971.

[23] A Greek folk song recorded by Theodore Alevizos and released in 1960 on the album *Songs of Greece*.

write. You write as though it were the last you were every going to write. And you talk of giving the watch to James?

I gave that watch to you, Marianne, because I loved you and I wanted you to have it, not because I wanted to bind you in any way. I will never have, and never want to have, a hold on you in any kind of way.

Keep the watch. And weather you like it or not you are always going to have me too because I am your friend. Just your friend. And you may break the watch into a million pieces or give it to who you please. It will make no difference.

I am glad you like to jersey I gave you. I like the one you gave me too.

I am glad you have descided to stick to Leonard. I knew you would even though I tried hard to sweep you off with me. You would not have been worth much if you had come, you know?

I wish you luck with Leonard. He sounds nice. I wish I knew him better. Go right ahead with him, Marianne. Maybe he will make you happy [...]

I am so glad you are coming out of your cacoon. It was not the deep freeze, for you have been growing inside all the time. I am sorry Axel never had the chance to see and know you as you are now too. But Axel experiences people, like an adventure or a journey, and passes on. I would not worry too much about Axel. The one I am so afraid for is Patricia [...]

Thank you for looking for a cook for me. I will probably take the nurse who is looking after Joyce. When I was married this would not have worried me at all. But now it is different. One has nothing to tie onto.

The sheep have just gone by along the edge of the harbour, their bells jingling. A donkey is braying. I surpose he is in love but he doesn't sound very joyful. Stormie Seas is lying deserted, very calm outside the window. The sun has gone down. It will be a new day tomorrow.

I'll write to you again tomorrow, Marianne.
God bless you,
Sam
There is so much I have not said.

*

13 and 14 February 1961, Spetsai.

Marianne,

The clock is ticking on the wall, Baba-Ianni[24] is twanging at his bars, the water is lapping outside the door and the lamps are sizzling quietly on the table by my hand

[…] The engineers are taking the engine to pieces today. Mastera Michaele, who lives opposite you, is doing the job. His grandfather has just died at 97! When his grandmother dies, who is 86, he is going to sell the house (I suppose it is hers) because his father-in-law, who lives in the house below his, is always nagging him. It would be quite a nice house to have.

The sheep are grazing on the quay outside the window […]

The sheep are grazing on the quay
outside the window - -

---

[24] Pet bird.

Looked at in the cold light of reason it was a pretty silly thing to ask you to marry me. You are a Norwegean, fourteen years younger than me and we have practically no interests in common. And yet, don't ask me why, I have never been so happy in my life as when I have been with you. You are the first person ever to make me wish to build a house with, far from the sea, to make lots of babies with, and together watch them grow up. This is no small thing and, having felt it once, I will probably feel it again [...]

I would like you now to forget that I ever asked you to marry me and just to know that you make me feel happy and then it can go on that way.
For two and a half years now you have occupied the innermost corner of my most secret places. Now you have asked me to open that door and let you out. I have done so, and anyone else can now walk in. But still, I don't know why. I am happy [...]

Lots of love to your mother, brother, eskime-aux, Peter, Elsa and, not least, to Marianne,
from Sam

*

17 February 1961, Spetsai.

Marianne,
I am writing to you because, even though you have walked out of my innermost door, you are still my favourite person along with James. I hope you don't mind.

Mastera Michaele has just been in to the house and together we have made out a plan to spend an astronomical number of drachma on the engine. He is willing to do the work almost for nothing if

I give him my shotgun. Apart from the fact that I don't want to give him my shotgun it is listed by the Greek Customs as being on board. But Mastera Michaele says that he will give me another one to show the Customs Officers if and when they make any enquiries. It sounded so ancient that I asked him, as a joke, weather it fired with a flint. "Oh! I took that off myself" he said. "Now it fires with a hammer and a pin. But when I pull the trigger it blows back and hits me in the eye!" […]

And I think I have a cook. I had a letter from Linette today saying she was studdying cooking and was frightfully keen to come. She must be keen because I had practically told her she could not come, that I wanted someone over 50 or a man […] When you were in my innermost recesses I was frightened, at such close quarters, of all the effort and business of keeping everyone else out. But now I am not even frightened of that […] Yolanda has a maid from Creete. Her old grandfather has just died at the age of 120. But he did not die from old age. Oh no! Not at all. He went into the garden to go to the loo. But it was very dark and he got hold of the horse's leg instead of the door of the loo. The horse kicked him in the stomach and he died of internal haemorage. Life is full of hazards […]

Doors wide open, sun streaming in. A lovely day, kind of a holiday, caique engines popping, songs, music, birds singing, no one working much, almond blossoms just bursting on the trees, onions, potatoes, artichokes, beans + lettuces all sprouting in the garden […]

Love to the Eskimeaux, love to you,
Sam

*

20 February 1961, Spetsai.

Marianne!

It is evening now and I am warming up some water on the stove for a bath in the big tin bath in front of the fire. Clean Monday![25] [...]

Sorry you are still worrying about the baby, houses and money. Don't worry too much about that. Axel seems to have some money now [...] After a bit of time has passed it might be an idea to take a job. Might be good for morale.

I had a letter from Axel yesterday. He has troubles of his own. Patricia is not coming out for a while yet. Her shoulder is giving her a lot of pain and her family are not well. Poor Patricia! Which ever way things go she is in for a lot of trouble yet. Axel gets involved in situations and when he has experienced them he passes on to the next. His work is justification for everything he does [...]

I am glad that you are fond of Leonard because I believe he is worth ten of Axel. And I think that if he is the person I think he is, then he will not hurt you. Good people do not hurt, Marianne, and they are so worth knowing.

So Axel Joacim Eskimo Jensen is now baptised! In Greece the godfathers have to pay all the church expenses, clothes, crosses and the lot. Please tell me what the customs are in Norway. And I am so honoured to be his godfather.

Hope you liked "Never on Sundays."[26] I have not seen it myself yet.

I don't know where Axel is planning to spend the summer. I think he was planning to spend it

---

[25] The first day of Great Lent in Eastern Christianity.

[26] *Never on Sunday*, directed by Jules Dassin and starring Melina Mercouri, came out in 1960. Mercouri and Dassin came to Hydra to film *Phaedra* in 1961.

on Hydra as he was having a studio built at the back of the house for Patricia's arrival. But whatever he does he will probably change his mind later […]

It is late now. The fire is out. The wind piping up. Sorry this letter is dull. Shall probably tear up part of it in the morning, Marianne.

Good night!

*

22 February 1961, Spetsai.

[…] I just put some prunings from the fig tree on the fire and it is cracking and spitting like a machine-gun, sparks flying everywhere and threatening to set light to the rush matting […]

I have just been out to the home of Lakis […] Lakis is a fat good-looking good-natured youth who used perpetually to serenade Eileen with his guitar […] We eat fried sparrows and tiny birds, fried by Lakis' mother, for a meze and drink ouzo. We also eat cheese made by Lakis' mother from milk from their goats, and bread baked by Lakis' mother from barley grown, sown, and reaped by his father […]

They told me that the boy who helps to keep the light-house opposite our house is missing. He not a boy really, being about 30. He got up at three o'clock this morning, climbed into his varka in his pyjamas, and chugged out to sea. No one has seen him since. Apparently he was a little weak in the head and loved a girl in the village, a pretty girl of 21. Her mother would not let them marry. Now the Harbourmaster is out with his launch looking for the varka […]

I had a tellegram yesterday in Spetsai asking whether I would charter Stormie Seas from 1st

April. This has created an urgent situation [...]
Must go now to get some coffee + then the bank.
A hug for the Eskimeaux,
Platonic love to you,
Sam

*

25 February 1961.

Marianne!

Just pulling out of Hydra on board the Saronis on my way back to Spetsai. Tooting of whistles, babble of voices, jangling of bells, and Axel has just got off the ship. We travelled down from Piraeus together and have had a long talk about all kinds of things, life on Hydra, philosophizing about life, Axel's book, Patricia and you. You know what life on Hydra is like [...] You probably know that his new book[27] is about a young artist and his wife on an island in the Saronic Gulf and how he does more or less what Axel has done on an island in the Saronic Gulf, and about the emotional and ethical problems envolved. You probably know that it is Patricia's collar-bone and not her shoulder that will not mend, that, if she does not come to Hydra he will go to Chicago [...]

I feel rather like a spy writing a secret report so you had better tear this letter up [...] I think I'll tear it up myself then my conscience will be alright and you will be left in the dark as to what is happening.

I think the April 1st – 10th charter looks as though it may come off. This means an early start and a rush to get ready. Leave here next Friday I surpose, slip on Saturday etc. etc. etc. but 10

---

[27] *Joacim*, Cappelen, Oslo, 1961.

days charter means $750, and $750 means ΔX 22,500, and ΔX 22,500 means £268.6.0 which is very nearly James' school bill for the year. Hey ho! What a sordid thing money is! […]

My chisels have gone x@!! – All the bad language I know does not make me feel any better […] Half of them belonged to my grandfather and must be 80 years old. The other half I have had myself for 20 years. They were lovely chisels but would be useless to anyone else. I carved your sandal with them. Remember?

The light-house keeper has been found. On an island halfway between Spetsai and Hydra, called Trikerie. He was building himself a monastery down by the sea […] A herdsman found him, still in his pyjamas, and they brought him back in a fishing-boat […]

Lots of love to you, Eskimo + family
Sam

*

1 March 1961. Sam, in Spetsai, consoles Marianne, who has received a discouraging letter from Leonard in Montreal.

Marianne!

This is from my upstairs window. Just offered the two Iannis half a day's pay each if they finnish scraping the two masts by tonight. The air is thick with shavings […]
I did not write to you yesterday. I wrote to James, home, five or six letters and then felt so bloody that I turned in directly after supper.

Ah, Marianne! So now at last you have heard from Leonard. I am sorry. You don't have much luck. And yet you have Joacim and he is a big hunk of luck and getting bigger every day. And maybe, when a little time goes by and the piece of you which is in Montreal comes back to you, and you are at peace again, you may feel you would rather have known him even for a short while rather than not at all. And that might make you happy. Who knows? […] About yourself, the Eskimo and Axel. Please! Please! Do be business-like about this, for Joacim's sake if not for your own. Axel thinks only of Axel. You have to think of the baby at least. Axel, as you say, wants a divorce and wants it quickly. Do talk to your lawyer (you are going to see him anyway) and get him to write into the agreement that he provides maintenance for the baby. You MUST, knowing Axel, get this written down. You are in a very strong position. You should, under the circumstances also get maintenance for yourself until such time, in the far distant future, as you marry again. Believe me, when Axel marries again, he will forget any verbal agreement he may make if he is at all hard up. The responsibility is his and you can and must make him face it […]

We started the engine today. Mastera Georgo arrived from Hydra two days late (he has been ill) and the engine started at the first push of the button and ran perfectly […]

I think of you so much, Marianne. I hope you are alright. It must be a great comfort to have the baby […]

My love to both of you,
Sam

*

Early March 1961.

[…] The last cook off a coaster I had snored like a fog-horn and his feet smelt so strong I could not stay in the same cabin with him […] Surpose you did think of coming it would be two months from the time you left Oslo to the time you got back again. If I were to pay you 3,000 ΔX per month that would be 6,000 ΔX. Your fare out and back would take nearly 4,000 ΔX which would still leave you with 2000 ΔX at the end of it. I would be 3000 ΔX better off than if I had taken the cook off the coaster or 12,000 ΔX better off than if I had taken a "yacht" cook and your feet don't smell nor, so far as I remember, do you snore! So do not think I would be doing you any favour by asking you to come. Rather the other way around [...] The only thing you have to think of is whether you could bear to leave the Eskimo with your mother for two months and whether you would perhaps be happier in Oslo.

Do say yes, Marianne!

Regards to your mother + Nils, love to you + The Eskimo

Sam

*

9 March 1961, Piraeus.

Marianne, Dearest Marianne!

Can't help wondering whether you will be coming out here for the 31st of March. It would be fun if you did but I don't really expect you will. I have been in Piraeus all day buying vast quantities of rope and paint and varnish. The agent at Turko Lemano payed me for the first charter so that is definite now.

As I had anticipated, the bottom of the keel has been eaten off and has to be renewed. This should not take more than a couple of days. We may be in the water again by Monday.

I hate being on the slip. The yards are so dirty.

You tread through oil and grease and tar to get to the ship. The decks get filthy and there is no water to wash them down [...]

These are busy days, chacing shipwrights, caulkers, painters, half of whom repeatedly say that they are coming and then never turn up. And then there are the shore jobs too, batteries to be remade, the agent to see, rope, paints, cable to buy and the consulate to visit for letters [...]

Marianne! Marianne! I won't hope that you are coming [...]

I have just come back from having supper with Gregorie, who was our sailor in the Bessie and who helped us build the Stormie Seas. His wife Fortinoula is plump and dark with rosy cheeks and the bluest eyes you ever saw on a Greek. Their little daughter of four has got the same eyes [...]

God bless you and your Eskimo very very much
Sam

*

14 March 1961, Piraeus.

Marianne, darling Marianne!

Got your letter this afternoon. You have no idea how much I love your letters. [...] I am glad that you have started work. I am sure that this was necessary and that the very fact of working will make you feel much more settled. And I am glad that Leonard has telephoned. All is not lost yet! [...]

I do not want to be with anyone else, Marianne, for a while yet. And my innermost most precious place is empty. And that is the way I want it to be for a while [...]

It must now be rather early in the morning. I had better get to sleep. We should be going in the water today. Shipwrights, caulkers, riggers, painters, electricians THE LOT!!! […]

God bless you both […]

Sam

*

15 March 1961, Piraeus.

Marianne!

And now the Stormie Seas is almost a ship again. This morning at seven o'clock while I was down in the galley having some coffee and making toast I felt a great lurch and shot up on deck to find Stormie Seas rushing backwards toward the water at a great rate. I swore and shouted because no one had told me we were ready to go in. But all went well and we sailed backwards for a time and gently came to a standstill near a buoy onto which we tied […]

It is worrying me rather becaused if there is no letter from you before we go saying if you can come for those two months then I shall not know whether to sign on someone else or not. But I doubt if you will come […]

Thursday

And today I got your letter. Silly of me really to think that you might come. Silly of you if you had come too […]

I wish I could plug you into my thoughts for a while. Words are so ambiguous. I am glad, Marianne, that you are happier now that you have talked to Leonard. Not long ago you would not have stuck to him the way you are doing now. There has been a change in you that I knew must come and I am so glad it has. You are a much stronger person than you used to be, Marianne, and I don't believe Leonard, or anyone else, would be so stupid as – well, perhaps you can guess what I am trying to say […]

Don't worry about a cook. There are lots of cooks. Fat cooks. Old cooks. Man cooks. To hell with cooks! […]

Babba Ianni is twanging the bars with his beak. Launches hum back and forth from the naval ships outside. Hellecopters clatter overhead. Stormie Seas is clear again. And the world seems a terribly, terribly empty place.

But it never seems empty for long and tomorrow is another day.

Love can mean so many kinds of things, Marianne. This is not a posessive love, that wants you. It is a big kind of love that friends and families have. I love you and I love your Eskimo […]

Sam

*

Late March 1961, Hydra.

Saw Axel today, Marianne. Looking well and brown. He had been up in the mountain picking flowers. The little house was empty when I went up there. The windows are warping and the glass remains unputtied. Patricia arrives in Hydra any day now I understand […]

I saw a dog which looked like Bilken[28] on the Kala Pigathia road. The small boys called out "James? Where is James? Is he with you?" And Stormie Seas sits in the harbour black and brooding. She looks finer than before with her masts taller and topped with spear-points. She came to

---

[28] Marianne and Axel's dog, left in the care of a Greek family on Hydra.

Hydra in under 5 hours nearly a knot faster than she has ever been before. The engineers have upset the timing of her engine I think […]

The caiques in the harbour breathe and pant and cough. One by one they come to life. The sky goes grey. Pale light filters down the hatch […]

This letter is getting too long. I tore up some of yesterdays. One should never write when one is feeling depressed. A big kiss to the eskimo and a kind of cold one on the forehead for his mum.

And love,
Sam

*

22 March 1961, Spetsai and Hydra.

Dear Marianne!

The wind is blowing a gale from the south east. Kyria Katie is whitewashing the outside of my house, keeps on bursting into the room splattered all over with whitewash giving instructions and demanding tins and other equipment in a shrill harsh voice. Mitso, Georgo and old Kapitan Lakis are putting the final touches to the paint on the Stormie Seas.

Yesterday a boy blew his hand off. Everyone is making bangs, the way they always do at Easter […] I offered to bandage it up and put sulphonamide on it but they, quite rightly, said that no one but the doctor could do anything for him. As it turned out the doctor couldn't do much for him either and they sent him off to Athens on the steamer. He had lost four fingers from his left hand and they could not stop the bleeding.

I asked old Capitan Lakis this morning how it had happened. He said the boy was up for stealing and was to have gone to the law-courts that day [...] So he had done it on purpose with a nitro-glycerine detonater that they use for detonating the dynamite with which they dynamite fish. Only he had rather overdone it [...]

Today must be SUNDAY. Last night we spent in Hydra. Today we came to Piraeus with half of Hydra on board, but no sailors [...]

Hydra was cellebrating Liberation day, dancing on the quay in national dress. We all went to dinner in the pink cafe. Fidel tells me that the old man who owned it [...] had a son who was mad and who was chained up upstairs for ages. He was taken to an asylum in Athens the other day.

Demitrie, Caroline[29], Axel, Derek (the cook) and a girl called Somebody DuPont all decided to come to Athens on Stormie Seas. This morning all but Axel turned up on the quay. Axel, I think, had a hangover. Patricia has had to have another opperation on her hand. It seems endless and she is not expected for some time yet.

Mitso was late getting up this morning and late on board. When he came he said that [...] his back was hurting and he must leave the ship. This five days before our first charter and still a mountain of last minute jobs to be done. I was angry. Georgo is only 16 and too young to come on his own. Derek has cooked in an R.A.F. officers mess and, so far as I can see, that is about the standard of his accomplishments.

There is a very good boy in Spetsai, Iannis Boffis, who is worth two of Mitso and is very keen to come. I will tellegraph him tomorrow [...]

Derek reading on his bunk. Demetrie and Caroline are sleeping in the after cabin, Somebody DuPont in the focstle. Grey and damp outside [...]

I seem to remember that on the 13th or therea-

---

[29] The painter Demetri Gassoumis and his wife Caroline.

bouts when I was very depressed and rather lonely I wrote you rather a stupid letter which I hope you did not take any notice of […]

LOVE, SAM

*

31 March 1961, Kythnos and Hydra.

I remember last year (it seems ages ago) watching the sailors carry the epitaph into the water at Kaminie.[30] And Axel was with Pat. And you were expected any day with Joacim. So little time ago. Tomorrow we should be again at Hydra for Easter to see Christ arise again. This year, no James. The two American boys are dear little boys and I do all the things for them I did for James […]

HYDRA SUNDAY

It is Easter morning, about one o'clock. I saw Axel today. He and Pat were coming to the Church at midnight but he did not come. Everyone says that Pat is well. Maybe you will be angry with me for telling him that I had heard you had a part-time job. He did not seem to know. You should have told me if you did not want him to know. Oh well!

Tonight I went up to David's house and had supper with Dimitri and Caroline and Fidel. Caroline's brother Jim and his wife are staying there. They are taking a house for 5 months this sum-

---

[30] On the evening of Good Friday, the *Epitafios*, which represents Christ's funeral bier, is carried through the part of Hydra called Kamini (or Kaminia), where it is borne out into the little harbour and immersed in the sea. The custom was established in the 1920s, when boats left for sponge-diving expeditions after the Sunday of the Holy Cross (the third Sunday of Great Lent). When the *Epitafios* is in the water, a prayer is sung for the island's sponge divers and sailors.

mer [...] I hope they do not catch Hydra fever.

At the monastery there was the usual fantastic celebration. The old Bishop, now nearly 90, being almost carried into the church by the monks + deakons, being vested with robe after robe, each more gorgeous than the last, the lights going out, the lighting of candles that spread like a forest fire till all the courtyard was alight. The chanting and banging of fireworks [...]

The Mayor [...] let off a bang right under the bishop and frightened the poor old man. When a shopkeeper objected the Mayor lost his temper and punched him. A fight started which had to be broken up by the police [...] Everyone was delighted by the ceremony [...]

There does not seem to be much more news from Hydra. Dinney, the Norwegian girl, her mother + baby went back to Norway yesterday. Iannis is here. David may be coming soon for a short visit. The Johnstones are due at the end of the month. Demetrie has bought his house. Fidel is fat and well and doing nothing. Bim and Bobby[31] are living at Kaminie.

Good luck and very much love to both of you.
Sam

*

2 April 1961, Kythnos.

Marianne,

Sounds of snoring and of frogs croaking in the swamp under a big moon. We are at Kythnos which you should remember.

A long sail today from Hydra. A good breeze to begin with which died away.

---

[31] New Zealander writer Redmond Frankton Wallis and his wife Robyn.

Axel and Pat were on the steamer which passed us as we were approaching Hydra. They came round to the ship later but I was not on board. She was looking well I believe. I fear for Pat […]

We came to Kythnos in the dark. The frogs told us when we were close enough to anchor. Tomorrow the Americans go by donkey to the village. It will be a relief to have the ship to ourselves. So far they have hardly set foot ashore […]

You have told me how things are with you and Leonard and I am happy that this should be so […]

There will come a time when I will meet someone else and fall in love with them, but I think I will not marry until you have married. Don't let this be a heavy thing on you. With me it is light and makes me happy […]

I walked up the valley towards the town of Kythnos yesterday. You remember the valley and the little boy that we could have done without. And I remembered you. And the valley was beautiful and it overlooked the sea. And the Stormie Seas rode so proud and gay. And I felt again all that I had felt with you. And I was so happy. And I felt that if the world passed away and if everything fell apart, I would still be happy.

[…] the one thing I would be glad of, that I am glad of, is the time I had with you […]

And now we are in Mykonos, and I must go ashore and post this letter.

Love to you.

Love to the Eskimo.

Sam

*

10 April 1961, Hydra.

Marianne! Marianne!

[…] the charter has finished […]

Yesterday I went to Athens and to lunch with the Stubbs. I collected the mail from the Consulate before lunch. If the engine is done on time they are all coming down to Spetsai for a few days on Stormie Seas, Joyce, Dick, Linette and the children […] The whole thing was so exciting that I did not realize until I was half-way back to Piraeus in the bus that there was no letter from you at the consulate. This is a good thing, I think, as a little time ago that would have been the first thing that I would have looked for […]

So good-night, Marianne. Take care of yourself. And take care of your boy. It makes me feel good to be his god-father. I surpose that he is walking now, nearly 15 months old. And you are 26 just about now. Happy Birthday, wise old Marianne!

*

20 April 1961.

Marianne!

I had just made up my mind to forget all about you. And today a letter came […]

I am so sorry, Marianne, that you feel lonely + I am sorry that you feel doubtful. Of course I feel lonely too and that is why I write to you. I have not been so lonely lately though. For the last four days, when we had no charter, I took Dick and Joyce Stubbs, their two children and Lenette down to Hydra and Spetsai and stopped again at Hydra and Poros on the way back […]

In Hydra, on the way back, while we were in the harbour, the Johnstones arrived. They had all, encluding George, put on weight and all lost their sun-tan. The Camerons had organized a great reception for them with paper banners etc. […]

Lenette re-organized the medicine-locker down the foc'stle. That is to say that we reorganized it together. She is a sweet person […] I am glad that I have a man cook this year. I want to be peaceful and to get things sorted out. And things would not be peaceful if Lenette were on board.

I took a good look at her this time. She is tall, and quiet, and dignified, and has very fine hands […] She is so very much one of my own kind, of the people that I came out here to get away from.

I am glad that you write me your grumbles, and glad that you are demonstrating in blue-jeans and jersey against city life. I would like to help you find a job in Greece. But it would be difficult even without the Eskimo […]

I think that anyone who lives in Hydra has got to be their own judge, be able to point the finger at themselves and say "What you are doing is wrong!" For that is the difference between Hydra and the other places. In Hydra there is no one else to point the finger. And for most people the fact that they feel like doing something is justification enough. Maybe you could live on Hydra, but, like everyone else, I think you would have a pretty hard time.

I am sorry that Leonard is in Cuba[32] and I hope he comes to you very soon. Cuba cannot be a good place right now […]

The cranes are creaking and groaning as they dredge the harbour. Dereck sniffs. The lamp swings as a ship goes by. The bulkheads creak and Baba-Ianni is fast asleep.

And now I have many letters to write, and such

---

[32] Eager to follow in the footsteps of the Spanish poet Federico Garcia Lorca, whom he greatly admired, Leonard Cohen went to Cuba in early 1961. He stayed for three months, during which time the US invaded the Bahía de Cochinos (the Bay of Pigs).

a short time.

God bless you, Marianne, God bless your Eskimo,

LOVE, Sam.

*

25 April 1961, Amorgos.

Well, Marianne!

I wonder how you are, and what news of Leonard. They seem to have put so many people in gaol in Cuba although, if one can believe the news, they seem to have treated Canadians well [...]

All our Americans (except one) are away on donkeys. They have gone for five hours on a rough road to see the monastery [...]

When you wrote the last letter (15th) you were lonely. I hope you are not lonely now. When I get lonely, I take you with me. I took you with me at Dhelos one early morning and we had a wonderful time. We did not look at the ruins much. But the flowers were everywhere and quite beautiful, poppies, tall yellow daisies, rough blue flowers like sea-lavender, thistles of all sorts and sizes, and thick patches of little mauve vetches like a heavy piled carpet wherever the grass was short [...]

And at Naxos yesterday morning I took you with me in the car to see the gigantic marble statue of Appollo where it lay unfinnished in a quarry on the far side of the island [...]

Down at the port again we bought some bottles of wine at 2½ drachmae a kilo (about 1½ drachmae a bottle). The bottles cost 2½ drachmae each and the man cut the corks out of a slab with his pocket-knife.

*

11 June 1961.

Marianne!

And now a letter from you, posted in OSLO on the 5th.

I am glad that you have heard from Leonard and that he is alright. As you say you will do what you have to do. And as you say, you have to think for the Eskimo too. You say the best thing would be to get your divorce and start to get married again. If you mean what I think you mean by this I don't agree at all and I thought you had learned more sense from what has already happened. That is to say, if you cannot marry Leonard, get a good job and wait until the right person comes along, as he will, or else, when he does, you will just be in another mess. Of course there is more than one person you could marry, Marianne, but for you, he must be one of the right kind and not just the first one that comes along that can offer you security […]

Lots of brotherly-sisterly, uncley kind of love to you –

And god-fatherly love to my Eskimo. And if you ever want to come back into my innermost of innermost places you had better be jolly quick about it.

Sam

*

19 July 1961.

Marianne! Marianne!

Back in port again […]

James comes out in 2 weeks time. That will be fun. I shall miss him when he goes away.

We saw an enormous shark the other day, a hammer-headed shark [...] One of the boys on board (19) and I went away in the dinghy to harpoon him. We the first excitement wore off I must say I wondered what I was doing as he was longer than our dinghy (our dinghy is eleven feet) and could have easily upset it if he had wanted to [...] Mitso managed to manoever Stormie Seas close enough to him and Dereck-the-cook twice hit him with a harpoon but the harpoon only bounced off [...]

Now, in ten minutes, new charterers come on board. So good-bye, Marianne. Good-bye Joacim.

I long to hear your news.

LOVE,

Sam

*

2 to 30 August 1961, Pireaus and Rhodes.

Marianne!

Our letters seem to have crossed, both written on the same day.

It is one o'clock in the morning now. We got in today at 12:00. I buzzed straight up to Athens to collect the mail. I was so glad to get your letter. Sad that you were feeling sad. I think that this is a most important time for you [...]

I was in Hydra two days ago. George and Charm seem well. They are resting on George's laurels, doing up the house, putting in a fire-place etc. but not writing. Martin has passed his exams for the Hydra High-School and Shane was top of her form. So they are, as ever, proud parents.

Leonard is in Hydra. I met him in the bank just as we were leaving and did not have time to talk to him which I hope to do when we go back there […]

Now it is seven thirty in the morning. Mitso has just gone grumbling off ashore to buy bread and peaches. Dereck is down in the galley brewing up coffee. It is hot and still […] James comes out tomorrow. Very exciting […]

In the consulate I bumped into Sybel Whinney who, when seven years old, used to look after James and change his nappies. He was seven weeks old then, living in a basket under the main boom when Stormie Seas was in Mina's cove at Poros. We were in Mina's cove again only yesterday and I saw Mina again for the first time in ten years. What a lot has happened in those ten years, Marianne. […]

Oh dear! Every day I have been meaning to write to you and every day it has seemed so impossible. Early morning is about the only time to write but we have been getting up early to avoid the Meltemi[33] and by evening we can hardly stay awake […]

James is on board, very well and happy […] I shall miss him when he goes as you can immagine. He lives on deck or in the water and really only comes down below to change his clothes.

We have been to lots of places that you know and are going to many more […] Mrs Stanning […] says Hydra is a "Tourist Trap" and does not want to go there. What they really enjoy are "Tourist Traps" anyway so I don't know what she is talking about. They have travelled around in busses with hordes of other tourists ever since they got to Rhodes and have enjoyed themselves more here than they have on all the rest of the

---

[33] Strong northerly winds that develop in the summer when high pressure forms over the Balkans and low pressure forms over Turkey. Meltemi come up in clear weather and blow hard. They often die down at night.

trip. Dereck has his mail there[34] and is mad to get there. James has the Johnstones. And of course Mitso has his family in Hydra so it will be a bit of a tragedy if we do not get there. I learned on our arrival in Rhodes that we have a new charter from Sept 18th – 28th. And most probably another after our October one which should take us up to the end of that month. If both those come off it will have been a very good year for us […]

Love to you, Marianne, and to the Eskimo
Sam

P.S. James very much wants a Norwegian knife like the one I got in Norway. If you could send one to him at […], London S.W.3. I would send you the money for it.

*

31 October 1961, Spetsai.

Marianne!

I have not heard from you for so long. I worry about you and wonder how you are getting on […] I hear news of you via George and Leonard but it is vague, second-hand, and none of it seems very good news. Please write and tell me everything that is happening and say if I can do anything for you out here. How is the Eskimo? Is your divorce going through? And did you ever enclude a clause for maintenance of Joacim?! I ask this as his godfather and your friend, Marianne. Axel is his father and that is the very least that he can do.

Are you still working with the film company? I think it is as well you did not come out here this year.

---

[34] On Hydra.

Our chartering is over now [...] We started cruising on 31st March and finnished 28th October (7 months), of which we were actually cruising 6 months and 6 days. Of this we were chartered for 150 days (5 months + 10 days). The rest was with friends. All in all a very good season [...]

Marianne, do you want the job of cook next summer!? [...]

35

---

[35] This drawing appears in a letter dated 2 August 1961.

At First Sight

Brian Sidaway

> Of the many things which the modern world has
> lost, one which it should deeply regret is the com-
> ing into a foreign harbour under sail.[1]

It was early spring in 1966, and an accident really or if not an
accident then at least unplanned. After a late lunch one Friday in
Pasalimani we had adjourned to a nearby yacht for a few drinks
more before the English girls had to be back to work at their shipping offices. One of the crew thought it might be fun to slip the
lines and let the yacht *gently* drift out into the harbour. No one
noticed. No one noticed anything until we were by now out of the
harbour entrance and setting sails. Still very quietly. No engine
had been started. Now that the sails were up we thought that we
might as well have a sail. We had all been more or less "shang-
haied." In those days there was no way of calling the office to say
we had been kidnapped.

The breeze freshened and it soon became "easier" and more
fun to continue to Poros and send the would-be mutineers back
by ferry. I won't at this time tell about that night in Poros except
to say that in those years there was a taverna along the waterfront
that had a reputation for its retsina and the dancing fishermen
and sailors from the Naval Academy. It was a large warehouse of

---

[1] From Charles Landery, *Whistling for a Wind* (Phoenix House, London, 1952, p. 74), in
which the quotation is attributed to Joseph Conrad, *The Mirror of the Sea* (Methuen, London, 1906). However, a search of Conrad's book fails to turn up these lines.

a building with one wall stacked from floor to ceiling with huge barrels of retsina. I don't remember the food.

Late the next morning it was decided that as we were already in Poros we might as well sail on to Hydra. That is the way decisions were made then.

There was not much wind as we motored slowly out of Poros toward "the gap" of Tselivinia. The morning coffees were taking effect now and it was noticed how still it was. Now as we passed Tselivinia we realised that a dense sea fog had settled between the mainland and our destination of Hydra. A very rare event. Serious navigation had not been an issue until now. The old sailors' cry went up: "Where the fuck are we?" Time now to look at the compass and plot a course toward the harbour of Hydra, wherever it was. Sailing in a fog is disorienting to say the least. No radar or GPS then. Just trust the compass, guess your speed and hope that you see something before you run into it.

~

At last there was some shape ahead. Solid land, a mountain, a cliff face emerging out of the gloom. Then suddenly we could see something. Crenelated bastions? Cannons? Cannons to the left and cannons to the right. Into the harbour of Hydra sailed the six lost sailors.

Like a watercolour painting with soft pale colours and blurred edges or like watching a photograph slowly develop in a dark room, there were houses, houses seemingly stacked upon each other rising higher and higher. It was magic. I do not think that we ever forgot our first sight of Hydra: this was something that might never be repeated.

It was so still and quiet with none of the usual port hustle and bustle that is the Hydra of today. It was my first night on Hydra and my first night at Lulu's and my first night sleeping in the cane chairs at Tassos' Bar.

~

In the years that followed I would become a regular sailor to Hydra. I was first working as a deck hand then First Mate, then finally a Skipper on a variety of sailing yachts.

A one-week charter would take in the main Saronic Islands with visits to Aegina, Poros, Hydra and Spetsai. In those days the individual characters of the islands were quite distinct. Aegina had Old World charm, Neoclassical houses and horse-drawn carriages plying the waterfront and excellent fish restaurants, which were the first stop. Then maybe next morning there was a visit to the truly beautiful Temple of Aphaia perched high on the northern tip of the island. They say that in ancient times you could see the sunlight flash from the helmet on the statue of Athena on the Acropolis. It is only a distance of eighteen miles so I believe it.

Next was Poros, where you entered the almost hidden narrow entrance on the north west end into a large well protected bay with many coves and dense green pines all the way down to the water's edge sheltered from the ever present summer Meltemi. Perfect to tie a rope around those trees and not have to worry about having an anchor dragging in the soft mud and grass bottom. On a full moon night at certain times of the year it was a wonder to swim among the plankton blooms. Diving from the deck of the yacht into the water would light up a trail of sparkling lights along your body. We would take turns to dive while the others would watch underwater with mask and snorkel. Screams of delight as we lit up like Tinker Bells with flashes of light streaming off our bodies and fingertips as we arced through the water.

Further down the bay, towards the town of Poros, the great grey dreadnought battleship *Averof* was a survivor of WWI and still somehow ominous. There were many tavernas strung out like lights along the quayside, ideal for watching the passing traffic as ferries, yachts and cargo boats slid by slowly in the very narrow channel between the island of Poros and the mainland opposite. Poros had always been famous for its "dancing" tavernas as the Naval Academy was just out of town by the *Averof* and the sailor boys and the fishermen had an outlet and nothing is quite like a wide-eyed audience of young tourist girls to stoke the egos and get their competitive dancing started.

Then on to Hydra, already becoming my home port. I now proudly flew the "battle flag" of Hydra wherever I sailed. I was getting to *know* the waterfront locals and more importantly getting to know the harbour. Hydra port is not a Great Harbour like San Francisco or Sydney. Hydra is more of a cove really. It is protected by an outer wall but it is tiny. It is the miniature scale of the setting with the towering stone bastions and great old *archontiko* buildings of the 18th century surrounding the port that makes it so famous. You don't want to "steam" into Hydra at any speed. Suddenly there is not room. Not room enough to turn, not room to stop a yacht with a couple of tons of lead in its keel. You learn to make your manoeuvres in slow motion. At any time there could be two or three other yachts in motion inside the harbour, all trying to choose a place to anchor or trying to retrieve a fouled anchor from the night before, all in the middle of the harbour. There is never a dull moment in Hydra harbour. You can spend a pleasant few hours watching the action while having an ouzo or two at one of the waterfront cafés. Like holding up the score cards at the Olympic diving, we would rate the efforts of the skippers. If a real problem arose there was always a willing Pan to help out.

What Pan, short for Pandelis, lacked in height he doubled in heart. Short, barrel-chested, with a great beard and the tiniest feet you can imagine, he was Pan. Pan, the unofficial Harbour Master. It was Pan that you went to if you needed any local knowledge. Pan and "Walrus" Niko (the moustache), Ilias the "water man" and "Captain" Giannis, a lovable scalawag who was a little retarded but still a functioning part of the waterfront activity, made up a welcoming team for any yacht visiting Hydra. Captain Giannis could catch a heavy rope and tie a bowline faster than any one I knew, and he got it right the first time. (Sailors will know what I mean.)

The island of Spestai was a different story. It was a little bit haughty to my mind but then it did have a famous old boys' school to its credit and old aristocratic villas to match the old aristocratic Athenians who still went there for their summers. White suits and straw Panama hats were the evening promenade dress code, and even some silver tipped walking canes. Very elegant, but not very friendly. The best anchorage was in the "Old Creek," as it was known. Here on both sides caïques were still being built and repaired with traditional methods. Huge skeletal frames on the water's edge were painted the orange-red colour of "red" lead or minion, as the locals called it. This poisonous brew stopped the woodworms and barnacles from eating the Samos pine hulls.

It was here in Baltiza Creek that the famous *Stormie Seas* was based. Built in Perama in about 1949, I think, she was at forty-eight feet on deck, a dark blue hulled schooner with sails "tanned" with red ochre. A beautiful sight under full sail. It had been built for an Englishman, Sam Barclay, and although it looked like a caïque, in fact below the waterline it was a pure Colin Archer designed Norwegian fishing boat. Heavy but seaworthy and fast on a beam reach, it could even go to windward as well as most schooners can (which is not well at all but I won't get into that here). The Greek sailors who were not aware of the *Stormie Seas'* heritage would be amazed as the traditional caïque does not actually sail very well. A big old "one lung-er" single-cylinder diesel now fitted to most working caïques had done away with the sailing arts and now the stubby mast was used only as a deck crane and sometimes to set a small steadying jib, to stop the rolling.

On any day back then you would see the large ketches, yawls and schooners of the wealthy under full sail with their uniformed crews working hard to trim the sails. There were not roller furling sails and hydraulic winches then. All was done by hand: hanking on the foresails, hauling up the mainsails, sheeting in the sails with a block and tackle. Maybe there was a powered anchor winch if you were lucky. The wealthy Greek ship owners of those times had a taste for these elegant sailing yachts. Now they have gone for the most part, replaced by ever larger motor yachts that are more like floating apartments in *Architectural Digest* rather than vessels designed by naval architects.

≈

The Saronic Gulf had become my backyard and now all these years later I still love to take friends out on a sail to explore the many little bays and coves that are not so well known. There is still a sense of adventure to anchor in some sheltered spot and swim ashore to explore, to find some long forgotten pottery shards or a large carved piece of some ancient stone building that seems now so lost and alone among the nettles, with nothing else around to say what this place might have once been.

Hydra is still like that too. To anyone arriving for the first time there is still a sense of timelessness. Walk any street and you will find pieces of carved marble fragments of some grand old structure: a piece of a marble column, a carved ornamental pediment now being used as a step, an old anchor so huge that you wonder how it was ever manhandled on the deck of a sailing boat. The beauty of Hydra is there to be discovered anew, to be seen with fresh eyes.

There is the first time for everything and though it was many years ago now that I first sighted Hydra appearing out of the fog as it did, I still see that look in the eyes of young people as the ferry makes that last turn to port and the amphitheatre of Hydra opens like a stage setting. So little changed after all these years.

Wine Dark Sea

Charlotte Mensforth

I sometimes think that Hydra was like a theatre, and the port, or as it was known, the *agora*, was our stage, for it was indeed built like an amphitheatre and we like so many actors were playing our roles. We would come down to that stage when one of the boats came in with the mail and we would collect our post, if any, and wait to see who our fellow actors might be that morning. Did we gossip, I wonder, and did we also drink? Of course most people did, for we were all acting out our secret dreams.

Some say the Greeks judge colour not by its tone but from its intensity. They call it thick and dark as a glass of Samos wine. So we would come and go, sit and watch the stage, but for me Hydra would always be the island of the intense blue sea. "Wine dark," they said. That would never change.

~

I first arrived on Hydra one September morning in 1961. In those days it was a big adventure to travel to Greece and I had been invited by an art school friend, Niobe, to visit her in Athens. She, like me, was studying at the Central School of Art in London. Foreigners in the late Fifties were still something of a novelty. She loved London and I in my turn used to sit fascinated at her table in the Common Room and listen to her description of Greece, of the islands and life there. It sounded so exotic and so different from post-war England and I knew immediately that it was a place I wanted to see, to paint or maybe to change my life.

Yet what did I know of Greece? – a few hazy notions of Greek history, a visit to the British Museum to see the Elgin Marbles, where we learned the three orders of classical column when we studied the rudiments of architecture at art school, that was all. Yet I had just landed a commission to do a poster for the London Underground and would soon have money, so I decided to buy a ticket and go to Greece.

In those days travel was not as simple as it is today and one did not hop on an aeroplane and in a few hours arrive at a remote island. If such a flight existed, plane tickets were expensive to those destinations. Niobe told me that a travel agency in the Haymarket, advertising Cunard and P & O Liners could perhaps help.

"Yes," they said, "there is a ship from Brindisi to Piraeus that takes on passengers." I bought a one-way ticket and the die was cast.

First I would visit Athens and then it was arranged for me to stay at one of the houses – set up, I think, by the Greek government – which offered lodging, an easel and a place to paint for a legitimate art student. The fee was ludicrously small, one could stay ten days and the house chosen for me was on Hydra.

"Very beautiful," said Niobe, when I told her about it. "Lots of artists go there. Hydra is really just a rock, but the colour of the sea: you wait, you will not believe it."

How I travelled from Brindisi to Piraeus on an old tramp steamer along the coast of Albania, that belongs to another story. We called in at Corfu, where a group of locals came aboard and sat in a group on deck, there were children eating grapes and the women had coins in their hair and I think somebody had a goat. I had never seen people like this before. The sea had already changed colour. It was a darker blue and I was in a different world.

I spent a few days with Niobe and her husband but it was hardly time to become adjusted to the strangeness of it all: a visit to the archaeological museum, a taverna in Plaka, traffic, dusty streets, sandals, the smell of sun on hot pavements and the Greeks, who had no hesitation in staring at foreigners. "*Xeni eisai*," they would shout and even point. "You are a foreigner." I suppose to them I did look different for in those days all Athenians were conservative in the way they dressed. "Do not worry about their stares," Niobe told me. "They are just interested."

It was early September and the weather was still hot. Niobe explained how I must take the little train from Monastiraki to Piraeus to catch the boat for Hydra and I immediately felt apprehensive for this would be the first time on my own in Athens.

All boats to the Saronic Gulf sailed at eight o'clock and by a quarter to eight it already looked to me like total confusion. How did I manage to carry my very English suitcase across the quayside? I did, as touts descended on the waiting passengers waving tickets. There were three boats, the *Portokalis Ilios*, the *Neraida* and the *Pindos*. I think that I chose the *Neraida* and struggled on board with my case and like everybody else grabbed a chair on deck. There were boys selling cashew nuts, hot *tiropita* – cheese pies – and families had already made little groups, talking and eating. It was three and an half hours to Hydra.

I still remember the magic of that first trip. I made it many times later and then with familiarity I took less notice of it all for we do forget how beautiful it was. Aegina, Methana, with its houses of blank windows staring at you, and then the straits of Poros, where the trees came down to the water's edge, their reflections in the water, which was like a transparent pool. Poros, white Poros, on the hill above the strait, then through the gap as the wind got up, and into the yet more vivid wine dark sea and there on the horizon was the rock that was Hydra.

I was met off the boat by an elderly Greek who spoke some English, and to my surprise seemed to know exactly who I was. He took my suitcase and carried it on one shoulder, and I followed him across the *agora*, up a flight of impossibly intricate steps to an old Venetian-style palace above the port. I think they called it in those days the Art School, and it was where I would be staying.

I remember my room with its tall windows and a view over the harbour. There was a familiar artist's easel in one corner, and scrubbed wooden floors, a bed, rough cotton sheets and a blanket. It was all very simple. I was taken downstairs to meet the Director. He spoke some French, as the older generation did in Greece in those days. He welcomed me to the island and said he hoped that I would have all that I needed and that I would perhaps later show him some of my work. I was then left pretty much to my own devices.

~

This early part of my stay passed as in a dream. I went out early in the morning to explore, climbing the flights of steps that led to the houses on the hill above the *agora*. There was no traffic, for Hydra only possessed one battered truck, which took the rubbish to the dump along the cliff. There was no noise of cars yet there was always the noise of people, the sound of a donkey braying, footsteps, men with their loaded mules clattering down the steps, women with baskets, children and stray cats.

I took my paper and watercolours and started to paint. The colours came strangely to those first impressions, colours I hardly recognised, transparent and delicate. When the sun is at its zenith, Greek colours become translucent, difficult to capture, as if the sun has stolen their very energy. I soon discovered the difficulty of trying to be alone in Greece: take out your paints and one is surrounded, like moths to the flame, by children and grown-ups, by men asking questions I did not understand. I tried to choose my spot with care, but it is impossible to have secrets in Greece.

Where did I eat? I hardly remember. There was one restaurant on the *agora* with rather untempting food. There were cafés with chairs that had cane seats, always set out in pairs, one on which to sit and one, I noticed, mostly used to put your feet. The cafés served very little food, just thick dark Turkish coffee, and I learned to ask for *ena metrio* or an ouzo, accompanied by some black olives or a piece of dried and extremely tough octopus, and always, but always, a glass of water. I think in those days there was no what I would call European-style coffee and there was certainly no Coca-Cola. There was a grocer's shop, part-café, on the corner called Katsikas', which maybe also offered bread and cheese. They stocked a few provisions, feta kept in open tins, the tins looking as if they were once used as petrol cans, perhaps they were; and there were sacks of beans and rice. There was not very much else to buy.

~

By the time I arrived in late September there were few visitors on the island; the Greeks had returned to Athens, and the old palace was nearly empty. There were a couple of girls also staying there from Germany who were art students like myself. They invited me to go swimming, and they took me along the narrow path that led to the rocks just round the corner from the port. You swam in water of the most beautiful and intense blue, the most beautiful water I had ever seen. As Niobe had said, I could not believe my eyes. Deep and clear, was it near green or sometimes purple? It was on that sunny morning that we met the son of the Mylonas family – Greeks from Athens – who owned a house on the island. Konstantinos, introduced himself; his father was an architect and his mother director of a dance company. I remember he invited us up to their house, "To meet Sylvia," he said. "She is English."

You could not miss the house from the port for it was one of the highest and the only one with a big picture window. Such a climb, and then, the view! I came to know it well for the family invited me to stay, suggesting I could be company for Sylvia, who seemed delighted. She wanted to stay longer on the island she explained, but had not liked the idea of being alone. My time at the old Venetian palace was drawing to a close, so what a piece of luck, I thought, and for the moment it suited both of us and I accepted.

∼

I did not see much of the Mylonas family during my stay for they were now mostly in Athens, but I learnt something of them or certainly about the architecture of Konstantinos' father from living at that extraordinary house. He was, I discovered, from the generation of architects who were going to build "beautifully" for a new Greek industry: tourism. Niobe had already shown me what later became my favourite café, by the Acropolis under the olive trees and facing Mount Lykabettos: I thought it stunning. "This is how they plan to build," she told me. I then heard Kyrios Mylonas had finished an hotel of a similar style on the hillside outside Athens.

The Mylonas house was old, but so far only one large room, the room with the magnificent view, had been transformed and the rest of the house remained unaltered. The room was very simple with low couches and very little other furniture but it was the ceiling that was so extraordinary; yet it worked, for it was entirely papered with grey egg-carton boxes.

Sylvia and I spent the next few weeks together. We lived in the room with the picture window and slept at the back of the house and tried our best to cook on a one-burner stove in a tiny kitchen.

"You wait … you see how I will make this house," said my architect host. I was learning about Greece.

Sylvia, I discovered, was a fund of knowledge and she spoke Greek for she had been visiting Greece for many years. We went walking to Kamini and the little beach at Vlychos, and we looked after the house and I found quiet corners to paint; she was great company for me then. We drew water from the well and only the large room had electricity. A neighbourly fisherman would come round to the house and Sylvia would hand out bread and toma-to to his hungry children and one day the father took us fishing off the island we called Whale Island. Some days we would walk the many steps down to the *agora* and bring back groceries from Katsikas'.

"Kyrios Mylonas says that it all goes on his bill," Sylvia explained.

So that was how it was.

∾

Often the tables outside Katsikas' would have foreigners sitting and drinking.

"When they are here the Mylonas are always on the beach," Sylvia told me. "They like to go every day to Mandraki, so they hardly socialise, but that couple, I believe, are two Australian writers. He is called George Johnston and the lady with him in the hat, her name is Charmian. I heard he is writing a book about Australia. The younger man is a Canadian poet called Leonard Cohen and the other two are Chuck and Gordon, dancers from New York. They own a house here and have painted their door black. None of the Greeks approve of the colour," she added, "but I rather like it."

I wanted to know more, but Sylvia though obviously well informed was not one for gossip. She only commented that she had heard the foreigners drank a lot. Sylvia rarely drank and she had always stayed with the Mylonas family. I did not take the questions further but secretly I was intrigued.

~

Now autumn was approaching and some nights the wind rattled against the badly fitting shutters and then the daily boat was late to arrive. There were warm days when you thought the weather would last like this for ever; but we both knew it was time to leave. Sylvia and I went back to Athens and through the Mylonas family I found a job looking after the children of a Greek ship-owner. It was an experience in itself and I stayed three months and saved a little money.

On my free mornings when the children were at school I would walk up to the Acropolis and sit at the lovely café or sometimes I would explore the little area above Plaka known as Anafiotika. Life with the family was not easy for I soon found out that I was not a person best suited to looking after Greek children. I was longing to leave and it was in Anafiotika one winter morning that I met John. He was sitting on the terrace of his little house cleaning a decorative oil lamp and we started talking; the house was filled like an Aladdin's cave with curiosities.

He told me there was quite a community of foreigners living in this area below the Acropolis and he had a little room to let, he said, and maybe there was a job teaching English. I soon disentangled myself from the family and moved into Anafiotika and thus began another life. We made a trip together to Turkey and brought back cloth from Istanbul, exotic prints with flowers and vivid colours, and I had clothes made up by the Anafiotika tailor. I became more exotic. It was as if the patina of a Surrey upbringing was slowly being removed. There were parties and we made visits to the Monastiraki flea market at the bottom of the steps by the *agora*, and people came to his house as a constant stream of visitors. I was also teaching English.

Was it really me? I hardly noticed; it was all so different and so very different from living with a rich Greek family who had a large apartment just off Syntagma.

John's terrace was like open house to the many people who passed along that dusty path and one of the friends who came to see us in those early days was Marcelle Maltais. Marcelle was a French–Canadian painter and had just come back from Hydra. She had to return to Paris she said, and wondered if John would be able to look after Mustafina, her favourite cat?

"And," she added as a sort of afterthought, "you can use the house when I am away."

I remember the enormous iron key she gave to us. Mustafina, a sprightly tortoiseshell, arrived in a basket some days later. So John and I had acquired a key, a cat, and if only for a short time a house on Hydra. This was how our weekends began.

∾

John had never seen the house, though from Marcelle's description I thought I knew where to find it. We took the train down to Piraeus and caught the early boat and then climbed the long flight of steps from the *agora* up the hill towards Kamini, along a street we always called "Donkey Shit Lane"; I do not think I ever learned its real name. We climbed with Mustafina in her basket up over the crest which overlooked the next valley. There was the house, quite unassuming from the path: one big central wooden door with long windows either side. You found the entrance round the back, Marcelle had explained. "Go through a door and into the courtyard. The key will open a second door into the kitchen."

Marcelle had been able to buy the house for a song some years ago, she told us, when she first discovered Hydra, but unlike the Mylonas house it remained unchanged. It was still a traditional Hydriot house, unmodernised and without electricity, for very few houses had such a luxury in those days. We pushed open the old wooden door onto a little courtyard and let an excited Mustafina out of the basket. This was her own familiar territory and with the large key we opened the door into the kitchen hardly knowing what to expect. It was a kitchen as kitchens had always been on Hydra, with its cistern for storing rainwater, a fireplace and a stone sink under the window. It was not until you climbed the wooden ladder to the room above to Marcelle's studio that you found the joy of the house. I saw that view which looked towards the sea, towards Kamini with Whale Island beyond. It was more intimate than the view from the Mylonas house yet far more beautiful.

~

The house became a sort of home to me. Sometimes John and I came alone, sometimes we came with two English friends from Anafiotika. We were all teaching English so we were only able to stay for a few days at a time. It was like an adventure to us, lighting oil lamps, a fire in the kitchen, learning the right way to throw a bucket down a cistern to bring up water: water collected on the roof from the winter rains that was always quite sweet and fresh to drink. We took picnics of feta and bread onto the hillside and walked along the cliffs by the sea. A quick visit to the *agora* to do some shopping was our only contact with Hydra life, for the tiny store near us at the top of the hill sold only paraffin and basic provisions; we were happy just staying up at the house. I remember there was often that same small group of foreigners sitting at Katsikas' when the morning boat came in.

"I think those are some of Marcelle's friends," John said.

"She spoke about them."

We left it at that.

~

Hydra came as an escape to another world for all of us after teaching in Athens and I began to feel that I wanted to paint again. I still had the group of paintings I did when first I arrived on the island and the ones I had painted when I was staying with the Mylonas family. I looked at them again: had I done these? They were so direct and strong and even Kyrios Mylonas had admired them. Somehow in Athens life was too hectic, or the life that I was living did not seem to lend itself to painting. Then one day I noticed Marcelle's easel in a corner of her studio: an accusation, a temptation or a reminder.

It was on one of the walks we took to Vlychos that we first found the ruins. They were on the right-hand side of the path in a large abandoned garden of olive and lemon trees overlooking the sea. It was a magical place. We would sit in the garden and wonder who had lived there and try to recreate the house.

For what reason, we wondered, had it been left to fall into ruins, for just a few walls of the old house remained and abandoned in the garden were still remnants of shutters eaten away by wind and rain. Wicked or not, for they were mere skeletons held together by a few iron rivets, we took three of them away and on Marcelle's easel and, with the powdered colours I found in a local shop and used by the locals for painting their boats, I started to paint. It was exhilarating. I painted a head of a woman in a large hat, and I painted a decoration of flowers and a bird of paradise. Much later when I returned to the island I was told the pictures had been found in the house where I had left them and sold as the work of an undiscovered primitive painter for a considerable sum. I have often wondered who owns them now.

Could it have been the visits to Marcelle's house that helped to keep John and me together? I do not know, but I began to sense how fragile was our joint life for we were companions in a sort of dream. He had his teaching job in Athens and he had his friends. I was flattered to be seen on his arm, to have his admiration, and I loved my new collection of brightly coloured clothes. I dyed my hair red to suit my mood and had a cloak with a fox fur collar we christened "Foxy Foxy" and we would walk through Athens watching people turn their heads to stare. It was all theatre and I was uneasy but I was swept away by this different world.

That late spring Marcelle came back to Greece. Mustafina, with her new litter of kittens, was returned to her owner and we were offered – by chance – a house in the valley, just below a tiny church. It had no sea view and it had just two rooms and there was a small stony garden. John said he was full of plans, so we built a dining table out of an old door and I painted a decoration round one of the windows. The little garden took on shape, but I think we both knew that we would not spend that summer together.

~

Perhaps it was the discovery of the taverna we all called "Lulu's" that made me question the life I was leading. Lulu's was totally Greek and was in a little back street behind the *agora* and was always crowded. Perhaps I had been there with Sylvia, I cannot remember, or did I go there first with John when we were spending weekends at Marcelle's house? They played Greek music and we drank too much retsina and often ouzo. An Hydriot would link an arm with you across the table and call "*Aspro pato!*" and you emptied your glass in one quick swig. I used to watch the sailors from the Naval School above the port dance *rembetiko*; they danced with the few foreigners and with each other. Once one of the boys leapt round the room with a laid table clenched between his teeth. We clapped and danced and laughed. I watched the boys dancing together. Was it the same as the gay world John had introduced me to in Athens? No here it was part of a tradition that was Greece. But this other side to life existed in Hydra too.

A boy would sit at the table of a likely friend and perhaps the friend had money, and a few nice presents were always acceptable. For after all, such a relationship was an old custom in Greece. The family considered it a good experience and no son could be married until all his sisters were taken care of and the dowry paid. Then he would settle down to married life and raise a family. I began to notice how certain cafés on the *agora* were used as meeting places by the dapper naval cadets. Like Athens, Hydra was changing for me; there were many Hydras, depending on how and where you looked.

~

How can we describe a place after so many years? Am I looking back at Hydra as I remember it, for I still have clear memories of its stark landscape, its houses and the wine dark sea, or are we looking back and merely looking for ourselves? The two are forever interwoven. That long hot summer I try to describe is, I realise, as much a picture of myself as it is of the people who lived there and an island I knew, all those years ago.

Summer came and every day brought more visitors on the morning boats and it was no longer the Hydra of the winter months. I was also becoming a different person. I was discovering that good weather was the norm, that swimming and living outside were part of everyday life; even the heat did not bother me for I was always busy at the little house in Kamini.

Once John came back from Athens where he had been teaching just as I finished the decoration around one of the windows. It was hardly serious painting but I was enjoying myself. When I met him off the boat I could see that he was excited.

"Darling," he said, "it is just divine. I have put down a deposit. It's French I think."

"But what," I asked somewhat confused. "What is it?"

"A grand piano, darling. We need the space for the piano. It will all be marvellous for entertaining."

"Entertaining": of course, I knew what he meant. And so that is how it came about.

But for now and I would stay on in Hydra. Yes, it would be best that way; it was bittersweet, for I knew that I had grown to love him, perhaps we loved each other, and yet it would be better that we separated, at least for a time. John, I felt, wanted his independence and perhaps I too would be happier. A grand piano and a large apartment could not disguise the way things were. I went with him down to the port to catch the afternoon boat for Piraeus and I believe he thought that I would join him later; perhaps I too thought that but for now I knew I needed to stay on, at least for the summer. It was a hard moment.

≈

I think that summer on Hydra began with meeting Magda, beautiful Magda who had opened a boutique at the bottom of Donkey Shit Lane. It was in an old house just before you turned onto the *agora* and her boutique was very different from anything you could find in those days on Hydra. It was elegant and it had clothes that she designed, and I think that there were antiques for sale as well. The clothes were mainly dresses, very simple, in bright colours but decorated with her own drawings of flowers and birds. The designs, she told me, were taken from the traditional decorations used in the old houses of Czechoslovakia, for Magda was Czech. She later taught me how to use the special paints, and that summer I wore and then kept for many years an orange cotton dress which I had made. It was in the style of what was called a petticoat dress, with very narrow straps, and across the top I had painted one of my favourite birds.

I worked for a time looking after the shop; Magda needed someone to sit in for her, but she would often come and talk and see how thing were going. Magda! I think she was the first exotic character I met on Hydra. Her background, it was said, was from one of the great families of a long-past and different Europe and she was someone you always noticed: prematurely grey haircut in a short bob, a squarish jaw and a natural elegance in all she wore. She had lived in Paris and spoke French and English perfectly, and Greek. Then there was the handsome Theodoros who came often to the shop, just to pass the time of day, he told me. I heard that they were married but she never said and I never felt inclined to ask. Stories circulated that Theodoros had once been to prison for a theft of money; others said that he had been wrongly accused. This was some of the usual gossip of Hydra.

~

It was about then, I think in 1962, that I also met Lisette. I had noticed her welcoming people off the morning boat. She was always elegant, but in a Fifties sort of way: blonde, with very red lipstick, espadrilles and shorts. I was told that she ran the guest house above the *agora* near the house where I had first stayed on Hydra. She had rather exclusive guests, and she was very English and I can only describe her as what we called in those days "Mayfair." Her boyfriend, she told me, had been one of the famous racing drivers of the time and when I went to visit her later in London she had rented a flat behind Harrods.

Lisette invited me up to the guest house to help, or perhaps to translate for the guests, for my Greek by this time, although a trifle picturesque from the vocabulary I had picked up in Athens, was now much more fluent. I began to spend a lot of time there.

I started to meet another sort of Hydra society – or shall I say visitor – who was quite different from Magda's many friends and certainly very different from the people I had met with John at Lulu's. These were well to do people from England on their first exciting Greek holiday and in the evenings they would sit until the small hours at Lisette's long dining table, talking of Hydra and the legends associated with the house. There had been scandals, even a suspected murder in the hills when a previous English family lived there. It of course fascinated the guests.

Lisette often arranged excursions for her visitors and sometimes I went with them. There would be a hamper of food and a fishing boat would take us to a cove beyond Vlychos where nobody went in those days. We plunged into the deep cool water with only a deserted shore for company. I remember Chuck came with us on one occasion, and we talked about Magda's boutique and the changes he had seen on Hydra. For me those were idyllic days.

It was about this time that Lisette offered me the job of cook, but it was just as well that she soon found another English girl, my neighbour, who had more experience; I would hardly have been able to live up to Lisette's exacting standards. However, I stayed on, meeting new people. There was one guest who worked in television and he was surprised we had no television yet in Greece, and he even considered some sort of a business on Hydra. His talk came as a sort of shock and made me wonder what would happen to the way of life there which had remained unchanged for so long. Yet Hydra had always been an island of merchants, of mercenaries, of Hydriots building boats to fight against the Turk: riches came and went. I consoled myself that Hydra would always remain the same.

≈

Even in high summer with all the Athenian visitors there were still the groups of foreigners who went to sit at the cafés along the *agora*, but now two bars had opened on the port. They were in the old boat houses where once shipwrights repaired the local fishing boats; now they were decorated with fishing nets and anchors. "It will make the place look more authentic," I was told. One bar was called the Portofino, where one could always find a motley gathering of people, people you knew and half knew, who had known the old Alexandria, those who had known Beirut, and those who had lived in Paris. Who were they? I hardly remember now.

They were Greeks who lived part time on Hydra, like George Lialios, or Panagiotis, even Theodoros would be at the Portofino. It was there that I met Bim, handsome Bim from New Zealand, and it was through him that I met Anthony Kingsmill, the English painter who was Marcelle's neighbour. They were all living above Kamini. There was Leonard, who had just won a big prize for poetry in Canada, and beautiful Marianne with the golden skin and flaxen hair; we were all neighbours. Sometimes I would see them swimming off the rocks with Marcelle, and sooner or later, in one way or another, our paths would cross.

⁓

I finished my window decoration, I had painted my pictures on the three shutters, but I was not painting. Perhaps I was using the heat as an excuse and was putting off the moment to take out my brushes again. There were too many other distractions. So when I met Marcelle one day on the rocks at Kamini I asked if I could visit; it was as if I wanted to reacquaint myself with the world of painting, to see how another artist was working.

I remembered her work from what I had seen the winter before, abstract painting of great strength and a certain elegance. Now as she showed me her recent canvases I saw that she had dramatically changed; she was no longer painting abstracts but representational pictures and Hydra was her subject. They were very still paintings, detailed and representational, but full of light. Whether this had anything to do with it – for I do not remember what she said – but on a previous visit Marcelle had had a dramatic accident falling on her head from her upstairs studio into the kitchen below, and perhaps it was the accident which had altered her vision, she did not say. She was well known as an abstract painter in Canada and the change did not altogether please her collectors, for this was the early Sixties and abstract art was considered the cutting edge of art.

"I woke up one morning and there was Hydra, and I began to paint."

I still remember something of her words. Maybe in my turn I would want to simplify and I knew abstraction was not my world: like Marcelle's new vision, it was colour and the things around me that I needed to interpret. I think by talking about painting she and I created a bond, for we would remain friends for many years and we unexpectedly met again much later in Paris. She was now calling herself not Marcelle but Marcella, and her show of new works had opened. There were paintings of Paris and still lives but it was mainly the paintings of Hydra that I wanted to see: the familiar house and the view I knew so well, the view towards the sea. This painting had a strange title, I noticed. It was called *Adieu Ma Vue*.

"Yes," she explained. "This is how I shall always remember my view, nothing can take it away. But now my neighbour has extended the house next door, and I no longer have it. But for me it is always there, in my painting."

Summer was ending, people were leaving, the guest house was closed and I knew that it was time for me to leave too. I stayed on a little longer at the house in Kamini; the evenings became colder and one had to sit inside, and I remember a small group of us used to meet at one of the only restaurants still open during the winter. It was halfway down the long flight of steps, and I know that the food we ate was the familiar menu of beans and lukewarm *moussaka*, but the place was cheerful and warm. There was Bim from Portofino, and Anthony and another face I now forget and we made a little group. Anthony was always the centre of any conversation for he was a wonderful talker.

He used to tell us of London literary life and the people he had known and I had the impression he had once been well connected. He had studied painting in London and then become a Chelsea lamplighter, the last lamplighter in London.

"The ideal job for a painter," he told us with one of his pixielike grins. "You start work when the light is beginning to fade."

I remember these evenings which often turned into a small group of poker players and I was persuaded to join. I was not a good deceiver but it did not seem to matter; it was the conversation and the jokes we had that counted.

"You should be painting too," I remember Anthony saying, and I knew he was right.

I went back to Athens and lived for a while in the apartment with its grand piano, then I went on a boat to the Canaries with Butterfly, my friend from Anafiotika. I would not return to Hydra for nearly two years, when my life would again be very different.

~

I took the boat to the Canaries with Butterfly and it was on that journey I met Jack, the man I would later marry. Jack was English and a writer and had been living in Ibiza, where in those days he told us, there was a community of writers and painters. From the many stories he told me, I immediately thought of the people I had met that long summer two years before on Hydra. Maybe the world is small, and we meet and find strange links with the people we meet in the most unexpected ways. We stayed together in the Canaries, and then Jack found a job as poet in residence in America and I went with him. When we returned, we decided to go to Greece. We were free, we would find a little house where he could write and I could paint, for Jack said Spain was becoming spoiled. They had now built an airport on Ibiza and it looked as if mass tourism had arrived in a big way.

Greece seemed so separate and different and we rented a little house across the straits from Poros in Galatas. Hydra would be too complicated, too demanding for us, I thought, but this would be familiar, a place I already knew. The little house we found was in a lemon grove and Pericles was our landlord. He was large and very short with a smile full of gold teeth and I am afraid we used to laugh sometimes at such a man with such a name. He had a very bossy sister who used to come and reprimand him when he was not irrigating the lemon trees or looking after the property as she thought he should. There was an old ruin down on the shore and Pericles said I could use this as my studio. Jack took out his typewriter and I began to paint.

~

After two years away from Greece I was still curious about Hydra and I think Jack for his part wanted to see the island I had talked about so much. Hydra was, after all, so near and I would try to find a few old friends, and perhaps look up Anthony. Jack asked me his second name, but as I never remember exchanging surnames, I had to admit I did not know.

"He is from Sussex," I told him. "He is called Anthony."

Jack was from Hastings and perhaps they would have friends in common.

Nearly two years had passed since I had been to Hydra, it was a long time, but as we came into the port it seemed like yesterday. We climbed the familiar steps up to Kamini, I remembered Anthony's house, and the door to the courtyard was open. A young woman introduced herself.

"Yes, he will be back in a minute," she said. "Charlotte, I remember you are Marcelle's friend. Anthony spoke about you."

We were shown into the little sitting room. Jack was always one to scrutinise the titles of other peoples' books and to my surprise I saw him take one from Anthony's shelves. I saw him look at it intently.

"Hugh Kingsmill," he said. "How unusual to see this book here. In his time quite a literary figure, but not much read now! Did Anthony know him?"

It was at that moment Anthony came through the door.

"Anthony," I said, "this is Jack. Jack, Anthony."

There was a pause. Jack looked at the man standing in front of us. They looked at each other.

"But you must be Anthony Kingsmill. I have just been looking at this book, not many people read it now. Don't you remember me, I came often to your house and met Hugh, your stepfather. You were only a schoolboy then, and we were at school together."

So began our many meetings. I would sit and listen to them talk. They spoke of their time together at school, though Jack had been a little older, and of a world before the war when Jack as a boy had known the Sussex countryside, and they talked of the literary world of Jack's former guru, Hugh Kingsmill.

~

We came many times to Hydra, and sometimes Anthony's great friend Leonard would be there. I asked about the people I had known on Hydra, and they told me that George Johnston had left, a very sick man, to go back to Australia. His book, *My Brother Jack*, was published and had been a great success. Now Leonard was wondering if his own talent did not lead to composing songs and playing the guitar and he had started trying out some of his new compositions at the island parties and everyone wondered what he would make of it. I was not there at the time but I remember Jack telling me how he and Leonard discussed this new project. Here was another poet, and for Leonard, I think Jack was somebody with experience, an established writer, but above all he was somebody who understood the way a poet thinks.

It was later that summer when Jack and I had been living in Galatas for quite some time that my cousin Penny came to stay. Jack's library of books had finally arrived from Ibiza, having rather picturesquely been sent on from Piraeus by caïque. All was now unpacked and sorted, and I had my studio for painting down by the sea. I knew Jack had been working far too hard to finish a commission for a book, and when suddenly he announced one morning that he needed a break I was not surprised. So it was decided that we make one of our visits to Hydra and look up Anthony. Penny had never been there and it would make a change from life among the lemon trees.

As we came into the port we saw Anthony on the *agora*. He had come into town to meet the boat and was full of his news. He had just been given a commission for a painting, he told us excitedly. It was to be of a nude, a young Greek reclining on a bed. Anthony had already met his subject. They had chosen the bed, the pose was to be exact, and no detail – his subject was particularly insistent on this, Anthony told us – must be omitted. The painting was for the new owner of Lissette's guest house, who wanted a portrait of his boyfriend.

Anthony introduced us to the boyfriend as we were sitting at Katsikas' on the *agora*. He was still good-looking in a flamboyant way but had only one interest in life: himself. We were then invited to a party at the house to meet the new owner. The house I had known as Lisette's guest house had been transformed beyond recognition, remodelled by an interior designer. There was not one oil lamp but twenty, and there were antiques and tasteful Greek curiosities from fifty flea markets. It was in the best of gay good taste. Seeing the rarefied atmosphere of that house, I was immediately transported back to Athens, to my life there, and then came the memory of the "other" Hydra too. Yes, it had been another world, but now that Jack was with me, I could see it in a different way.

Anthony started on his new commission and we did not see him for a while. Then we heard that after the first few sessions the model was always too busy to pose or he complained that the canvas was not right. Perhaps Anthony was paid a little but the portrait was never completed. I had perhaps been tempted to come back to Hydra with Jack. But no, the *agora* was still a theatre, and Hydra a place of dreams. Nothing had changed.

With the hopes for the portrait gone, Anthony began to find his small income from his London gallery hardly enough to pay the bills. Even buying a tin of sardines for the cats which I remember so vividly from his drawings, Spatso and Katy, was becoming a burden. We heard much later that Leonard had helped him out and financed him on a visit to New York when he wanted to see a special exhibition. Yet even Leonard, with his success, would leave the island. Hydra was unique, it was beautiful, but perhaps for many it was a gilded cage.

∼

It was May of 1967 and I had already a new group of paintings I had done in my studio by the sea. I painted the lemon pickers harvesting the lemons by our house and I began again to paint my first still lives; Jack had a contract for a book. We would have some money and all was good that morning as I was walked into Galatas to buy some groceries.

"Kyria, Kyria! The police, the police! You have to go to the police in Poros!" I remember my neighbour calling urgently.

Jack and I took the little boat across the strait. The man who was sitting opposite us at the police station was without expression. I managed to understand his Greek.

"You must go from Greece," he said pointing to a piece of paper on his desk. "It is an order from Athens. You have three days to leave. Kyrios Beeching is being deported."

We had no recourse, for Greece had been taken over by a military coup. Had it something to do with our visit to America when Jack had expressed his views on the Vietnam War? Was it because he was termed an intellectual and therefore dangerous? We never knew. How could we pack our things: Jack's manuscripts and library, my paintings, in so short a time? Jack took my hand.

"We will manage," he said.

We contacted the British Consul and left for Turkey.

Mustn't Grumble

Penny Eyles

The internet and e-mails are the work of the devil but occasionally something interesting creeps into my inbox, bypassing the barrier I have built by suggesting that I do not open my e-mails hourly, daily or obsessively and that a letter, a telephone call or even a text would receive a more immediate response. Anyway, one grey wintry day in London an intriguing e-mail arrived from 69°39' north 18°59' east. I opened the *Times Atlas of the World* and found Tromsø. It was very, very far north, above the Arctic Circle and sounded cold and dark. A Dr. Helle Goldman from the Norwegian Polar Institute had written to ask me if I would contribute to a collection of essays about Hydra during the late Sixties and early Seventies. Then I remembered two small girls with straight blonde hair and pale golden brown skins scuttling down the lanes in faded cotton dresses to swim off the rocks. One of them was Helle, who, with her sister, her beautiful Danish mother and American father, lived in a house near me, across the street from the bakery.

So I began trying to resurrect memories of that long ago two years I spent living then leaving then living then leaving that island where everyone said they were leaving to travel somewhere somewhere more idyllic, less fraught, cheaper, or go home to earn some money, do a proper job, wait for funds outside the American Express in Athens sitting in the cafe next door in Syntagma Square in central Athens drinking a *metrio* – a very small, strong coffee in a tiny cup with mud at the bottom but eked out with a free glass of cold water and maybe even a *croque monsieur* paid for by the limited amount of drachmas they still had or had borrowed or even owed but managed to hang on to – to find love, escape a broken relationship, take the kids home for a proper education or just look round at faces in case a friend or even a friend of friends briefly met might have a room to rent, or even a house on another island, where there might be some crumbling neglected hovels abandoned by all the family who used to live there but now preferred life in Athens or Thessaloniki, where they could definitely – oh, yes, absolutely, definitely – finish the novel, screenplay, poem. Inevitably, several days later they would still be seen on the port of Hydra, sitting outside Katsikas', the grocery shop and café where everyone used to see everyone sipping a cloudy ouzo, and yes the *Portokalis Ilios* or the *Neraida* had left without them for Piraeus again. But definitely tomorrow.

∽

That was all fifty years ago and since then I have travelled and worked with and met many people, but it was still surprising on a recent and my first visit to southern India to hear a familiar voice as I came out of of a bookshop called Idiom in a narrow street in Cochin. There was my cousin Charlotte, a painter living in Ibiza, and as amazed as I was and whom I had not seen for over a year. It was she who introduced me to Hydra.

We had travelled by train on the very unexpress-like Orient Express to Athens, during which time Charlotte, who could create a smart handbag out of an old t-shirt, and I crocheted garments in thick white cotton, which was very fashionable at the time. Charlotte was making a bikini using something called *Les Formes* to contain the bosoms and cover the nipples while I was crocheting a dress. At maybe Munich some returning Greek people squeezed into our compartment, along with a fridge, which to accommodate we just lifted up our legs and continued crocheting while they fed us bread, olives and baklava.

In those days – the late 1960s – the voyage from Piraeus to Hydra took about three and a half hours either on the *Neraida*, which was – and I don't want to hurt its feelings – something of an old tub or the *Portokalis Ilios*, a large and more stately vessel. On both the bar served sandwiches: a piece of ham slapped between two slices of very dry white bread wrapped in tracing paper but actually quite tasty. The ferries used to tie up at Aegina, then Poros, with lots of shouting, bundles, and locals and tourists getting on and off, little three-wheeler vans, vegetables, newspapers, mail, motor scooters, women advertising rooms to let, and then on through the gap between Poros and the Peloponnese and, in the distance, Hydra, arriving at the harbour wall alongside the naval school and opposite the big, high, grey stone wall of the Koundouriotis house.

There were no cars or vans, only donkeys wearing wooden panniers to carry luggage bundles or belongings or even people. They were led along the harbour past grocers and cafés and people sitting sipping things. In winter the wind and rain whooshed and splashed across the cobbles and people huddled inside or scurried as fast as possible up narrow twisting lanes off the harbour – the most famous being Donkey Shit Lane. However, the population of Hydra – donkeys, locals and foreigners, some who came and went and regularly came back as well as a few who survived permanently on the island – was probably outnumbered by cats, who could be thin and sly or thin and starving or big, scarred robber baron cats or plump, moderately well-cared-for and loved cats like Spatso, the one with whom I shared a house with Anthony Kingsmill, an English painter, plus Katie and Thomas and various others who spotted a good thing and tried to get in through the door to the small courtyard or over the wall until chased out by grumpy Spatso. I have two black and white paintings of her on my wall in London: black with four white feet, stout and glowering.

However, birth control for cats was not an option and even if there had been a vet on the island we could probably not have afforded the operation or even merciful euthanasia of the increasing miaowing feline population and no one else wanted yet another kitten, however sweet or needy. The house of our neighbour Dorothy, a blonde German woman and previous partner of Anthony's, had become completely overrun with cats, to the point that it was probably a health risk. She arrived one dark, wet, stormy night, banging on the courtyard door where we were feasting on a small piece of roast lamb with roast potatoes and mint sauce and hoping that no one would call so that we could divide it equally between the two of us.

Anthony reluctantly unlocked the door. Dorothy was wet, shaking and crying outside. She had tried to get rid of her brood of cats by taking them in a sack to a ruined house and throwing the whole lot down a deep empty well. Some time, or even a day, later she swore that one of the cats had arrived back at her house pointing an accusing paw. Seeing her distress we naturally invited her to stay the night in case any more cats returned and of course we shared the roast lamb.

We soon faced the same dilemma – and this is a disgraceful, horrid story – but with myself, Spatso, Thomas, Katie, plus various other fosterings and adoptions and Anthony there was not enough to feed anyone or any more cats. So I went up to Michali the grocer's shop just above our little house and bought cans of the tinned fish the cats liked. Anthony acquired some sleeping pills and we mashed them up with the fish for their supper. The unwanted cats and kittens gradually fell asleep and – we hoped – died during the night, but just in case they hadn't, early the next morning we loaded the comatose, possibly already dead, cats into a sack, adding two heavy stones and tying up the neck. We walked quietly down to the nearest cliff; Anthony whirled the sack round and flung it out as far as he could so that it wouldn't get stuck on the rocks below. It hit the water and disappeared just as a small fishing boat chugged around the corner. It was a very, very close thing for us, the cats and the fishermen.

⁓

Not only were there no roads on Hydra, no cars or vans except maybe the rubbish truck, but there was no natural source of water. Beneath all the houses were cisterns into which rain ran down off the roofs. Some were big, some small and some leaked or during a dry period simply dried up. When that happened the only thing to do was buy it from the very expensive supply that came in the water boat heavily loaded and very, very low in the water, puffing across from the Peloponnese. Saving money by not bathing or washing was one option and of course a swim off the rocks was fine, but in rough weather and winter storms, and even when it was winter and calm in winter, the only person that one was likely to spot in the sea when walking along the coast from the harbour to the next small bay, Kamini, was Donald, a very tough Englishman, snorkelling for octopuses, for which he had many recipes.

I cannot remember why Donald had washed up on Hydra. He lived in a small stone house which had been abandoned or was being argued over by various branches of the family who owned it. I am not sure if it had electricity and it was a big event when he built an outside toilet to the right of the house – a bit of a stumble across a short stony path on a dark, windy, wet night but inside the house was cosy and organised and I have photographs of Rea, his first wife, and their small child Melissa, who must be nearly fifty now. I used to stop off for cups of tea, a biscuit and a natter when I was walking – it was a breath of Englishness.

Donald lent me books as he rescued those abandoned by visitors on holiday and he used to look after some of the houses belonging to absent foreigners. In fact he was the odd job man and I was the below stairs scullery maid one summer for the houses rented out to holiday-makers, changing beds and humping huge bundles of sheets and towels on my back up and down narrow lanes to one of the donkey men's wives for washing. I cleaned the kitchens and emptied the fridges and if anything had been left Donald and I divided it up between the two of us. One group of young Irish women had left some packets of Pom – powdered mashed potato – which we thought odd. Did they think there were no potatoes in Greece? Anyway I put my share to good use, whipping it up with hot water, pepper and some Vitam, which was margarine, plus slices of tinned corned beef from Michali's shop. Delicious.

All the grocers shops used to smell the same: olives and olive oil, dried salted cod in barrels, called bacalao, retsina, kasseri cheese or feta. There is one small store in London, in Bayswater, on Moscow Road next to the big Greek Orthodox church, called the Athenian Grocery, where the aroma always reminds me of Hydra food shopping. The main challenge was to get a freshly baked loaf of bread up Donkey Shit Lane without picking holes in it because it was so delicious, warm and soft, and crusty outside, and once the baker had finished for the day the locals and we foreigners could take flat metal dishes of lamb and potatoes and herbs to be baked in the remaining heat in the oven, then scrumptious and cooling, and carry this feast home. The vegetables were rather a sorry lot, waiting the next delivery from Poros or Aegina or Piraeus, but big fat tomatoes, onions and potatoes could be relied on and of course tinned sardines, tuna or mussels, tasty with olive oil and garlic, and when mixed with spaghetti and leftovers could be turned into a spaghetti omelette with a few eggs. Sounds revolting? It was not.

Today I have been walking in southwest Cornwall. It is April but the wind is howling and the waves are wild and tall but along sheltered, narrow, high-sided lanes wild garlic is growing. On Hydra during my first autumn I wondered what all the headscarfed Greek local ladies were doing on the hillside outside the town, bent over so that the tops of their black stockings showed beneath their aprons. They were picking dandelion leaves which, when boiled and served with olive oil, lemon juice and pepper, made a dish called *horta*. It was free, although a little bitter. After a time I think Anthony became less than excited by *horta* even with tinned corned beef. When the autumn rains came the locals, who knew where they grew, bought down baskets of wild mushrooms to the port. These were a real treat fried in olive oil and served on toast.

We were surrounded by fish but they were in the sea and I don't remember any great seafood meals. Waiters were always waving lobsters at the tourists but the prices were extortionate and the lobsters looked rubbery. Instead of a menu, we used to choose from a tempting display of fresh fish and meats, and vegetable dishes cooked earlier, in a cold glass cabinet in front of the kitchen. Unfortunately, our orders would arrive garnished with olive oil and lemon juice but overcooked and leathery. My favourite was a greasy chicken and chips dish from a restaurant at the bottom of Donkey Shit Lane opposite Katsikas', and of course there was Lulu's up a back lane from the port, where, as in all the other restaurants, the tablecloths were plastic, a white paper sheet was plonked on top and then a plastic basket with cut lumps of bread, white paper napkins, knives and forks. Small thick glasses followed, tap water and a beaker of retsina or a metal-topped bottle of the cheapest of the cheap Kourtaki or smarter more expensive Domestica, opened with a corkscrew, which Anthony insisted on ordering – and then another despite our lack of funds and I gradually discovered after the first few months of delight that he liked to drink too much and visits to Lulu's became a strain for me. At certain moments he would almost physically change from being a witty, interesting, intellectually idiosyncratic companion into a vicious, argumentative goblin, pointing his finger and calling anyone with a different point of view "Dove."

I used to leave and walk home. Lulu's was also not only cheap, but famous for plate smashing, a practice which, on looking back, I found rather odd and a bit too violent and threatening. It could either follow or precede dancing the *hasapiko* – joining hands in a circle or a line and moving right and left. Some of the foreigners became very good, particularly an elegant woman called Virginia, who lived near the port, off a side street, and I think came from Rhodesia rather than Zimbabwe.

Virginia and I had a strange adventure. One summer evening on the port I met someone – maybe it was Virginia – who asked me if I had seen P., an American artist from New York who lived high above the town with his wife M., also an artist, who had thick, long, black, curly hair, and their two very small children. He might have gone on the boat to Athens, taking the children, the younger just a baby. A neighbour had been up to their house and was alarmed to see that all the mirrors had been covered in black paint. M. was apparently on a small beach only accessible by sea. Virginia found two fishermen with a boat.

It was a very dark night, warm and calm, and as we approached we could see in the distance a figure in white sitting under a tree. The fisherman waited by the boat as Virginia and I walked towards the white figure. It was M. To our horror we saw that she had shaved off all her beautiful hair; she had done it badly so there were small black tufts all over her head. She was completely still and looked straight ahead towards us, staring blankly. We said we had come to help. She didn't acknowledge us or even signal that she could hear us. Finally we managed to persuade her to get into the back of the boat. The two fishermen were scared, as were

Virginia and I: M. appeared calm but we did not know what she might do. The boat was small and we were out of sight of the port and couldn't see any lights anywhere.

When we arrived at the port, Virginia went home, taking M. with her, to wait while I ran to the telephone exchange to try and contact Donald's wife in Athens and get her to go to the railway station where P. might be trying to catch a train with the two children. Only some locals had the luxury of a landline so the only option was the telephone exchange, where you gave your required number to the operator and waited patiently, especially if there was a queue of people in front of you, to be called to a booth while listening to everybody else's shouted conversations. I found Rea and rushed back to the port and turmoil. M. had attacked Virginia in her house and the police had taken her down to sit at the café opposite Katsikas'. I am not sure if there was a doctor on Hydra but when I saw M. they were trying to keep her quiet and secure. She was very distressed. I was told the police sat with her all night and she was taken on the first boat next morning to a hospital in Athens. I think she had a severe case of post-natal depression. I never saw any of them again.

∾

I think I lived in a little bubble when I was on Hydra – the odd newspaper, letters from home collected from the post office and occasionally a telegram or a notice that someone had been trying to telephone you, although how that arrived I cannot remember. I am embarrassed now by my ignorance of the fact that the colonels were in power and appalling things were happening to protesters in Athens and elsewhere. Perhaps I just didn't know or it wasn't discussed that much. Our one source of news was from a small, rather inadequate, radio belonging to Anthony and the only English language station we could pick up was the US Air Force broadcasting from their base in Athens.

One particular event had both Anthony and me glued to that little battered black wireless: when American astronauts on an early space mission went round behind the dark side of the moon, losing all contact with mission control and the rest of the Earth.

It was planned but no one knew whether they would disappear for ever or be able to return, not their families, the space scientists, the President, the American public or even Anthony and I on a small Aegean island. No one else on Hydra seemed remotely interested in this adventure, or maybe they were hidden away, crouched round their own little battered radios. We waited and waited until we finally heard the news that the astronauts had emerged from that hidden blackness and we gave a little cheer.

∾

I have no idea what the Hydriots thought of this strange floating community who arrived from all over the world and rented, occasionally buying, abandoned houses, furnishing them with whatever could be found and using bed sheets made from white seersucker with a thin blue stripe, even wearing them as kaftans. Mainly the Hydriots seemed tolerant and friendly towards us and after all had probably got family who had emigrated and whom they may have visited. There were also Athenian families who came over in the summer to stay in their large family mansions. I used to visit and occasionally stay with Angeliki Stefanou in the Koundouriotis house.

Angeliki was a wonderfully feisty, brave woman, crippled by polio as a child and in a wheelchair. She had to hoist herself with some help onto the back of a donkey to be taken up the hill and used to entertain in the large courtyard because she couldn't leave the house without the paraphernalia of a donkey and the wheelchair but she always wanted to know what the *demi-monde,* that is, us rag, tag and bobtail, were up to. The house had wonderful wash basins and lavatories – large porcelain Victorian constructions engraved with blue flowers, with wooden seats and substantial pull chains that needed a sharp yank down. Every summer when Angeliki came so did her great friend Mina and if they weren't on Hydra they would go to Mina's family house on Aegina. Mina had a dog called Short and Stout, a rescue dog. Both she and Angeliki did a lot of work for an animal welfare charity in Athens, raising funds as well as offering practical help with abandoned pets. In Athens, Angeliki drove a specially adapted Mini, rather perilously keeping a wheelchair in the back, and Mina drove a Citröen 2CV with two doors and deckchair-like seats in the front. She and Angeliki used to travel all over the place; I think Mina even managed to drive to England in the Citröen – that journey possibly without Angeliki. If for reasons of mobility she could not get into a hotel for the night Angeliki told me she would just sleep in the car. She was tough as well as brave.

Angeliki and the rest of her family, who were all part-owners of the house, eventually decided that the expense of its upkeep was too much and now it is owned by the country. At roughly the same time there was a catastrophic fire and Mina's family house on Aegina was nearly completely destroyed. She did up a gardener's cottage in the pistachio orchard which surrounded the ruined house. I do not really know what happened between the two very old friends but after they lost both their houses there was a change in their relationship. Angeliki could no longer go to Hydra and Mina had lost her house and their friendship became tetchy and bitter. Sadly, they are now both dead.

So is Anthony, who eventually turned up in a council flat in London very near me. I am not sure how he got there and so many years after we parted I didn't particularly want to see him. I was working long hours on a film being shot in London so he never found me and very soon after I had a phone call from Bill, of Bill's Bar on Hydra, who told me that Anthony had been taken to the Whittington Hospital, at that time a rather bleak place, where he died. A good friend, who was fond of Anthony, came with me to his funeral in a rather grim red brick North London church, where his brother, a delightful man, was the vicar. I was surprisingly upset when I saw a photo of him in the church porch, very youthful and smiley. The service was simple and short and afterwards we met one of his sisters, a nun, a very forthright woman who, when I admitted that I hadn't wanted to see him, said, "Well, Anthony could be a bit trying." All that remains for me of him is a painting he gave me of his first wife's shoes in the bottom of a cupboard, done by him after she left him.

Other paintings done by Anthony still exist. When I first met him he worked hard and would climb up to the studio attic in the morning, staying up there muttering until lunch, and afterwards or the next day destroy what he had done as he thought it was no good, which I found a bit annoying, especially if I had been sitting for him. He did landscapes too: the view from the attic over to Kamini. Andreas Focas, a friend and painter with a studio in Plaka whom he admired, would come over to eat and discuss their painting problems. Pandias Skaramangas, who has a house perched over the port, used to join us at weekends and is one of the survivors still visiting, as is Daniel Klein, at that time a hovel dweller and student philosopher/writer, whom I recently saw in London on a visit to his publisher and whose book *Travels with Epicurus* is prominently displayed in a lot of my favourite bookshops. While I cooked, peeled potatoes or opened tins of mussels they would sit around with glasses of Kourtaki, debating the opposing nature of platonic and erotic love. I didn't think I was expected to join in.

One man who did supply me with educational reading and who lived partly in Athens was an American called Bill Finley, who didn't believe in and as far as I could gather had never had, something as boring as a job. His family had supplied him with a limited income enabling him to travel all over Europe, Morocco, Mexico and the rest of the world, even one day to my doorstep in London with a suitcase from which hung bits of garments because he hadn't been able to close it properly. Fortunately he had already made arrangements to stay with another friend in London and just wanted to make a phone call. I think after a few days the friend moved him on to Morocco. But despite all his shortcomings he did lend me the most wonderful range of biographies, frequently of very unpleasant people like Hitler, or writers and artists, which he used to order in hardback as soon as they came out. We spent many hours talking and he told me his life story, which I still have written down somewhere: wealthy childhood, brief early marriage, later a liaison with Nancy Cunard of the Cunard shipping line, various relationships with men including Malcolm Lowry. When I met him he was with a young Athenian medical student and I never knew him to be in a relationship with a woman.

He was thin, with a strange squint, not much hair, a mixture of garments, mainly decent, and a deep, rich, gravelly voice which deepened and became more gravelly the drunker he became. He used to roar. That was the problem. Finley drunk was to be avoided at all times. Sober he was fun, but dangerous when drunk. He used to carry – rather daintily – a plastic bag containing probably the latest biography he had bought and a little change purse. One day he was waiting on the jetty at Kamini for the small boat that carried people to the port, but as he stood there, plastic bag in his hand at his side, he suddenly disappeared feet first straight down with a plop and scarcely a splash into the sea, completely vanishing until, like a cork, he plopped up again, looking a little surprised and very wet.

In Athens he could be found regularly in a bar called Apotsos, where certain literary expats met to drink and eat little plates of olives, stuffed vine leaves and delicious small sausages called *loukanika*. I arranged to meet him there one lunch time, having just got off a night flight from London. Finley was in drinking mode. I was exhausted and it was very, very hot. Eventually all I wanted to do was go to the small hotel nearby, where I had booked in for the night. But I had to think what to do with Finley as he was becoming very incapable. Lunch time was over and I had to find a taxi for him. We lurched out of Apotsos but it was siesta time when taxis used to either disappear or be occupied or not want to go where you wanted to go, not that I even knew where Finley was living as he could be a bit itinerant. Eventually I propped him up against a wall and left to try and find an empty taxi. It was a fruitless search but when I returned he had vanished. With great relief I set off to my hotel but as I went round a corner the scarecrow figure of Finley weaved towards me.

He was an experience and I wish I could have done something with his life story, which we recorded and I typed out. As I recall it was a catalogue of appalling behaviour interspersed with accounts of delicious meals. Besides booze Finley enjoyed good food.

$\sim$

Today I am back in London; it is late April and although sunny there is still the same east wind that has been blowing and chilling us for weeks. I am checking my will and about to eliminate some of the bequests – the friends or relations are either dead or their fortunes have improved so I am going to cross them off the list, all of which has made me think about lost friends from Hydra who were really friends and whom, if they were sitting in a café, I would feel comfortable joining without feeling I had to be invited or we would go on an expedition together, like Jeanette, an English guide who had a family house overlooking Kamini. She was a rider and several times the two of us took mules or donkeys along stony tracks to Episkopi, the small deserted village at the end of the island, dismounting when it was more comfortable or less precarious to walk than ride and then avoiding small adders who were just starting to emerge from between the stones on the track. Sometimes we crossed to the other side of the island and clambered down to a small deserted beach, where we left a cheap bottle of Kourtaki retsina to cool in a pool while we picked shells off the rocks and prodded out their insides to munch with fresh bread.

Picnicking in this deserted place was peaceful and calm compared with the seething cauldron of the port, particularly in the summer, when yachts and gin palaces were parked along the edge and their owners and guests sipping gin, nibbling expensive snacks on deck or wafting off to lean back on cushioned chairs at a café. This theatre was always interesting for someone who likes snooping, watching who was with whom and who was going to dine where and with whom, or the tourists heading for the growing number of jewellery and whatnot shops, which even late at night would suddenly throw open their shutters when they heard a cruise ship's *toot toot*.

Another escapee from this hullabaloo was Nike Hale, a Greek–American woman who had family in Athens. She lived in New York with her much older American husband, who had been curator at the Metropolitan Museum in New York as well as a distinguished teacher of anatomical drawing. She used to leave Robert on the port with his newspaper and meet me on the jetty in Kamini in one of the small boats, which, despite plans for a quiet ladies' outing with a picnic and maybe a bottle of retsina to help us in our discussions about life and relationships and things in general, would inevitably arrive with a boatload of small children, her son and daughter, Alexander and Evelyn, and a family of small blond bullet-headed rumbustious, tough little boys. She used to apologise profusely for this invasion as we set off to a small island – really a large rock – nearby and the boys immediately dived into the sea and clambered up the rocks. Occasionally, mid important discussion about life et cetera, she would fish one out. Fortunately we never lost any of them. I did visit her and Robert in his beautiful old family house on the East Coast, near Boston. It was being repaired and done up by a young Australian to whom Nike had taken a fancy. She would cook lunch for Robert in one side of the house and then on the other side cook supper for the young Australian or possibly vice versa. It seemed a sophisticated arrangement but I do remember Robert showing me a very sad poem and I have a black and white photograph that I took of him sitting alone in his side of the house.

∽

There were not that many English people in that collection of itinerant *demi-monde,* as my friend Angeliki christened us, but one day I met a young lad from somewhere in the Midlands. For a while we sat in one of the port cafés and talked. It was like slipping on a pair of old carpet slippers. We laughed and nattered and nattered and laughed – no need to explain because we came from the same background, which was home to both of us. Previously, when I got on the bus marked ATHENS from the air terminal building on Cromwell Road in London, I used to feel very pleased to escape from damp, grey, boring old England, to be flying off to somewhere where everybody and everything was fascinating and exotic, unlike our own *mustn't grumble* culture, which is of course an instant excuse to do exactly that. My short period on Hydra forty-five years ago, in the late 1960s and early 1970s, was wonderful in many ways – an education, but what is done is done. The streets of little red brick semi-detached houses and the mutterings and grey faces early in the morning when I buy a newspaper from the corner shop or even a croissant – these foreign habits have crept in – are home. We could do with a bit more sun – the weather is terrible but *mustn't grumble.*

However, today it is not raining though cold and autumnal. Beside the entrance to Highbury and Islington tube station is waiting a tall elegant woman with bright red hair. Is she one of those small skinny little blond girls dressed in a faded cotton dress from the house opposite the bakery at the top of Donkey Shit Lane?

George

Angelika Lialios

"Ancient columns and sculptures of Gods, that's Greece," said my friend Barbara as we drove through eastern Europe in my little red Deux Chevaux en route from Germany. Of course, the sculptures were not lined up behind the border, as she had envisioned in her eagerness to explore Greek culture. Instead we crossed into a landscape of olive trees and a road dotted with tomatoes and melons that had fallen from the trucks ahead on the curving mountain routes. The roads were bumpy and unpaved and what we assumed to be little romantic miniature churches adorning the mountain side at intervals we later discovered to be shrines to those who had underestimated these treacherous tracks. We continued our journey safely to Ioannina and Meteora, through pomegranate and pistachio groves until our way led us to the Peloponnese and from there to Hydra. If we had read a little about the history of Hydra we would have known that the island had always been a place of rebels and independence. During the Ottoman occupation its merchants were among the few allowed to keep their ships and continue their trade. The liberty backfired on the occupying Turks because it was the naval leaders of Hydra that played a large part in the revolution of 1821.

The sense of freedom on Hydra remained and it became a centre for poets and artists where creativity flourished. For two young girls freshly out of art school who were looking to escape the rules of a rigid German society it was a place of marvel. Hydra had me under its spell form the moment I laid eyes on its beautiful amphitheatre-shaped port. My friend Barbara and I rented a small room in the bay of Kamini, a short walking distance from the main town of Hydra. We soon discovered that when venturing out we would stumble across the same people day by day.

Before long we had many an acquaintance on this little island. One was Felix, who became a regular dinner companion. He was Norwegian and a writer and he was one of the irreplaceable elements of our first moments on Hydra. With him we learned the artists' habit of "floating" through the evening. Meetings were not arranged but pre-dinner cocktails in the port, followed by dinner, followed by more cocktails meant that you were more likely to end up at a table of 20 than alone. Pretty soon we knew almost everyone on the island except: "George! You have to meet my friend George."

Felix and George had known each other for a while. Felix introduced us when George joined our table at Tassos', one of the popular coffee houses on the harbour front. George was recognizably Greek but untypical in every way. Born in Munich as the son of a Greek diplomat and a Greek singer, he had only moved to Athens at the age of ten. His family had an estate in Patras, where they took refuge during the war years. Later he went to study music in Vienna at the Music Academy, following in the footsteps of his father who was as much a composer as a politician. Charming, polite and reserved he addressed us in fluent German. I think we already fell in love that first evening but we married much later, in 1981. To many George was the linking element between the foreign and local communities of Hydra.

He had an almost magical ability to blend into any society. He could walk into the forbidden section of a Hindu temple, closed to foreigners, without evoking the attention of the surrounding visiting sadus with their tridents, the same way he could walk into the glamorous parties of Edgar Kaufman, unshaven and in an old shirt and jeans. I still remember the evening of the latter event clearly. It had been my birthday and we had been out at Vlychos beach celebrating very casually at a taverna. Bill Cunliffe, the owner of Bill's Bar, caught us on our return to the port and asked if we were not joining Edgar's party, a question that, without doubt, contained a trace of mischief. Like George, I was not very formally dressed. Wearing what Bill called my *Einmachgummihose* (pickled rubber pants), I walked between dark pools lit by floating candles on both sides of the path as we entered Edgar's. Waitresses in long white dresses, draped at the shoulder like those of Greek goddesses, served lobster on silver trays. Edgar loved our quirky arrival so much that we became regulars, even at his more closely knit parties.

Many of George's friends date back to earlier years. He had first arrived on the island long before me, in the year 1959, and here is how he describes it.

~

The port was empty. The groceries (the Katsikas dynasty on the right and the Sourelis on the left), the vegetable shop and the butcher, at that time still in the centre, closed at 1 p.m. and only some coffee houses on the quayside were open. There would sit the few foreigners living or dropping in on the island, shirts off, sunbathing. But the fascinating thing was that Hydra lived like two centuries ago and we experienced this as living in different times simultaneously. The port was like a stage with few, so to speak, *dramatis personae* and the local population, whenever they appeared at all, acting as the chorus of an ancient drama commenting in sheer amazement on the ways and behaviour of these strangers. I myself, being Greek, was partaking of both sides. Local women would hardly ever be seen.

The locals would not spend any time in the port except for shopping. Few men could be seen in the typically Greek coffee houses. A new local power station, sending D.C. current from sundown till midnight, was installed in today's marketplace. Butcher, fish and vegetable shops were right on the waterfront where other commercial premises were unoccupied.

The group of strangers, some with houses on the island, others on a prolonged visit, were gathering at Katsikas' grocery, which served wine and some *meze*, and was headed by Charmian and George Johnston, who decided who was allowed into the circle and who not. The grocery had a back store-room, where we could sit in the wintertime for a glass of wine before dinner. There I first met Anthony Kingsmill and Demetri Gassoumis. I think it was Leonard who introduced me. I joined this congregation quite as a matter of fact, though they wondered who I really was and made some odd guesses. An Athenian staying over the winter was an intriguing phenomenon. (One guess was that I could be a remittance case, i.e., one whose family paid to have stay away.)

So in the morning I would sit at Sotiris Douskos' small coffee house in the corner opposite Tassos', where no foreigner was welcome; chattering people would only disturb the meditative silence of the patrons, who were all elderly and serious persons. No foreigner would even dream of taking a seat there. I, though not a local, was accepted there because I was Greek after all and silent. Inside there was, in a glass casement, a coloured statue of Napoleon. This, a restaurant and the Lagoudera bar were the only places in use on that wing of the port. What now are shops had in older prosperous times of the island been the store rooms of the residing ship-owner-and-merchant class.

Sotiris took a liking to me and took me to a small tavern run by a jolly man called Grafos that had good retsina and good local food. Still only Greeks were the patrons. Sotiris, a man in his sixties, had the evenings out. He had told his wife before the wedding that he would always be home for lunch; in the evenings, never. That was when he liked to have his wine and start singing. I had to second him. Singing in public was hardly what I liked to do but with Sotiri pressing me I had no choice. The evening spent, I would go home, have another glass of wine and go to bed. There seemed to be no other entertainment until one evening, after having had my fill of singing, I turned toward the port. Not a soul to be seen, ghostly it seemed. With a sigh I started up Kala Pigadia Lane when suddenly I heard *bouzouki* music next to the market entrance.

To be more precise, *rembetiko* music. *Rembetis* is a marginal person of unconventional behaviour, to put it mildly. The main dance, the *zeibekiko*, is a highly individual solo dance and I first became better acquainted with it in 1954, when I had come to Greece with my car, a necessary proposition if you wanted to visit such places as they were way out of town and at the time not frequented by normal society.

The music differs from the demotic Balkan–Oriental sound as

it uses the western scales of major or minor tonalities. The instrument *bouzouki* was imported from Asia Minor but the music developed in the cities of Greece, mainly Athens, Pireaus and Thessaloniki. It was something in between the Balkans and the West. It had not yet made its way to the radio programmes, which played strictly demotic and opera. Only the third was playing classical music, a sound which to the average Greek ear was sad if not outright funereal. If you heard classical music on the first programme you could be almost certain that death had struck the political proscenium.

So up the steps I went and there it was: the local entertainment joint, men only and none under thirty. There was a juke-box, next to it a small dancing space, and a free table next to the counter and opposite the juke-box and the dance floor. No one would sit there but me. It was too exposed. From then on I would spend my evenings there after supper. The dancing was outstanding.

Time rolled on quietly; the event of the day was the arrival of the boat at 11:30 and we would be sitting at the coffee house by the quay watching the arrivals. Apart of course from the locals who all made quickly for their houses the port was again deserted with any new comers wondering where to go. It was a time when often young people (perhaps on a gap year before university) would step off entranced by the sudden appearance of the town as the boat took a sharp turn into this horseshoe-shaped harbour and decided to disembark and then eventually even to spend the winter. Life was cheap in the golden years of the century and a house could be had for $10 the season. Empty houses abounded and at that price they could afford to also buy the essential furnishing and a kerosene heating stove. I spent one dollar a day for my two meals, including wine.

The search for a house to buy proceeded and produced nothing of interest and I let it be for after Christmas. I got invited to the Johnstons' for that occasion and spent a nice day. All the selected members of the foreign community were present. When the days of festivities were past I told the local person who functioned as real estate broker to show me what was for sale. He told me that he had something but that it was at some distance. "How far could far be?" I asked myself, and told him to go ahead. So we walked for some ten minutes up "Donkey Shit Lane" to a house beneath a church.

He opened a ragged wooden door with a big key and I stepped into an overwhelming mystery house. He went on and on showing me around and the more I saw the more I loved it. That evening I told my new friends in Katsikas' backroom and tried to draw a plan of the house. It was evidently impossible. I had to see it again and got the key to go there by myself. As I opened the door a tarantula dropped onto my shoulder, then onto the floor and ran away. I proceeded to the interior. There were goat droppings on the ground. It had obviously been used as a stable. Again I walked all over the rooms, steps up, steps down, into a maze.

It was partly a ruin and partly magnificent, but way beyond what I had imagined to buy. All the same I felt at peace there. As I walked into the semi-darkness of that large ground floor I wondered if I wasn't mad. Clearly, the investment would be no loss but the cost of refurbishing promised to be immense. Yet so was the attraction and the urgency of repair was more than doubtless. The roof was damaged, rainwater had already caused destruction down two floors, a wall was leaning out; in short, it would soon collapse. I had to save it. I asked my heart if I was acting out of greed or with sincere love for the object and decided for the second. It was worth saving.

The next day I took the road to Kala Pigadia and up to Kiafa. The region was full of ruins and looked like a ghost town. It was a shocking sight. "Where have I come to live?" I wondered, now really worrying but the moment I entered my empty ruin again all fears were gone and I experienced a wonderful feeling of peace. I was at home.

By the time I became the legal owner it was March 1962. Easter was celebrated at Margarita Lymberaki's house, which was not far from where I lived and there I had already met our good old Angeliki who kept house there and did my laundry. I did not suspect yet that this would become a long-term engagement. Meanwhile, my daily routine, sitting at Sotiris' coffee shop and letting my mind get immersed with insights, went on. Angeliki gave up her job with Margarita and moved into the little house she owned across the riverbed. That was it. She was to be my house keeper for almost the rest of her life.

I have not mentioned any of the many, many persons I met on Hydra, all with questions cultural, political or existential.

∽

These are just a few meditated notes that George made. The memoirs, which he had written for personal recollection, remain unfinished. There are indeed many interesting things he could have said especially about the many Greek artists on the island and about the history of the house he bought. If my recollection is correct, it is one of the old captains' manors and once belonged to Antonios Oikonomou. Oikonomou had a less fortunate fate. As one of the first in favour of revolution, he tried to rouse his fellow islanders to riot but was killed by his pro-Ottoman countrymen before reinforcements could arrive. The house remained, however, and among its guests was King George I, who visited Hydra. It is just one of the many manors once belonging to Hydra naval leaders that can be found on the island. Characterised by their thick walls, they stayed cool in the summer and warm in winter and their barred windows and thick iron-clad doors kept out pirates and plunderers. Deep cisterns, in which rainwater could be collected, lay under the ground floor and provided the inhabitants with drinking water at a time when Hydra had no natural water supply of its own.

George kept his house in much of its historic shape. He redesigned the library with a coffered ceiling that matched the style of the old manors. The shelves were quickly filled with philosophical and classical texts. No television or internet intruded here. At times staying here truly felt like living in a place where past and present collided.

Hydra Reflections

Valerie Lloyd Sidaway

It's an odd feeling to read a novel that is, in part, set on a Greek island that just happens to be the island where I have spent most of my life. In *Sea Change*, the writer Elizabeth Jane Howard describes a much earlier period when things were simpler. It was the late 1950s. As Howard's characters progress through the scenes, I suddenly find I am *living in* the very house she is describing. I am taken through familiar rooms and onto the terraces, as seen from another person's perspective and in another time.

I am already nostalgic about the house as I know one day I may have to leave.

∾

I arrived on the island in the spring of '72 and spent a magical summer. The winter was quite different. Only a few foreigners were willing to stay. Some of us did not have the funds to leave anyway. Those were the heady days when you gave little thought to the far future. I knew I did not want to return to Sydney and reside in the suburbs.

I first rented a small house with only a bed upstairs and an outside kitchen with a three-burner gas top and a cold water tap. There was a "throw down" toilet in the corner. By the end of summer the owners wanted it back for it was a *prika* house – a dowry – and it was going to be occupied. After much searching I decided to take over a house that an English painter and his Canadian wife had leased in the next village. It was a bigger house with very little furniture, bare light bulbs in each room and a refrigerator, which was a big plus.

Before this I had only an old wooden icebox. This meant carrying a huge block of ice up the many steps. Usually I bought half a block and dragged it with a rope over the cobblestones along the harbour front and up the narrow lane. I carried it in a canvas bag the last part of the way and arrived home exhausted.

The small ice factory down in the port was in a large old warehouse and in the room, suspended in mid-air, were large beams of wood attached to ropes and pulleys that clanked and rattled and out came the huge ice blocks. I'm sorry now I didn't take more interest in all that clanging

~

Katsikas' was the main grocery store, where we would go to fill up our large wicker-covered wine bottle – *galloni* – with retsina. Often when I questioned the price ("*How* much?") the shopkeeper lowered it. He was a kindly man. There were two brothers and both were used to dealing with the crazy foreigners, some who ran up large bills whilst waiting for their money to arrive.

There was a song written about this shop by an English lady, Eileen Barclay. She had lived on the island in the 1960s, along with expats George and Charmian Johnston, Australian writers whose three children were raised in the local Greek lifestyle. The song went something like this: "Who's in whose bed now, who's having a God damn row in whose bed now ... Sitting here at Katsikas' waiting for the mail, waiting for the checks to come ..." It was a simple folk song that related some of the drama in the foreign community. The tune was quite catchy, best sung by Eileen with her guitar, which she played for us on occasion when we met her in 1967. At that time she was working as a hostess on board a large private motor yacht called *Henniesta*, temporarily based in Piraeus.

In her earlier days in Greece Eileen had experienced numerous adventures with her husband Sam Barclay, which included the building of his caïque schooner. At twenty, Sam had joined the Royal Navy in the Second World War. He later volunteered for service in the British–Greek Levant Caïque Flotilla, which was engaged in intelligence operations and commando raids on

Axis-occupied Aegean islands. In 1948-49 Sam built the schooner *Stormie Seas* in Perama. That's where the hull and decks were constructed. Some of the finishing details were done elsewhere. In November 1949 Sam was involved in the Albanian Operation of the CIA and MI6. It was the first covert Anglo-American operation of the Cold War. Eileen and their family dog, Lean-to, were both aboard.

Subsequently they both sailed together with their son James on *Stormie Seas*. In 1966 I almost became cook on their boat, which was available for charter, when the Australian Jon Smith was skipper. We were alongside her in Freatida, now named Zea Marina, in Piraeus. I was relieved not to take on this difficult job, as the galley was claustrophobic. It was a great boat on deck; my partner and I spent many amusing times on board when she was in harbour. Jon Smith was a likable rogue and had many stories to tell. At the time we were taking care of a yacht that was owned by the Viscount Lymington, a really nice man whom we hardly ever saw.

～

On Hydra, life in the early 1970s was modest. Days were spent shopping for food. Picking up fresh bread and vegetables was a daily event. There wasn't much choice for fruit in the wintertime.

There were two cinemas then, one outdoors in the summer with deck chairs you sank to the ground in. Smoking was allowed and dogs and cats wandered through. In winter there was an indoor movie house in a space next door, a huge stone-floored freezing old storage room. There were movies every night and the programme changed twice a week. If you were wise you waited until Wednesdays to go as that was the night the boys from the Naval School went. They marched in uniform along the port and broke rank before entering. It was much warmer on those evenings as we all huddled together. The small wood burning stove only worked sometimes and made little difference when it did.

The movies were D grade and usually about Hercules or similar classics, what we called the "Blood and Sandals" epics. Often there was a spaghetti Western from the Fifties, before Sergio

Leonie, or a Greek black and white singing-and-dancing-at-a-taverna movie.

I recall going to the movies with Leonard Cohen and Anthony Kingsmill, the English painter, one evening in the dead of winter. We saw Vincent Price in the movie *Dr. Phibes Rises Again*, a campy film with Art Deco sets. We voted it the best movie we had seen at our local cinema. It was a gelid night and we later went for a hot drink at Tassos' cafe and then on to Leonard's house were we chatted into the early hours.

The movies cost seven drachmas and you could get a steak and chips for twenty-five drachmas – a dollar. My rent was sixty dollars a month and still I was trying to budget myself to thirty drachmas a day, including paper and pencils to draw with. There was no television then. I didn't even own a radio.

The painter I took over the house from sold me his old tape deck and left one tape, which I had to repair. It was Leonard Cohen's first album. I only had a couple of books. I found *The Magus*, by John Fowles, intriguing and it kept me entertained. I read it twice! The other was a rag-tag paperback missing its front cover: *In Search of the Miraculous*, by Ouspensky. This demanded a lot more study and re-reading and took me to other dimensions. It became an absorbing adventure on the long cold nights when I slept in the living room on an old wooden bench, in a sleeping bag with many blankets on top, as the temperature in the bedroom was below zero. The only heating I had was a small gas fire, which in those days was a round tin disk with a small burner in the centre the size of a light bulb. This was attached to a gas bottle that I could only afford to light for three hours a day. The outside bathroom was cold and damp. I was lucky to have a *thermosyfinos* for hot water, which was turned on only when needed. The small kitchen, in another outside building, had a white marble sink and cold water. I would cook my meal and dash into the living room to eat. To get warm, I went for long walks when it was not raining.

Living conditions had not changed much since Leonard arrived on Hydra and bought his house in 1960. The island and the way of life inspired him. It was a very idyllic place then, a much quieter time. Leonard used to chat with the local tradesmen and made friends with them. Many of the expats that were here then were writers and painters escaping the mores of suburbia. They felt that on Hydra they were free to explore themselves. The Seventies were similar to those earlier days when creative people had time to write, paint, talk, drink and have affairs. They too were discovering who they were. Leonard spent many months on the island at that time, using it as a writing retreat and a respite from city life.

It was at this time, the early Seventies, that Helen and Brice Marden bought their small cottage high up on the mountain, facing west, overlooking the spectacular landscape of mountain, sea and the village of Kamini below. It was a different aspect of their lives, away from the sophistication of New York. The Mardens were generous of spirit and introduced many painters, art critics and other such folk to the island. They gave dinner parties set in the garden under large old almond trees. The guest list varied. Helen was a natural cook and never seemed fazed by the enormity of finding ingredients for a dinner party and having the food and wine delivered by donkey. These events produced humourous evenings sparked by the diversity of interests and opinions, and there were many differing opinions.

I dropped by their house one morning and found Brice on the upper terrace surrounded by coloured paper shapes, or it might have been canvas, scattered across the old paving stones. He had been commissioned to design stained glass windows for the Basel Cathedral. At that moment he was deeply involved with what colour represented, its meaning. I left him puzzling over the arrangement of colour in the clear light for which Hydra is renowned.

≈

In the following years there were more people of varied nationalities staying through the winter. It made social life much more interesting. However, the long wet windy nights remained the same. I remember one evening in particular. We were all bemoaning the ever-lasting cold weather and needed our spirits raised. Suzanne announced she was going to have a party. This was to be at Leonard's house, where she was living. But you were only invited if you agreed to give a performance. It was decided that a small theatre event would take place as Suzanne had a large room in the lower part of the house with a raised floor at one end that was to be the stage. (This brought back memories of Marianne, who had transformed this dark, damp basement into a spacious, attractive room.) The offer of an evening of entertainment was well received but it was doubtful if all would keep their promise to take part.

The night arrived and everyone came, a cast of about eighteen in all. I happened to be part of the first act since I had created a skit that opened the show. Dressed in a long black velvet strapless gown with a full skirt and a blue silk sash across from shoulder to waist, plus a silver crown, I was to represent Queen Elizabeth II. Accompanying me was Athena, the tall, captivating daughter of Demetri, the painter. She was dressed as Prince Philip in suitable black attire. Athena stood beside me with her back to the audience whilst I gave my opening speech, which alluded to two gay gentlemen who owned what we considered a luxury villa on the island and who wintered in Ceylon, and also referring to my Philips radio.

"In the absence of the reigning queens of Hydra, my husband and I hereby welcome you all to this evening's mid-winter night's theatre … When I am at home, to entertain myself on long winter evenings, I like to turn on my Philips."

As I turned and raised my right hand to do so, Athena turned around and unzipped my dress at the back, and it dropped to the floor. Underneath was a black French corset, stockings and black knee-high boots. We kicked our legs from side to side in time with the music from *Cabaret* … except that the person who was supposed to put on the vinyl record at this point miscalculated the timing so there was a delay of some minutes before the music caught up with the act.

Demetri Gassoumis came next. He stood mid-stage and performed *L'Uomo Vitruviano* – *The Vitruvian Man* – Leonardo da Vinci's depiction of the ideal proportions of the human body, according to the Roman architect Vitruvius. Demetri carried out the motions in a silent act of concentration and symbolism. He was an excellent painter and a great teacher. He enjoyed explaining the techniques of drawing; his discussions on this and other subjects were never dull. His passion was understanding colour.

He studied painting at what is now known as the California College of Arts. One of his teachers whilst in San Francisco was Richard Diebenkorn. Demetri lived in one of the grand old houses of Hydra, which he rented. His studio was vast, with a high wooden criss-crossed ceiling and huge arched glass doors leading onto an inner terrace. The light bounced in from north and south. The property was said to have been an old carpet factory and then a schoolhouse, before being bought by an American sculptor, John Lefarge, who remodelled it to fit his needs.

Deidri Dowman, Demetri's Australian girlfriend, was a creative young woman and a talented assistant who worked with him on his larger paintings. Her part in this theater party was to dress as a court jester. She sat at the front-side of the stage in a colourful costume that she had designed and sewn herself.

The next act was Demetri's youngest daughter Cassandra, who shyly performed the yoga sun exercise, very slowly and precisely. Yoga was her new discovery. Then came Douglas Pilbrow, who mimed a man on a crowded bus. He swung and contorted his body, swaying from an invisible strap. This went on for such a long time that I hoped he was going to get off at the next stop.

Christina Kingsmill followed with a lovely song by Leonard Cohen: "Famous Blue Raincoat." "Jane came by with a lock of your hair, she said that you gave it to her …", she sang in a tender voice, unaccompanied and not forgetting the words of the long song.

Larry Hulse … I can't recall what Larry did on that stage, but I remember him for the laughter and joyful disposition he brought to our diverse group.

Fran Benninghoven, Christina's mother, was from Chicago and had been involved with the Bauhaus movement. She was a sculptor, a maker of objects and a big fan of Brâncuși! Fran read a poem. She owned a charming house in the village of Kamini, overlooking the sea, and would invite me for afternoon tea and serve tiny sandwiches that she took great care to make.

Suzanne, aah, the enchanting Suzanne, had set the stage with an antique dressing table with mirror and candlelight and soft curtains as in a boudoir. Dressed in a soft blouse and skirt, she entered slowly and seemed to drift across the stage. She arranged herself at the dressing table with her back to the audience, as a slow blues melody played. Suzanne took a brush to her hair and then slowly removed her blouse, revealing a slender naked back. She then donned a light silk negligee top. It was an enchanting scene, an intimate, feminine moment. The audience was mesmerised!

The act I missed because I was changing backstage was the snake-charming performance by Lily Mac's children, Sergei and Natasha. Together with Sergei's father, Alan Parkin, they had constructed a basket with a snake, which was tied to a supposedly hidden string and somehow raised from within. They were suitably disguised as Indian fakirs. I was sorry not to have seen this magic.

There were three offbeat Frenchmen in attendance that evening, who were all talented. Bernard had painted very realistic eyes on the eyelids and foreheads of the other two men which gave them an extraordinary power of expression. Jean-Noel was a brilliant artist and if you gave him any medium he could create the most fascinating object or painting. He later designed sets for the French theatre and opera. Guy was an eighteen-year-old painter.

Anthony, the English painter who married Christina, we could not manage to draw on to the stage. This man of many words was silent! It would have been a fine moment had he recited a verse by his favourite poet, Wordsworth. After all, he knew all of the poems well and on nights of revelry he often drove us to distraction with his endless quotations. We had all been shy of performing but having exposed sides of us we had not shown before we were warmed and upbeat.

On the walk home that winter's night, the full moon made the white-washed houses luminous. It was so bright on my terrace we could see each other's faces clearly. Small scops owls hooted in the pine forest below. We called them sonar birds because they sound like sonar bouncing out into the night, answering each other across the valley with deep whistles.

~

In the Seventies there was very much a village life still. The town crier would come to Kamini and we would hear him to announce events like "The electricity will be turned off at nine tomorrow morning for an unknown time!" or "The town council will meet to discuss whether the goats should be tethered or allowed to run free on the mountains and eat all the thyme!"

The *papoutsia* man, a small, frail, elder gentleman, would walk the alleyways with shoes and slippers for sale. These were tied to a wooden stick that hung over his shoulder. His soft rolling call – *"Pandoflas! Pandoflas!"* – echoed through the lanes, bringing the ladies of the island to their doorsteps to take a look at the slippers. The little man who sharpened knives and scissors hauled a heavy grindstone wheel in order to apply his trade, which would be welcomed these days. Jimmy "the ragbag" sold clothes from dead people's estates. I have a black and white photo of him, staring into the camera. He always liked to stop and have a talk when on his rounds of the village. He told of returning from America, where he had worked very hard and saved a small fortune. Back on Hydra he gave a party and invited all of his old friends and lots of new ones! This lasted many weeks, until the money was gone. These long ago peddlers offered their service in a simple manner and in return hoped to make a modest living. I miss all of these good, kind folk.

The small grocery shop in Kamini was run by Kyria Kalliope, who had a cleft palate and fascinated me by the way she rattled on about small things. She cooked lunch for some of the local workmen and they looked forward each day to her good home-made food. Her husband Vasilis was a little deaf and he often short-changed. It was a game one had to play on a regular basis. He had been one of the many men on the island who had spent time away at sea in the merchant marines. There were three oilcloth-covered tables in the store where one could sit and enjoy an ouzo or retsina. These are the things one feels the absence of now: the fresh goats' milk they would deliver by donkey each day to your door and the banter of husband and wife, and the joyful workmen after a fine meal, anticipating a long siesta ahead.

Then, of course, there were the ghost stories. One concerned a house in Kala Pigadia owned by Derek, an Englishman who bought ruined houses and slowly fixed them up to be sold. This was hard and labourious as he did most of the work himself, being a capable carpenter. He once told me the story of the long wintry night he had finally had enough of weeks of huddling through freezing evenings alone at home so he thought he would have a night on the town. On this night of eating and imbibing much retsina with Greek friends the revelry went on into the early morning. He finally staggered home up the long steep cobbled lane, crashed into bed and fell fast asleep.

The next morning, stepping out on to his terrace to chase yowling cats away, his Greek neighbour said to him, "That was quite a party you had last night!"

He replied, "What do you mean?"

The neighbour said, "The party at your home – there were people singing and all the lights in the place were on for hours."

Not thinking too clearly Derek did not continue the chat. Later, other neighbours commented on festivities at his abode late the previous night. He told them he had not been at home and they must be confusing his house with another. But they insisted and related many of the antics and details of the event. There were people making much noise out on the terrace, they said.

When he later rented the house to an American lady, she left after one night, complaining that she could not sleep there because there was a ghost in the house and someone snoring loudly in the lower bedroom. This was a well-known story among the locals.

∾

After surviving that winter I experienced my first Greek Easter – *Pascha* – on the island, yet another wet overcast day. The celebrations in the large private church connected to my house went on for three days; there had been weeks of bell-ringing before. On the Friday evening – *Megali Paraskevi* – there was a tentative knock on the front door. When I opened it there entered a line of black figures that proceeded onto the terrace overlooking the small harbour. These were elderly ladies who came to watch the *Epitafios* being carried down to the sea and the bearers of the ornate flower-decked canopied "bier of Christ" wading into the chilly water. The congregation stood on the shore of the curved natural harbour holding their hand-made yellow beeswax candles. It was a wonderful vision to behold.

This appearance on the terrace had obviously been a privilege these ladies had observed for many years. They stood solemnly watching the event below with an occasional remark.

"Kyria Maria, can you see? Have they entered the sea yet?"

Kyria Maria obviously had the better eyesight. After twenty minutes or so they all filed back into the church. "*Efcharisto, efcharisto*" was the thankful chorus as they left. This ritual is observed to this day, though with fewer ladies in attendance.

~

Many eccentric characters found their way to Hydra. Along with painters, writers, poets, musicians, there were people like Bill "the lines-man" from Arkansas. In America, lines-men are employed to climb telephone poles and make repairs to the wires. Bill's daily outfit was faded green overalls with many pockets. From every conceivable place hung many different sized keys, small tools, tiny scissors and other paraphernalia. He was a chubby guy with a merry face when he smiled, a lost soul nevertheless. It was difficult to escape his rambling mind once he had cornered you. He was around for a long time and we got used to him; then he left and suddenly you missed him, you missed the jingle-jangle sound he made when he walked.

Betty Anthony, from Boston, had studied Sanskrit and although wealthy lived a spartan life. Like Fran Benninghoven, Betty used to invite me for tea and after searching through her almost empty refrigerator served me very individual sandwiches made from long forgotten pieces of cheese or a lonely sardine in hot chili sauce. Betty played a magnificent golden harp, which she informed me had its own passport. The sound of her playing drifted across the valley during siesta, when all else was quiet. On hot summer afternoons the notes floated lightly through the air and resonated above and around our terrace. On one occasion I was invited to be present whilst she played. A small group of us sat perfectly still and silent in a large sparsely furnished upper room. The harp's melodious sound travelled across the hillsides, calming a flock of goats in the field next to her house. Years later I remember the instrument leaving the island in its big black case.

It was carried by several men down the many steps that led to the harbour. It was too delicate an item to be transported by mule. Betty's arthritis made it impossible for her to play any longer so, sadly, she shipped it to a new owner.

We appreciated folks who liked to entertain, especially in wintertime. Felix Thoresen, the Norwegian writer – "I'm better known in Russia," he insisted – was one such person. He liked to give dinner parties in a haphazard manner. One evening at Vera Lei's house, which Felix rented for the winter, we were all crowded round a table that took up most of the small windowless room. There must have been nine people tightly packed together; as it was a chilly night we appreciated the warmth and closeness. After much food and drink an argument broke out between two of the guests who disliked each other.

I said to Felix, who was sitting next to me and smoking as usual his cigarette in a holder that he held ostentatiously, "Why do you invite people who hate each other?"

He replied in a very upper class British accent, "My dear, oh, oh, oh! How else can we entertain ourselves if there are no interesting discussions?"

He had a waxed handlebar moustache and red hair that reminded me of a British colonel. He had a certain affectation: after a few drinks he would chuckle – "Oh, oh, oh!" – and slowly fall backwards off his chair, glass in hand, a trick he managed to perfect without breaking his neck. This was the Felix I knew. There was, however, another Felix who had quite another and much darker disposition, so I have been told.

≈

It was cheap to rent or even possible to get a free house during the winter months. Harold and Anne Ramis came one summer and stayed the winter. Harold was writing ideas for television satires and creating scripts for movies yet to be realised. He was a struggling writer then. Later he hit the big time with movies like *Ghostbusters* and *Groundhog Day*. They returned to the island for many years, usually in winter for six months at a time. We spent numerous evenings together, discussing life and the probable future. Harold said to me once, "If you want to be someone else, change your mind!" Meaning, think differently. They were intriguing and appealing company. I remember at one time saying to Harold, "When you're rich and famous, Harold, you won't talk to us anymore" – an old cliché. But he did speak to us! He often invited us to see the movie sets in Hollywood when we visited Los Angeles.

Harold had lots of dark curly hair. His first summer on Hydra he was desperate to have a haircut. Not trusting the island lady hairdresser or the local barber, he begged me to cut it for him. I was used to cutting my own hair but not other people's. With his gentle husky voice, Harold coaxed me into giving him a trim. This became a routine that his wife Anne okayed as I was the only woman she would allow to do so. I was fond of Anne, who had her own inner world that was difficult to penetrate. She was always fully covered, wearing a long dress, and in summer was never without a parasol to protect her from the harsh rays of the sun. She must have been the first person I knew to be aware of the damage it did.

Film stars, royalty, aristocrats and ambassadors were among the grand visitors to the island. Prince Charles and his bodyguards came several times. He remarked on the architecture and was fascinated how it evolved quite naturally. He was the honoured guest of a wealthy Greek shipowner and would arrive by launch to Hydra. The large luxury motor yacht would moor over by the Peloponnese. One late afternoon after an all-day boat picnic, the British Ambassador, a charming man and full of fun, who owned a house on the island, was climbing the steep steps of "Donkey Shit Lane." Sun-burnt, hair in disarray from the sea and salt, in wet beach clothes and having drunk much wine, he saw Prince Charles and his escort descending the steps. Even in this dishevelled state, ever the diplomat, he approached the Prince and introduced himself in the formal manner, as etiquette required. He reminded Charles that he had met him before on a previous occasion. They enjoyed a pleasant chat before going their separate ways.

≈

When the summer Meltemi wind from the north blew for weeks it could easily change your mental state. It was best not to tackle any serious matter because nerves were frayed. When the wind blew from the south – the Sirocco – the sky turned hazy with what I called Qaddafi dust. The red desert sand from Africa covered everything – plants, laundry on the line – and filled your hair and ears. Rain turned it to red mud. Too bad if you had just white-washed the house.

Then there were those balmy summer days spent swimming and lazing around in the sun. Rising late in the morning after all night at cafés and the island disco, I would go to a secluded rock with cheese, bread and a bottle of cool water to read and doze. During languid afternoons I watched dragonflies – "sky hunters" – skim the water and perform aeronautics, manoeuvring straight up and down, or sideways, and hovering like a helicopter. Much older than dinosaurs, dragonflies have been known to migrate across oceans. In some species a single dragonfly can eat up to one hundred mosquitoes a day. Their brisk colour and agile flight are admired in the poetry of Tennyson and the prose of H.E. Bates.

Some somnolent afternoons were spent in siesta even though cicadas – *tzitzikia* – were making a terrible racket, after a while you didn't hear them and then just as suddenly you tuned in again. I was often awakened by the cry, *"Mariaaaaaaah! Mariaaaaaaah!"* through the window opening onto the back terrace. The woman's raucous call came from up the mountain, down into the valley. I never did find out who Maria was – perhaps a daughter lost in play. Those days few people had a telephone.

One hazy day we were entertaining friends from New York. He was a professional jazz musician and played tenor sax and flute. His English wife had been an actress. There was a knock at the door and in came a sparkling, gamin nine-year-old with long dark hair and gleaming white teeth, two missing in the front. Her name was Simone. She came from Switzerland and spent the summers here. Surprised by the visit, we asked how she had gotten to our house.

"By donkey," she said. "I borrowed him from Four Corners."

This was a grocery shop halfway between the main harbour and the village of Kamini, on the inland lane. She had obviously observed the muleteers give instructions to their animals. The *brrrrrrr!* for stopping the donkey is very important if you wish not to end up in Vlychos, the next village. A sharp loud *eehh!* usually gets its little legs moving. Turning left and right can be more tricky. To climb aboard one had to find a small wall or bench to step on first.

We had lunch on the terrace overlooking the sea. We were shaded by the big, old lemon tree and the ancient grapevine whose masses of foliage and bunches of ripe red grapes kept that part of the terrace cool. After lunch it was time for Simone to leave, no doubt to return the donkey before the shopkeeper's returned from siesta to discover it was missing. It was also nearing the end of her holiday, when she had to go back to Switzerland and school. We asked her if she would be sad to leave the island.

"Yes!" she said, "because there are no donkeys in Geneva!"

≈

Hydra constantly brought my attention to nature; this remains one of the reasons for being there. There are lots of rosemary bushes surrounding our old traditional house, the flowers a delicate light lavender shade. The bees are abuzz when they are in full bloom. The honeybee, *Apis mellifera*, is a fascinating insect. When a worker bee has located a food source or a nesting site it performs a "waggle dance" that involves running through a small figure of eight pattern. The distance between hive and target is encoded in the duration of the waggle runs. The more excited the bee is about the location, the more rapidly it will waggle to gain the attention of the observing bees. They also adjust the angle of the dance to accommodate the changing direction of the sun. Taking sightings similar to navigation, the bee takes a line from the hive to the sun and then indicates the angle from the sun that the destination is found. The bee has an internal compass knows the location of the sun as it arches across the sky.

Barn swallow, common house martin, white wagtail, European robin and great tit, which is black, white and yellow, are among the small birds that visit the island. On April mornings and evenings the great tit sings his heart out protecting his boundaries, and calling for a mate with a wonderful loud call for such a tiny bird. There are also collared doves, imported pigeons, different kinds of seagulls and chatty, quarrelsome house sparrows and tree sparrows. Sparrow hawks and occasional large sea eagles, with enormous wing spans, circle over Vlychos beach. If you're lucky, sometimes you can hear a nightingale. Each season brings different migratory birds. I once saw a hoopoe in early summer feeding in our back garden, which is more like a small field with sixteen almond trees as well as orange, lemon and wild fig trees, and several olive trees. One huge olive tree is over 150 years old and has two large trunks angling off in a V shape; my arms cannot encircle either trunk. The cats use it as a play centre.

~

In the late afternoons, when we felt cool after a swim, we often played softball at the local football (soccer) field, a large area of small, rough buff-coloured stones and hard ground. Pan was the organiser and if we did not have enough players he would scout the harbour for visiting young tourists to fill the positions. Gregory Corso and Buckminster Fuller were guest lecturers at the summer school run by John Zervos on the island of Aegina. When Gregory heard about our softball game, he challenged us to a match. Gregory was the captain of their team and he was sure of a win. It was a hot and dusty day and our rag-tag crew was keen to go. After an hour or so of play, with much bantering and haggling over scores, the Hydra team managed to pull off a win. Gregory was his usual rebellious, irascible self and not a happy loser. It never occurred to us to take a photo of the teams. Nobody carried a camera, but I still have the softball bat we used.

Corso had lived in Athens in the Sixties and spent a winter on Hydra in the early 1970s. He and Anthony Kingsmill spent time together and tried to out-drink and out-quote each other. Quite often I took to avoiding them, especially when they were inebriated. My nickname for him was Coarse Corso. I was too young to realise that his advances and attempts to make conversation were just his way of flirting.

One evening I was having a quiet meal at the "half-way taverna," which was on the inland lane halfway between the port and Kamini and had no name. I was reading a Greek comic book. I am very bad at languages and I'd been advised to start by reading comic books and children's books for simple sentences. Gregory was sitting alone at another table trying to get my attention.

Finally he called out an expletive: "– – – *comic book!*"

Gregory was disgusted that I was reading a Greek comic book instead of Homer or other Greek literature. He was, after all, a Beat poet as well as a great cynic and was known to make those kind of remarks. I would have been kinder had I known what to do with the comments thrown my way. I was no match for his variable mind. Gregory, I found out later, had experienced a difficult period in Athens, when he was struggling with a serious drug problem and alcohol was a way out. My compassion missed the moment!

Many other poets wandered through Hydra. Irving Layton stayed a while when he visited the island in July, 1975. I loaned him a book, *Inside Mr. Enderby*, by Anthony Burgess. He came sheepishly to the house one day to tell me he would have to get me another copy as it had been washed away by a wave. This happens all the time on the rocks if you are mindless for a moment when a ferry boat passes. Five minutes later the great waves reach the shore and many a tourist, and much bathing gear, has been swept into the sea.

Irving and I often spent time together. All I knew about him was that he was a poet from Canada and he was a friend of Leonard and Suzanne. He stayed in their house whilst Leonard was away. I don't know what we talked about, as I was not well versed in poetry. I *was* a good listener.

One morning when I had gone down for a morning swim, I found crumpled pieces of paper with unfinished lines of poetry tucked into a crevice in the rocks. They were poems of unrequited love. Irving had had a huge crush on Suzanne's latest au pair, a young foreign girl. He was a relaxing soul, easy to listen to and a good companion. He did replace the book he lost with another. He couldn't find *Mr. Enderby* in Athens, so he gave me *The Mani*, which Patrick Leigh Fermor had written on Hydra at Ghikas' house. Before leaving the isle to return to Canada he gave me a book of his poetry, *Seventy-five Greek Poems, 1951-1974*, in which he inscribed a warm message.

~

The summers seemed endless then. There were days when the sea was so calm and quiet, the surface reflecting clouds and deep blues and greens. On such a day I was sitting on the edge of a flat rock reading, and listening to the silence and an occasional gentle lap of the sea. Suddenly it was raining flapping silver objects and I was sharing a space and a strangely timeless moment with a frightened school of young *gavros* – anchovies – that must have been chased by a large hunter and in alarm had leapt into another dimension. Fish get quite nauseous when out of their element so I swiftly returned them to the ocean. To connect with nature in this way, to be immersed in its colour and vibration, even briefly, is magnificent and it's why I liked to go for walks alone into the landscape.

That season there were two large turtles that used to swim close to the shore. I would watch them come to the surface and float. Often when sailing we would see them on their way to Hermione. One October, after the tourists had departed and the swimming spots were empty and tranquil, a cormorant popped up beside me in the glassy sea. It was not at all disconcerted finding me there as it had already located me under water. It was I who was surprised: it's rare to view such a specimen up close. Moments later, a flash of green iridescence sped by just above my head, the bright sparkle of a kingfisher and then gone!

~

Painters speak of a special light in Greece and Anthony Kingsmill captured this in his landscape paintings. He explained to me how he prepared the under colours to reflect light into his finished canvas. One summer a friend gave him a ticket to Paris as he yearned to see the Picasso exhibition showing there. Before he left he asked my assistance in preparing a couple of canvases for paintings. He had a commission for a landscape of "houses and seascape" looking towards Kamini. Then he left for Paris. I prepared two canvases to the exact size of his drawings of an earlier work and had traced the drawings onto the canvases in readiness for his return, as he had asked. A week or so later, I received a telephone call from him asking if the drawings were completed. He said he was delayed and that I should proceed to apply the toned coat and instructed me what colours to use. His palette was minimal. He wanted an imprimatura: a light wash of ochre, letting the drawing remain visible. Then I was to mix certain colours in order to build up his under-painting to the window frames of the houses. Every week he called to give me new instructions and each time I got more nervous, repeating that no matter what paint colour he told me to mix it was not going to be the same as he would prepare. Painting by phone was not going to work: he must return and finish them himself.

He remained in Paris, got locked out of his hotel for not paying the bill, and rang his more wealthy friends for assistance. This went on for several weeks. Finally he reappeared in London. The painting lessons from Paris ended. After begging him for years to instruct me in painting, that was how it finally came about.

Everyone who knew Anthony had a story to tell. Although he could drive you crazy with his antics, we all missed him when he left the island. Just like the bee pointing to the pollen, Anthony would do a little dance that led to the next bar. I remember the little skip he would do when feeling joyful.

≈

The reason Anthony entrusted me to prepare his canvases was because I had had good training from Miriam Young Hart, wife of Dick Hart. She gave my first lessons in oil painting on Hydra. Dick Hart was an excellent watercolourist and etcher. Both were Chelsea Art Club members. Miriam was a fine teacher and a good friend. They owned a small house in Kamini with a sea vista and spent many summers here enjoying the many different aspects of the island. It was Miriam who taught me to prepare a canvas with rabbit skin glue and the many finer points on how to apply paint. She never touched the canvas herself – she sat quietly and talked me through the process. It was because of her I spent many contented hours alone.

Some time later we became a proud owner of Anthony's painting of Lulu's taverna. It was a gift from an American millionaire who owned a beautiful yacht that we worked on. The painting had previously been owned by Leonora, an attractive blonde woman and an intriguing character. She owned a house very high above the main harbour, with a spectacular view. She lived with her younger lover David; I later found out that they were married and had been companions for a very long time. I happened to be on Donkey Shit Lane one evening and heard the tinkle of little bells. Down the steps came Leonora in a white dress and her necklaces, of which there were many, jingling.

Leonora was quite a personality and had lived many different lives. The story told was that she had been the last mistress of Batista, the Cuban dictator, before the Cuban Revolution in 1959 overthrew him. She managed to escape Cuba with a bundle of cash and some jewels. She spent her later years in a convent in Portugal, but not as a nun. It is said that David was close by, in a monastery; they used to meet in the garden.

They were part of the older crowd. That circle of friends included Chuck Hulse and Gordon Merrick, who was one of the first writers to enjoy literary success with a gay-themed book. They served cocktails of Bloody Marys at their Sunday brunches. These were good for hang-overs from the previous night. The younger crowd went on boat picnics and held barbecues on the beach at night and went for moonlight swims. The older folks gave cocktail parties and swapped stories. We did mingle with them at parties. There were always numerous social events in the summertime. Alexis Bolens gave the biggest and best party in mid-summer, with many international friends invited.

In those days everyone mixed together, young, old, rich and poor and there were lots of attractive people. This, and the fact there were no cars on the island, was what had appealed to me when I first visited Hydra in 1966. Sailing to the island on a yacht called *Vega*, an eighty-foot steel-hulled ketch, with a captain called Mad Mike! We had entered – a term I use loosely here – a race, which started in Piraeus. With a motley crew, much wine and strong gusts of wind that broke the bowsprit, we arrived safe enough.

Subsequently, I often came to stay on the island and met the foreigners living there. Brian was off sailing around the Greek islands so he would spend much time at sea. In 1968 we were, for a while, in Malta working on yachts and then we travelled through Italy to Spain and Majorca. Then on to Gibraltar, where we joined a wonderful Californian couple on their forty-two-foot steel-hulled ketch and sailed to the Caribbean, along with their Labrador dog, who was great company on the voyage.

We returned to live on the island in the early Seventies and I found the house that was to be home. Brian had returned to sailing and spent that winter in America. The view from any part of this old island house is spectacular for it sits high on a rocky ridge overlooking the sea, with a westward view towards the sunset. It is aligned so the sun in winter shines on the house all day as it arcs across the sky. Without the winter sun, these stone houses get very damp.

~

I never tire of the scenery. From the terrace there is a panorama spanning the mountains on the left, the hillside over the valley below, the picturesque harbour and the sea looking outwards to the Peloponnese. People come and go, men work on their small colourful fishing caïques, the sound of music trails after boats going by, seagulls circling.

As Leonard said, "I came so far for beauty."

What I Come Back to

Alison Leslie Gold

The place

If you dropped your wallet in the central square it would still be there the following day. Untouched including contents.

Someone I haven't seen in twenty years sits at a nearby café table. Without fanfare, we resume a conversation begun when last we met.

The old bakery is known as the old new bakery; the more recent, the new new bakery.

The tinned evaporated milk brand called Gala Nounou has had the same two-shades-of-blue-and-white label for as long as I've been adding it to my tea and Nescafé. Except for a few changes. Before the Socialists were elected in the Eighties, the milkmaid's alabaster breast nursed a plump baby. Then the blouse was buttoned and the baby and breast were replaced with an armload of white tulips. Also a small, resting cow was erased completely.

Roosters do not abide by any rules when they crow and do so all day long.

I buy paint by number (as I always have) from the hardware shop. My kitchen floor is #26. My small bedroom floor is #62. My large bedroom floor is a mix of two parts #21 and one part #26. My windows and shutters are one part #38 mixed with one part white enamel. My interior kitchen doors/windows are yellow #18.

A mangy, feral cat with a crushed foot appears at my door like clockwork visit after visit somehow knowing that I've arrived, meowing hoarsely, insisting I feed her. I do. I've tried to love her but have failed. She's called Olympia: O-*limp*-ia. Also, like clockwork, my neighbour brings lemons from her tree. The bag is so full I can hardly lift it.

A cemetery in the hills with a view of the sea is where my great friend Lily rests. I visit bringing news good and bad, wine or coffee, my latest publication (if there is one) for her comments, a wild flower or two, fresh bread. With the tinkle of goat bells nearby, we while away the day. My friend's conversation, even in death, is music with lyrical flights of idea in four or five languages, sometimes simultaneously.

Sparrows jabber along with the sunrise.

Guests and visitors have haphazardly mixed red-coloured books with those that are blue or green, yellow or black. Darin, my Virgo writer friend (who white-washes and otherwise fine-tunes the house as well as finding junk that he magically transforms into makeshift white-enamel bookcases), will be furious that his colour-coding has been altered.

The sea here is so salty and buoyant that my son at age four walked boldly in and swam, having had no previous experience. Even on a blazing hot day, if you can find a bit of shade, a breeze will always cool you. Lily taught me: this same breeze will keep a watermelon cooler outside a refrigerator than in.

The house

Ann Rivers, the poet who kept an eye on my house when I was away (and who remains a still point in this turning world just as she was then), was my Greek chorus:

> One unfortunate circumstance inheres in the fact
> that the girls failed to water the garden with the
> result that when I went to prune the rosebush, I
> found it moribund. Ditto the jasmine.

> The Water Co. recently replaced your meter, as of
> 13 August reading, zero. Doing so, they uncov-
> ered a leak in the pipe, necessitating the plumber.

I've watered the plants and fed the cat.

The electrician has for sale a mauve-coloured, push-style telephone which, with the wall connection, would cost approx. 8,500 drachmas. The "phone jack" would consist of a clear-plastic cube you insert in the wall outlet when the phone is in use, and remove when it's not in service.

Your cistern was cleaned in 1986.

Irrespective of what Loussis told you last autumn, he no longer sews awnings. For that you would have to go to Ermioni. Last summer, he told me he did such work only in wintertime. One reason I waited. Perhaps by the time you arrive you'll find him in a more cooperative mood.

Your house is becoming a way-station of sorts.

This is to reassure you insofar as possible about your plumbing. The plumber pronounced the old toilet tank inoperable.

The plumber has tonsillitis. If he's not well soon I'll find someone else to change the washers.

The wall outlet alone costs in the neighbourhood of 1200 drachmas When I enquired, the electrician's wife was unable to guess what he would charge to install the phone.

Your house is doing fine. There has been no rain leaking in, but let's await some torrential downpours for any final judgement.

The outside tap is leaking, a leak the plumber promises to repair before you arrive. The telephone connection may or may not have to wait; possibly an inconvenience. It takes no more than a jiggle, however, to coax it into service.

It was 36 hours without electricity.

The carpenter has yet to put in an appearance, but judging by his past record, it may have to be someone else who does the trellis repair. Less felicitously, requiring the electrician's services. Also there's a minor plumbing repair the plumber has agreed to undertake, but not until Easter's done.

The wife of your guest is, whether you know it or not, hyper-allergic to cats. Vig herself is an easy cat who stays outdoors and is less likely to raise hackles and dander. There should be no objection to feeding her.

The plumbing job is completed, but not paid for. By the time you faxed I had mobilized the Municipality only to discover it was not their problem but that of the house whose pipes had rusted through.

It is the season of funerals and also the time at least one woman gives vent to a hysterical fit of screaming.

On 7 September the meter read 15,844 kilowatts and 18 tonnes of water.

Two long sandbags have been left in the foyer of the old part of the house.

The house is snug, all save one small puddle under the kitchen door. This after our first substantial rain.

Wiring shorted out.

Friends/songs/springtime/1971

I first set foot on Hydra's stony surface wearing red and white bowling shoes and very dark glasses. I was dissolute, adrift, often inebriated, irreverent on principle, had not forged an identity of my own, doubted I ever would nor thought it mattered if I did or didn't. I was not alone.

Exhuming those haphazard days is bittersweet. It was the end of the Sixties, the Vietnam War was raging, I was recently divorced and had an unquenchable thirst for spirits in a glass. I was twenty-four; my son, Thor, was four. We'd sailed from New York on the Greek ocean liner *Queen Anna Maria* that landed in Piraeus ten days later under a full moon – June 21, 1970. I had planned for a month on a mythic island that accidently turned out to be Hydra. We stayed two years, left, and I have been returning since.

This rock-hard place was/is/will always be breathtaking, life-altering, doubtlessly ensnarling new victims just as it did me. Its Sirens tend to tease out tender seedlings of art/writing/music/creativity/Eros from between otherwise dry rocks. This proud island harbours pockets of worldliness that have left fingerprints in many pies; it's an aphrodisiac, rife with intrigue; its enchantment can draw one toward oblivion. Or so it was for me.

I had one cassette tape in my little player when I arrived and played "What Have They Done to My Song Ma" about a thousand times. Melanie sang about what they'd done to her brain and how she was half insane. I don't know why I had this piece of music or what (if anything) it was saying to me about life/my life/the world.

∽

Lily Mack: I was taken under the wing of this mesmerising Russian with the mind of three geniuses rolled into one, in her early forties at the time. Lily was the original untameable spirit, one of the first foreigners to own a house on Hydra, so alluring (green eyes, tawny hair) that rumour was that more than a few smitten men followed her to the island. The locals called her Angelina because of her many acts of kindness and generosity. Overlooking the sea in Kamini village, her house was – as we said then – a two-cigarette walk to the port along the coast road. She arranged for us to rent a newish house above hers owned by a friend for a pittance. After mind-numbing repetitions of Melanie's song, Lily admonished me. One piece of advice she gave me through our long friendship: Never coarsen. If only she were here to tell me if I have or haven't.

After a while I acquired a few friends (some of whom I'm calling by their real names here). The first were among the resident foreign colony as I didn't speak Greek. My Greek neighbours were always tolerant; always had a smile or a greeting or some food to share; in time lasting friendships (and occasional conflicts) were forged.

Christina Benninghoven: the same age as me, from Chicago, full-figured, tall, peaches-and-cream skin, had had problems at Sarah Lawrence College, she bragged, for wearing a gorilla suit to graduation. She fell in love with Anthony, a gnarled Englishman, who was twice her age, half her height.

Anthony Kingsmill: a poetry-quoting, drinking painter who, when actually able to complete a masterly painting, often lost it in a poker game. Usually to a close friend. Anthony and Christina were lovers and lived in a ramshackle white-washed house with several cats belonging to his former lover. They'd decided to marry if Christina was pregnant, and, if she was, were sure the child would be a girl they would name Emily. That spring, in 1971, the island strewn with yellow daisies as far as the eye could see, they had gone into Athens for a pregnancy test. Because some of us often passed out together when we drank too much, Emily was of common interest and we wondered what they would decide to do.

EMILY YES STOP WEDDING TOMORROW MIDDAY STOP BRING EVERYONE STOP COME JEANETTES, read the telegram.

Jeanette Read: in her late twenties, had fallen in love with Hydra, bought a half-ruined house in Kamini, imported much of her British family there but had to spend most of her time and energy in Athens and elsewhere earning money to feed her family and repair her house.

The news: traversed the island by mouth as no one I knew had a telephone then. Someone at the bakery was against the marriage: She is young. He'll bully her, go out and get drunk, and not come home. Lily was for having Emily as she was for all women having all babies, had even tried to persuade me to have another "miracle," as she called children, beginning with her own two.

Rie (pronounced ree-ah) Goldman née Albertsen: red-haired, Danish, a captivating woman my age whose mother had been an Olympic gymnast and father a Resistance hero during the war. She and her American husband, Robert, formerly in advertising, and their two beguiling, flaxen-haired daughters, Johanne, three, and Helle, five, were enchanted with Greece and had been living on Hydra for about five years. That spring Robert was away in Turkey doing something mysterious.

While news of the telegram was spreading, Rie joined me for coffee at Tassos' Kafeneon, dropping a tomato-filled canvas shopping bag at her feet. I was seated in the left-hand-upper-corner at the café, drinking a celebratory beer across from Christopher Pearl. I'd occupied that same seat at that same table religiously (my office, my church) behind sunglasses since my arrival on the island the year before. Christopher, Rie and I huddled around the table, discussing the news. Rie admitted that she loved ceremonies and wanted her children to witness one. We thought it a good idea to travel to Athens together, she, her kids, me, my son and my au pair. "Bravo!" said Christopher, not mentioning whether he would also go.

Christopher Pearl: an Australian, thirtyish, thick, mahogany-coloured hair, good-looking, son of a renowned Australian journalist, could write, paint, act and joke all at the same time, was drinking tea. Lily hoped Christopher would father my next "miracle" and occasionally balanced a portable record player on my windowsill while it played romantic Russian balalaika music when Chris would visit after dark. When Thor first noticed Christopher at the port, he had gone up to him and asked, "Could you please look after my mother so I can play?" Christopher obliged.

Once Chris asked Thor what America was like. Thor replied: "America is the good guy country." When Chris told him he was from Australia, Thor informed him: "Australia is the bad guy country." Chris then enquired as to what Thor thought of Greece. Without a moment's hesitation, because Greece was made up of so many islands, Thor announced, "Greece is the broken country."

Dominick: Fresh from Kastello (or Baby Beach), Dom, my au pair, lumbered over with my son Thor, who was golden-haired, with singing eyes, sun-tanned, dangling limbs. English, slim, dark and brooding, a few years younger than me, Dom had been fleeing what he described as "a stifling upper-class upbringing" when he chanced on Hydra and my son. Some mornings when Thor would wake up very early, Dom would look in on me and seeing me, as he described me, "fast asleep, on, not in" my bed, he and Thor would go down to the beach for a swim in the "lazy benign sea lapping the shore, the two village cockerels crowing and the sun coming up" (as Dom put it in a letter years later). Then back for breakfast. (Not long afterwards, Dom abruptly departed the island to visit his parents in Malta and didn't return. I lost track of him for thirty years. When he resurfaced we managed a teary reunion.)

Thor seemed more like a member of Rie's family than mine, as I was dark and raven-haired. Dom glared at my beer bottle while he described how magnificent the sea had been. Thor told us that Norwegian Marianne Ihlen, the lovely, ash-blond muse to many men, especially Leonard Cohen, had a cluster of men of various nationalities swarming around her at the beach. She, along with her lovable and leggy eleven-year-old son, Axel, had been swimming with Thor and Dom all morning.

Thor ordered a *portokalada* (an orange soda), showed me a fistful of coloured beach glass discovered among the pebbles on the shore. One cobalt-blue piece was shaped like a wishbone. He handed it to me, then demonstrated how he and Dom had almost captured a little octopus. "It came this close before it shot away."

Johanne and Helle: were a dozen yards away fishing with a net and a string between the small boats. Fishing with and not with them, holding a net and a string with a hook on it (several small, still living, fish he'd caught thrown wiggling on the ground), was a skinny, Chaplinesque Greek of indeterminate age called Captain Giannis who sported a half-grown moustache, wore baggy pants rolled up to his knees, held up with rope. Captain Giannis had the mind of a child and fished all day at the port. (Everyone on the island kept an eye on him, made sure he had food.) Seeing their mother and Thor, the girls wandered over. Helle pulled over a chair, the fish net still dripping, Johanne plopped onto Rie's lap. When told the news of Christina's pregnancy, the children wondering if they would be allowed to see the baby born, or, as Johanne put it, "When Christina lays her baby."

Marriage was a hallowed business to them. Thor and Helle had wed in winter under the Goldmans' grape arbour. Because Thor was a little sluggish during the solemnising, Johanne (who they'd decided could live with them forever) clutched one of his hands while the bride gripped him by the neck and Robert recited a melodious ceremony.

∾

It was almost noon. Local Greeks, a few tourists and various members of the foreign colony criss-crossed the port to or from post office, bank, grocery shops, vegetable market, bakery, pharmacy, paint shop, electrical shop, OTE, where telephone calls were made.

Talk was about the wedding, other news received by mail, money that hadn't come. Anne Rivers: aloof poet, with elegant, erect posture wearing a ruffled white blouse, walked by, didn't sit. So did Rick Vick: son of an English judge, the sexiest man on the island with piercing blue eyes and a pirate's ink-black hair. Rick was light on his feet, wrote poems, scoffed at money. He sat down at nearby Katsikas' restaurant/shop with Phaini Xydis: the most carnal, funniest, best cook, most generous woman on the island, daughter of a Greek ambassador. Henna-haired Phainie was wrapped in a metallic, tent-like sarong, wore a ring with a large cockroach embalmed in plastic on her middle finger.

Nancy Major: rumoured to be the composer of "How Much is that Doggie in the Window?" and "Que Sera, Sera," huddled several tables away with her daughter, Phyllis, and son-in-law, Jackson Browne, over a *meze* and ouzo. Across from them was Muriel Wilde: a famous, white-haired, Canadian war correspondent in her seventies with crepey skin who had retired on Hydra, drank brandy in the morning, ouzo in the afternoon, scowled non-stop and raved about politics, unsteadily waving her carved cane to make points.

Lily, with three beautiful young French friends in tow – Katya, Jean-Nöel and Guy: imaginative artists who could make art out of anything and everything – leapt off an arriving caïque before it landed then scurried up the lane toward who knows where. Also climbing out, once it had tied up, Sinclair Beiles: South African, editor and Beat poet, friend of Corso, Ginsberg, Burroughs and Greek artist Takis, his face flushed and waxy. Sinclair marched toward the post office in order to send off another 10,000 word express opinion letter to the editor of a Greek newspaper that Lily had translated into Greek for him earlier. A beautiful Swedish woman in hand, muscular, tanned Pan Lambesis jumped onto a small boat and began rowing out into the harbour.

The children thought it practical if we all spent the night at Rie's place as it was closer to the port, had handy extra beds, would make it easier to catch the ship at dawn. We adults agreed. "Bravo!" Chris once again offered, who knew why.

Dom persuaded Antonio, a fisherman with a bristly moustache who looked like Socrates, to take us to Kamini by caïque. Dom and I stepped onto Antonio's boat and the children went off to fish some more, envying Captain Giannis' catch. How did he do it? Fish seemed to jump onto his hook. Our white boat with blue trim putt-putted slowly out of the harbour, hugged the rocky cliffs. Antonio offered me a cigarette, took one for himself. Lit them both. Across the glassy blue and green water lay the spine of mountains on the Peloponnese. We passed Kamini village, putt-putted further on to a small dock adjoining my temporary rental beside Kastello, where we got off. This was a makeshift dock at which another fisherman, this one resembling Lily's husband, Alan, docked weekly to deliver a large block of ice since our house had an ice box rather than a refrigerator.

As I hadn't "dressed" in a year, I wondered if I still knew how. Here was a good reason for an ouzo. Passing through my little kitchen into my bedroom, I poured an inch of mirror-clear ouzo into a glass, added water and watched it go cloudy. The aniseed flavour burned its way down. Within seconds my skin became swan's down. I dug up an old Ted Lapidus shirt in passable shape despite a missing button – I could easily sew on the button on the ship – and packed a purple and poison green faux-Pucci silk dress that came in a can.

The shoe situation was hopeless since I only had bowling shoes and sandals. Thor had nothing at all dressy, his Shetland sweater and cut-offs would have to do. I filled my silver flask, got a handful of drachma bills and a credit card from under the mattress, also my lucky nugget-size piece of marble from the Acropolis, re-hid my passport and hoped I'd remember where this time. I'd shower at our hotel room in Athens since, if I turned my water heater on at the house, there was a chance I'd get an electric shock in the shower that had been repaired by Robert, sometimes a would-be electrician as well as a celebrant. (Or had he been trying to murder me?)

I kicked the chicken that had wandered in out of the kitchen, closed the windows, fed the kittens and kicked them out too, didn't water the plants. Better to bring some extra underwear. (Untidy on the outside always, I wore real Pucci underwear from Henri Bendel on principle then.) I told Dom not to let the cats back in and that I'd see him later and began the trek on the back road, down, up, down, up, aptly nicknamed "Donkey Shit Lane," past large swatches of knee-high yellow daisies sprinkled with a blood-red poppies.

M.: I passed Kalliope's shop and the old bearded priest hurrying somewhere, then passed M. sitting sideways on her donkey, swollen ankles dangling. A wild-haired, soft American wearing a housedress, she was married to a talented African–American sculptor. They had a small child. Word was they'd left the Midwest, where they'd been ostracised. M. had a breakdown on Hydra in winter and was just out of the Piraeus asylum. (Had it been thirty years later, she probably would have been diagnosed with postpartum depression.) I acknowledged her with a wave but couldn't understand a word she said, her jingles resembling Eastern sayings, nursery rhymes, also imprecations. Sadly, the shock treatments didn't seem to have cleared her mind.

Halfway to the port on the back road was Rie's rental owned by a gay gallery owner from Düsseldorf. I sat down to catch my breath before lighting a Papastratos cigarette. Rie was stomping her laundry in a big, red plastic tub, slacks rolled up to her knees. The children called us from the grape arbour demanding that we come down and watch Helle "laying babies." The poor kittens were squealing under Helle's shirt while Thor, the dad, and Johanne, the midwife, gently extracted one ball of orange fur at a time. We played with the kids and kittens, then, went inside so Rie could finish the laundry. I took off my shoes, rolled up my slacks and walked around with her while we smoked and yakked.

After the laundry was hung, Rie fed the children. I read them a couple of stories then wandered onto the terrace to smoke and watch the sky go darker and darker damson until I could no longer tell where the island ended and the sea began. There just weren't unbeautiful nights on the island, nor unbeautiful days. When Dom arrived, we mothers decided to be sensible and go down to the port for just one tiny sip of retsina. For luck. We'd return early as neither of us cared to face dawn travel with a hangover. Dom and I contemplated the stars while Rie dressed and she and I made our way downhill on Donkey Shit Lane.

Virginia Newton: sat at Lulu's taverna drinking retsina that came from a barrel. She was also eating red mullet, pausing to smoke one strong cigarette after another. A Belgian originally, she had been in the Wrens in World War II, had been a decoder and travelled across the U-boat infested Atlantic, had lived in Africa with a husband for many years, had arresting Windex-blue eyes that matched the pale blue pastel corduroy slacks she often wore. Probably my mother's age, she remained alluring, albeit a bit frosty. I sat with Virginia and we discussed the wedding.

Rie joined a table with folks I didn't know. Two young, handsome Greek sailors began to dance, holding and twisting a hankie between them. One had a gardenia flower behind his ear. Virginia joined in. My drinking friend Bill Finley, older than my father, tall, slim, dark hair clipped close to his scalp, wearing a black cashmere V-neck sweater, took a seat with us, ordered retsina.

William Le Page Finley: at one point Bill laughed so hard his uppers fell out of his mouth and under the table. When he picked them up and slid them back into place, we saw that a front tooth was chipped, giving him an added sinister air. Part Irish, part Native American, with a raspy voice, Bill was alcoholic, a reader of non-fiction only, had lived in Mexico during the war, Paris in the Fifties, Tangier in the Sixties and Greece in the Seventies where his $200 a month fixed income still went far. He swore he was homosexual, was having an affair with a young Greek medical student, but had once lived in France with Nancy Cunard, heiress to the Cunard shipping fortune (he twenty-four, she fifty-one), as well as with a wife in Philadelphia who had died.

Someone shut Lulu's front door, cigarette smoke filled the room. As the night wore on the dwindling few clustered around a single table, the top of which was empty orange metallic retsina beakers, small glasses, an overflowing ashtray.

Philip van Rensellaer and Youla: impeccably dressed, as handsome as movie stars, Philip and Youla joined us. Philip came from old New York moneyed society, had grown up on the Riviera, at the Waldorf Towers, had travelled in Rolls Royces all his life but had hardly any money of his own. Tennessee Williams called him "a male Blanche Dubois." Youla, a still young shapely Greek with untamed orange hair, had appeared out of nowhere having been married to a wealthy gentleman in China and recently divorced. Youla thought Philip had money, Philip thought Youla had money. They shared a house below Marigoula's shop, were hoping to install babbling fountains in its garden. Despite never-ending panic over cash flow, they somehow got by until Philip took too many pills on New Year's Eve and was taken to the asylum in Piraeus and given shock treatments.

Lurching out of Lulu's, we were braced by chilly air that smelled of burning firewood. We breathed out pale clouds, walked to Tassos' for coffee, brandy or both. Beginning to flag, Rie made us all promise to push her up the hill.

A spilled jewel box of stars shimmered in the blue-black sky as we wound up the two hundred or so foot-worn steps that were illuminated by pale pools of moonlight. Up, up, up. If one lost the momentum, all was lost; sit down and stretch out and that's usually where you found yourself in the morning, nudged by a muleteer or a priest heading down from the monastery. One or another of us stopped occasionally to strike a match and light a fresh cigarette. Philip, Youla and I were literally pushing Rie upward.

We noticed a string bag lying on the steps, examined its contents. Two potatoes, half a loaf of bread, a can of imported French asparagus. A few steps further lay a hardback copy of Speer's *Inside the Third Reich*. Nearby, a beam of yellow light rising from the stone. Youla saw the body in time or we'd have fallen over it. There, face down, torch clutched in his hand, was Finley. He was fast asleep, snoring softly. We deposited groceries and book beside him, shut off the torch and continued uphill.

The cocks had started crowing, a donkey made gastric braying sounds, both echoed back and forth against the mountains. Giannis, the short baker with the sweet smile, was just opening his shutters when we reached Rie's house. The children were asleep. We sat outside for a nightcap, witnessed a shooting star …

≈

The next thing I knew Rie was shaking me where I was curled up, fully dressed.

"Hurry! The children are dressed. Does Thor have shoes? Just sandals? That'll do. Here. Coffee. Move!"

She handed me a cup. Dom was already drinking coffee. I pulled on my bowling shoes and looked out the window down the mountain toward the sea. The ghostly white ship could be seen in the half-dark against the Peloponnese in the distance. There was a chance we could make it but not without panic. I hated the Kingsmills. Bag, cigarettes, sunglasses, adrenalin, nausea. I raced ahead for tickets while Dom and Rie herded six little legs down the mountain. I noticed that Finley was gone from the path.

I clutched our tickets as the ship sailed into port. The gang seemed very far behind. "Hurry up!" I yelled. "Come on!"

The white ferry docked, Rie and Dom held children with both hands, were running, it looked as if Johanne's tiny feet weren't touching the cobblestones. It seems impossible, but, yes, everyone ran aboard just as the sailor ashore threw off the great braided rope and the *Neraida* began to glide out of the harbour. This vessel often didn't do well in rough weather, was famous for rolling and roiling while passengers vomited into what looked like Chinese take-out boxes. I hoped the sea wouldn't take us on a wild ride this time.

We settled around a table covered with a white cloth in First Class. I put on my dark glasses. Dom and the children ordered tea, bread, butter and honey. I looked at Rie. How did she do it? She was combed, beautiful, made-up and relaxed. She was a rare beauty, a pale face straight out of Norse mythology. I ordered a beer and a white coffee and lit my first cigarette of the day, felt the ship's engine throb. The sky had gone tawny, the sea was ghostly still. Bit by bit, cold beer and coffee pulled me together and I began to feel elated. Rie, however, was in decline and asked if we minded if she took a cabin in which to sleep for a while as it would be a long day and Johanne hadn't seen a car in a year. Of course we didn't mind.

Wearing an ill-fitting green wool suit that looked, and probably was, pre-war, Virginia joined us. She confessed she hadn't been to the mainland in almost two years. Though we were all fond of the Kingsmills, how could they make us all face Athens? The sun flooded the horizon and the day warmed up. We moved out to the open deck, looked for as yet unravelled orange and blue plastic string chairs that would actually hold our bodies. Finley was sitting in one in a shady corner reading the Speer book and sipping a brandy. He was mystified by a lump on his head. A lone old woman in black was curled up, asleep, on two chairs face-to-face.

Beer led to retsina, retsina to ouzo; the next four hours rushed by in celebration. By the time we reached Piraeus even Dom was celebrating and Thor gave him, for once, rather than me, a disapproving glare. Rie re-appeared, collected. Once the ship docked she and her kids dashed off to the Blue House Hotel, promising to meet us at the church. Dom, Finley, Thor and I taxied up to Kolonaki to find flowers and champagne. We gathered large, scented bouquets of roses, gardenias and a couple of bottles of imported champagne.

~

Pandias Skaramangas: Greek, Anthony's age, from an old shipping family, also slight, a bit gnarled, either very rich or not rich at all, I never knew, a raconteur, ruminant, womaniser, charmer, was Anthony's Best Man. He'd given Anthony the suit he was wearing. Pandias owned many of Anthony's paintings that he'd won at poker.

I was Christina's Maid of Honour. The simple wedding ceremony went on. Thor carried a bouquet of spring flowers down the aisle of the small Anglican Church behind Anthony, who was hung-over but had managed to slick down his hair alongside Christina, who towered over him, and would soon have a protruding Emily. She held fast to his arm. Pandias and I were a few steps behind, suddenly aware of the gravity of it all. The Vicar lisped through the service while Finley snored and other Greek and foreign friends from Hydra looked on from their pews, hot and uncomfortable in make-shift city clothes, already missing the scented light of Hydra.

Trapped in the ancient elevator at the Blue House Pension, Johanne, Helle and Rie missed the ceremony. Their shouts went unnoticed during the long languorous hours of Athenian siesta. Happily, they made it to Jeanette's apartment in time for us all, especially the children, to strew an almost naked, creamy Christina from neck to ankles with rose petals, and handfuls of strong-smelling, velvety gardenias to prepare her for her groom. The combined floral perfume was so overpowering, I can smell it still.

Six months later angelic little Emily came into the world.

The subsequent marriage was a disaster.

Island cats

Fleeing responsibility at that youthful time of life, I kept renting, though the house prices on Hydra were paltry. Always in Kamini near Lily, always within seeing and hearing distance of the sighing sea, without a single premonition of my future. As I neared thirty, I was involuntarily wrenched from alcohol's tightening noose. At first I doubted I could ever return to Hydra and remain sober, but a year or so later, Thor and I visited Lily for Christmas. For the first time I actually saw the beauty of Hydra. "Bravo!" Lily exclaimed many times, seeing that sufficient ballast had lowered my centre of gravity enough for me to live without sedation.

With two hands now empty, I began to write and sketch, I stopped biting my nails, stopped smoking. New ferries came to Hydra: the *Mania Express*, with its sexy, one-eyed captain, the orange-coloured *Portokalis Ilios*, said to be a former gambling ship. Finally, the large and shabby *Mikini* as Greece began to purchase smoke-belching hydrofoils from Russia that could make it to Piraeus in under two hours.

Lily found a house for me guided me when I bought the old, small fisherman's house with lime-green shutters, a tiled roof, a 180-degree westward view that included mountains on one side and the sea spread out before me, on the hillside directly across from hers. From then on the written word replaced ouzo and Papastratos. I came to experience the writing life as sexy, as inebriating, intensified on Hydra, as I once experienced the drinking life, though night became day. Lily gave me a skinny sapling that grew into a sturdy apricot tree. It blossomed and bore fruit for thirty years before it died, outliving her by three years.

I'd sworn that I would never adopt a cat. Once, a renter of mine adopted nine cats. When I arrived, I found nine little faces meowing plaintively every time I opened my front door. I then made it a rule that anyone staying in my house would be evicted immediately if they adopted a cat. If one had to feed cats, one must do so outside the gates of the house.

One winter night, though, the wind howled, the rain fell in buckets. I heard a thumping on my kitchen door. I opened it to find a drenched cat so desperate to get out of the rain she had been throwing herself against my door. I let her in, told her, "Just for tonight." She stayed six years and died before my eyes on my terrace.

From that stormy night on, whenever I would return to the island, day or night, rain or shine, winter or summer, I would drag myself up the last forty-one steps, insert my key into the lock in the front gate, swing it open. I'd then hear a light thump on the terrace in front of me. Unfailingly, from out of the branches of the apricot tree given by Lily, my cat Vigilante would emerge and leap onto the terrace. She would stand looking at me. If cats could cross their arms to indicate "It's about time!" she would have.

The worker is due on Sunday. He turns up on Tuesday but has not brought the right tools. He reschedules for Friday, so I take the sea road toward the port for coffee. A black cat crosses my path. Another cuts in front of me. Still another follows later as I make my way down to dinner and walk past the usual chickens and donkey and women gossiping.

At the Rolloi café, where I like to drink coffee these days, next to Tassos' (café stations having reconfigured religiously many times over the forty-five plus years), a black cat rejoins her litter of noisy kittens. One kitten climbs into my open backpack bringing more doses of bad luck. Black cat, bad luck, except in Japan or the UK, or, according to James Joyce, who swore black cats brought good luck. "He watched the dark eye slits narrowing with greed till her eyes were green stones ... then he poured warm bubbled milk on a saucer and set it slowly on the floor. – Gurrhr! she cried, running to lap [...] He listened to her licking lap."[1]

The sleek green-eyed mother cat follows me home, darting under my feet, almost causing me to stumble. I clasp the cobalt-blue wishbone-shaped piece of beach glass always in my pocket for luck. And, yes, feed her.

I'm wary of the promised change in luck, whether good or bad or even bad good luck or good bad luck.

One island tree

I noticed a tree growing in a coffin-sized space between my house and the adjoining house behind mine. I could swear it wasn't there before. It was a sad-sack tree, about the height of my roof. When I got close enough to examine it, I recoiled as it had a sour smell.

Glancing at it again on Sunday, the tree had shot up three more metres.

Made enquiries. My next-door-neighbour, Giannis, shrugged:

---

[1] *Ulysses*, James Joyce, Shakespeare and Company, Paris, 1922, p. 54.

"Of course, it is an ailanthus tree. Not really a tree but a weed."

More information acquired: the ailanthus is known in China as "the tree of heaven" but also as a foul-smelling tree that grows at break-neck speed, reaching heights up to fifteen metres in twenty-five years. The species is "short-lived" and rarely survives more than fifty years. Fifty years? By suckering, the tree can clone itself indefinitely, making it practically immortal.

But why had it appeared out of nowhere? Its branches are greyish; as the tree shoots up, they become pendulous. The odour reminds me of cashew nuts gone rotten. I, along with Anne, my then caretaker, Greek chorus, begin the task of dealing with this albatross/tree/weed as its roots threaten to destroy the stone wall of the old section of my house.

> The builder is out of town this week; or, has a sick child. His opinion is that the roots are invading the construction, but without x-ray equipment, how to locate each rootlet?

> Yesterday the builder and I went to your house together to survey the problem. The first thing I noticed was that the tree has sprouted again. He, the builder, can of course, simply chop it down once more, but that may not be the way you care to solve it. He can entirely pave over the area between the houses. For drainage he suggests running a pipe through the house, along the wall where there is already a ledge which will help, if not conceal it, make the pipe somewhat more aesthetic in appearance once sealed over.

> I contacted the builder about the job as now described to uproot the tree, fill the hole and pave it over. His figure for doing that is 30,000 drx.

> I did raise the issue of the tree again, the response ran to the effect leaves needed to fall and sap descend before the job could be done, after Christmas.

Showing how fast it grows, the ailanthus is back since it was lobbed and you left. I'll ask D. to chop it back whenever it appears.

Your new water reading stood at 7/0 on 2 October, and your electric meter at 15,344 kilowatts the same day. Sorry to report the ailanthus tree has once again sprung up, beside the spot the builder dug and cemented over. As you may recollect, these wild plants are willful; I've been doing battle with a fig bush for years.

It should have been called the Rasputin tree. We sawed it down, poisoned it, dug it up, smothered it. It grew back; grew taller; wouldn't die.

Then, out of the blue, just as a new conundrum, creeping mildew, began visiting my kitchen ceiling, the ailanthus tree vanished and never returned.

What I come back to

Finally the drowsy days of rain end, a rim of sunset can be seen against the soft curves of the Peloponnese. Lemons from my neighbour's tree have fallen onto my road and steps.

Doors have swollen from the rain. The door to the old part of the house won't open; the door to the front gate won't close. During the downpour, the leak under the metal spiral stairway to the newish upstairs studio – built when my neighbour erected a second story that obscured my sea view and broke my heart – stopped, but water from the kitchen ceiling dripped onto the table where my papers and fresh bread are.

When the sun has dried everything, I fill in a crack in the terrace above the kitchen with acrylic sealant shot through a tube with a kind of cocked gun left over from the recent cleaning, resealing of my cistern, and listen to goat bells high up in the hills. My neighbour stops by to bring me a sack of fresh lemons. The third in a week; enough lemons for an army.

After scrubbing my dirty laundry in the red plastic tub with soft cistern (rain) water and soap, I hang it piece by piece on the line that's strung across the terrace. A couple of indigo-coloured plastic clothespins crumble when I pinch them, exhausted after doing their work through a long, baking-hot summer. The sun is still strong, though it is now October. If I can get myself to put on my bathing suit, I'll go for a swim. Almost before I finish hanging the last bits on the line, the first have already dried. I walk to the sea and have a languid swim in the silky water.

Olympia, the hobbling tabby cat, hasn't visited once. I've seen her at two different tavernas, fat and swaggering, oblivious to my lack of affection at last. Perhaps it is because I still pine for Vigilante, also a tabby, that I haven't warmed to Olympia, who is most likely Vigilante's second, third or fourth cousin.

One time I glanced over at Tassos' café from the Pirate (my latest station of the cross) and saw Tassos' crusty old father sitting in his usual chair at a side table, sipping something. I commented, "Amazing that Tassos' father is still alive," to be told, "Tassos' father died twenty years ago. That's Tassos you're looking at."

Begrudging: After shaking her head – *"Tipota!"* (Nothing!) – a fatuous smile at the corner of her mouth, the bling-laden, hard-working employee at the post office shrugs and thumbs through the poste restante bins. She finds mail addressed to me from someone who has been dead for at least three years.

Inescapable: The volume of normal meowing increases to a howl, piercing, screeching, bawling, doleful, whining caterwaul. Which cat is this? I peer into the black velvet, polished night, shine my torch, glimpse only a cat's raised rear end, tail curled, the cat unidentifiable, the grating yowl, frequent, urgent, persistent on and off through half the night. Why not! Cats can always sleep all the next day.

Unfailing: Sandbags and cement are delivered by a donkey that leaves hunks of dung among my neighbour's fallen lemons in front of my gate. The scent of jasmine, second cousin to the olive, silent, unassuming, climbs – floats – past the far-away tinkle of goat bells from high up in the hills through my open window whether invited or not, almost overpowering the friendly aroma of the offering left by the donkey.

Village Girls

Johanne Rosenthal

I plucked the long, brown, carob pod, hanging at eye level, and brought it to my lips anticipating its sweet crunch. *Thwap!* The pod flew from my hand and landed feet away. My gentle, auburn-haired mother had slapped what I had assumed was carob from my hand.

"We're not on Hydra anymore," she snapped.

With a turn of the kaleidoscope, my world twisted and I understood. I understood exactly what she meant. Now living in Providence, Rhode Island, we were light years from Hydra. Hydra: where edible fruit sagged heavy over garden walls. In Providence low walls were often lined with broken glass to discourage the weary from sitting. The Mediterranean sea water was buoyant with salt and held us warm as a velvet blanket. Here the rough Atlantic tossed us and chilled us to the bone. Once my sister and I had run unhindered down the lanes, bare feet slapping the smooth stones, keeping an ear out for donkey bells. Now our mother tightly gripped our hands admonishing us to watch for cars, warning us from speaking to strangers. A stranger. What a concept for village girls. We were in a new and dangerous land.

Like a message in a bottle, Hydra experiences are never truly lost. They float on the tide and often return to you at the most unexpected of times. Snippets of memory are passed in the dark alleys, glowing like candles in the the night. "I remember your mom," a soft voice called under the street lamp. And a story unfolds as we walk and the ghosts of old Hydra weave through our legs like cats. I can see through Alki's telling, my parents young and madly in love, the old kitchen, the woven chair seats, the bittersweet marmalade that I apparently ate by a dabbing a finger into the jar and smearing it, painterly, deliberately across my face, my curls and dress, very much enjoying the effect. Rie's light-hearted reaction to my sticky creativity deeply affected the young Greek woman who told me the story. She fiercely wanted to be the type of mother who could so placidly and lovingly enjoy her own child's antics. She described my parents' romantic love for each other and another puzzle piece slipped into place. They had been doting lovers before tearing down the temple walls and leaving the rubble and bitterness that cluttered our family.

~

My first clear memory of the Rock is waking from sleep, hearing muffled music and laughter, the scent of roses pinked the air. There I lay, wrapped in my parents cast off clothes, placed carefully in the wide, cool, stone windowsill of a taverna. When Rie and Robert would spend an evening dancing and drinking they would often bring my sister and me along, and when we tired they would cocoon us in soft garments and deposit us in the windows, later carrying us up the hill to home.

In tavernas when the dancing began rose petals would be sold from trays. In honour of a beautiful woman or an agile dancer, one would purchase a handful or as a show of largesse a whole tray would be bought by an admirer and strewn on the dance floor for the dancer to trod upon. Our mother was both beautiful and an accomplished Greek dancer. One special evening an admirer bought not a handful but all the petals they had in the taverna and threw them at her feet in a grand Greek gesture of tribute.

Once, when Helle and I were tiny, our parents left us alone at home while they danced the night away. Helle and I awoke befuddled and sticky with summer sleep. Wanting our parents, we decided to go and find them. Not being savages, we knew not to leave the house naked. Helle (the practical one to whom, in later years I gave Father's Day cards in honour of her role as man of the house) carefully tied bright scarves to our wrists and ankles, adorning us for our walk to town. As we tripped the dark steps to the port, our bare feet sliding on the shining, satiny stones, a voice called out to us. It was the moustachioed police chief of the island. He called us by name and we went to him and explained our quest. He took us gently by the hands, wrapped us in policemen's jackets, left us nursing cups of cocao at the station and headed to the bright taverna. Spotting our parents, he called them over and sternly explained to them that we should be at home in bed and that they as our parents should be there as well.

Perhaps this explains Helle's and my own later passion for military jackets of all wars, and stretching it even more, wrapped in oversized men's jackets on that sticky summer night as we sat without a worry in the world, perhaps – just perhaps – it led us both to fall for and marry men in uniform, me a soldier in Israel and Helle a pilot in Tanzania. Both of us seemed to replicate in our unique ways our Hydra womb. What is a kibbutz if not a small community of misfits, dreamers and expats, a village, an island in the waving fields of Israel. Then there is Helle's pivotal time in Tanzania, which viewed from a bird's eye contains all the elements of our golden days on the Rock: foreigners banded together in primitive conditions, raw natural beauty and spotty plumbing.

~

Hydra was a paradise and as such contained both snakes and apples. The temptation to lose yourself in drugs or alcohol, the easy sex and beautiful lost souls that arrived daily on the ferry, the lack of mooring from cultural taboos as the expats were a tribe of their own.

On Hydra lay warm nights, silky turquoise water, blinding sunlight that softened to lavender at dusk. Our parents were drawn to this rock where you could live well on a dollar a day and still consider yourself one of the glittering ones. My father planned to write the Great American Novel. Silence was enforced as he sat at his Brother typewriter, the only sound the clicking keys, his face stern and stony with frustration as he wrote and rewrote the same sentence. While he struggled to capture the beauty of Hydra in words we would slip out with our mother to escape his moods and trip up the mountain to pick almonds or wander the sea road to the then barren Vlychos shore.

His father had sought freedom from his turbulent homeland of Poland, longing to build a life and family in the promised land of America, whereas Robert sought to escape not persecution but the stifling atmosphere of 1960s Worcester, Massachusetts, where his father had settled the family.

In 1910, fourteen-year-old Abraham Piwowarski set out on the final leg of his arduous journey across Europe on a steamer from Liverpool to Ellis Island, arriving a freshly minted Abe Goldman. Robert reversed his father's pilgrimage and departed on a ship from from New York to Liverpool in 1965 on his nascent journey of discovery. Calling himself the wandering Jew, his Gypsy feet led him through Palestine, Turkey, across Europe to Denmark, where he met our mother, finally settling on Hydra.

≈

In the bright cool mornings my mother would send me – a toddler – to the baker to buy the daily bread. I would dress in a t-shirt (nothing more) and trot the path half-naked on my little tip-toes and when I arrived the baker would tie a string around the steaming bread and then carefully tie the other end around my middle finger so I wouldn't burn myself. Then I would run home with the breakfast loaf that we would smear with honey and eat with bowls of thick white yogurt scooped from a clay bowl. Eden indeed.

As a result my nickname was Johanne Bare-ass or the somewhat less annoying Apple-arse. I was deeply annoyed with this embarrassing title. I went to Leonard with my problem. When my dad went on his covert trips to Turkey and America, Rie and Leonard would spend time together. It tickled him to take us out to eat at tavernas and have these two towheaded girls order from the menu in perfect Greek. After ordering, Helle and I would adjourn to under the table to eat our dinner with the stray cats, continuing whatever fantasy game we were playing, which gave my mother and Leonard time to speak as grown-ups. I went to Leonard's house to vent and he volunteered to find me a new nickname. After careful deliberation and perhaps a cup of cocao, creamy with condensed milk, he chose Jennifer Juniper. The single by Donavan had come out in 1968 and was hugely popular at the time. I marched home and announced my new moniker to the family.

As luck would have it Donovan sailed into the Hydra port that summer on a yacht. He came ashore and held an impromptu concert for a small group of us. Leonard kindly convinced Donovan to sing "Jennifer Juniper" to me at the end of the evening. This cemented my nickname and my father lovingly called me Jennifer–Juniper into his old age although the name Bare-ass still made an occasional appearance.

As a child of Hydra I saw the adults who were dashed on the rocks, whose children were scattered by the siren song of the island. We were among the lucky few, my sister and I. Our parents left Hydra before they crashed. Our mother, although an alcoholic, took seriously the responsibility and burden that comes from raising children; this kept her like a tethered kite during our years on the Rock. When we left the island she had the perspicacity to quit drinking. It was then that her creativity flourished in fanciful quilts and embroideries. On the island her cosy eider-downed beds drew the weary chilled drunks in the early mornings as her vats of lentil stew and huge bowls of pasta drew the starving artists and wandering hippies. Our table was open to all, and she sat in the kitchen with a compassionate ear, listening to the woes and infidelities of her fellow expats much in the way that in later years in Providence our house was the hearth around whom many warmed their hands and laid their burdens. Alison Gold learned the price to pay the piper for those hot meals and warm beds, it was little me, never able to resist a nap, who would invariably climb in bed with her and after an hour or so pee the bed. Poor Alison.

≈

My father continued to live there on and off for decades. Hydra called to him although he never realised that great novel but like many an expat he sat at the tavernas and alluded to great works he was just about to finish.

"Another Greek tragedy," my father would intone quietly when we passed an unattractive local girl, but it seems to me that the true Greek tragedies were the expats.

There was madness on the island that blew through people's lives like the hot Meltemi winds of summer, as those winds arise on placid seas and wreak a havoc with a boat's course, so Hydra wreaked ruin in seemingly placid lives. One foreign woman cut her long tresses lock by lock, snip by snip, hanging them over branches until she was bald and the garden decorated carefully as a Christmas tree. She was shipped off the island, but what happened to her young children? There was a man, a poet, who beat his wife terribly, there were drunks to be found in the dawn passed out by the side of the road. The Greeks shook their heads at our wild ways. Even as a child I was aware of the furious game of musical partners being played. It confused me this switching loves for a day or a month. The au pairs provided distraction and buffer to the gangs of foreign children with hung-over parents but recently I hear (from the lips of now adult children) they were providing a different type of distraction for the fathers as well. From a child's point of view the island was hard on adults – writers or painters, famous or anonymous, there was no distinction for us children.

The very real magic of Hydra floated about us – the insistent buzzing of cicadas, drifts of pale almond petals, the anise of ouzo licked off our fingertips after a quick dip in our parents' glasses, the sting as you brushed against nettle plants, the not so gentle pinch on the cheek by black-clad widows. Lemon blossom winds invaded our dreams and we woke to goat bell mornings.

≈

Shopping at the old *agora*, our mother Rie brought two baskets: one for her groceries and the other for me when my legs tired on the walk home up the mountain. "I'm too heavy to walk," was my refrain. Helle and I would feed the fish while we waited for her on the port. Once a throng of Asian tourists recently disgorged from the ferry surrounded golden-haired Helle and me and snapped pictures of what I can only presume they thought were two clas-

sic Greek children fishing off the port. We looked like ragamuf-
fins, with our make-do fishing line and bare feet. No respectable
Greek girl would ever have been caught doing something so base,
and unshod yet.

Stop the presses. I must point out, as I hear Helle interjecting
and objecting in my head, to that description of us, which may
paint a negative picture of our mother's parenting. Let me set the
record straight: each morning we were dressed in freshly laun-
dered, sweet-smelling clothing, hand-sewn for us by our aunt in
Denmark, Helle's namesake. Our hair was brushed at least once a
day, twice if we went swimming.

On our way home from shopping, I would insist on greeting
each flower we passed with a crouch, a wave and a gay *"Yassou,
loulouthi"* – "Hello, flower." The village women would spot us
from above, winding our leisurely way up the mountain and wait
in their doorways, trays in hand, offering glasses of cool water
from the cistern and a spoonful each of mastic-flavoured "submarine" spoon sweet, to dip in the water and quench both thirst and
hunger. Often the women would grab me (the baby) and take me
into their house, waving Rie off. I would be passed from person
to person, sometimes house to house and returned magically in
time for dinner.

≈

In late winter or early spring (depending on whether you are an
optimist or pessimist) of 1971-72 something terrible happened.
That terrible thing ended not terribly at all but with two small
scars and a tale to tell.

Helle, Rie and I had gone to visit a family friend, George Lialios. Maybe Robert was there too but he never figured in the story
and I don't remember him. Most likely, since it was a chilly night
in the rainy season, Robert had left the island in search of entertainment. At George's home that evening, I found myself alone in
the living room. Not quite alone. George's dog sat there. This dog,
as I remember, was black, with small brown markings around
the face and paws. Perhaps because this dog was the first dog
I was attracted to, I still fancy this type when I spot one. The

dog sat with his chest puffed out, looking a right noble canid. I knew what I wanted more than anything. I wanted to put my arms around his neck, lay my head on its chest and gently hug him. I walked over, knelt down and put my arms around his sleek furry neck. Suddenly I felt as though there had been an explosion, though at the time I didn't know what an explosion was. It felt as though the world turned upside down and shook very fast. Silence. And then Rie and George and adult feet running into the room. I heard crying – mine? Helle's? The dog had taken a very nasty bite at my face. Later Rie described my cheek hanging down, a deep puncture under my chin and lots of blood. I don't remember any pain. But I do remember a deep burning guilt that it was all my fault for hugging the dog.

As with our other death-defying stories of Hydra, the waves were high. No boats ran to Piraeus. The doctor had not yet returned from his winter-long drunken stupor with the monks (I guess that was a true Hydra sign of spring). To the rescue came Red-Cross-Chris-Cross and his trusty medic's kit. Red-Cross-Chris-Cross had been a Kiwi medic in Korea and was emotionally broken and terribly kind to our family. He used butterfly bandages to pull my cuts together and iodine to combat infection. The next week was *Apokries* and the islanders were dressing in costume for the Greek Orthodox carnival festivities. Rie stuck chicken feathers in a headband that she sewed for me and covered the rest of my face with iodine. Iodine stains the skin a bright reddish purple. My costume was a Red Indian, as they so narrow-mindedly said in those days.

George kept the dog. We all continued to be friends. And island life continued.

≈

On Hydra you made do or you left. There was no imposing your will upon the island. The parameters were set. Our magnificent island that cradled us was, after all, an isolated island when the seas were high, with spotty electricity, dodgy plumbing, floods in winter and searing temperatures in summer. We lacked phones and medical care and if you craved ice-cream in those days you would need take a ferry to the mainland to satisfy that craving. A great equaliser, the island imposed its will on those who arrived. If you wished to stay more than a few drunken days on the island then you must agree to the terms set out or depart with your hang-over and souvenirs. No trust fund would save you from the mosquitos, or the ache in your calves as you carried the day's provisions up the mountain.

At Easter-time the bakeries would sell *tsoureki*, a round braided loaf of sweet bread studded with dyed red eggs and sprinkled with sesame seeds. Helle and I were given the honour of running along the rain-washed lanes down to the port to buy the holiday bread. After buying the yeasty loaf we dawdled on the port looking at the donkeys and mules waiting patiently for their next load. We were particularly drawn to a large reddish-brown mule standing apart from the rest. He had a desolate air about him as he gazed somewhat dramatically into the middle distance, a four-legged French Lieutenant's Woman. Upon closer examination we saw a hint of wetness at the corner of his eyes. That cinched it: he was crying. To cheer him, Helle and I broke off a piece of the warm bread and held it up to his velvety lips. He nibbled the proffered hunk of bread until our hands were empty and a bit damp from his warm breath. We broke off another hunk and offered it to him, and so it went until the whole loaf was just a memory and our pockets were full of red-dyed boiled eggs. He seemed happier but still downcast. So Helle and I peeled the eggs and fed them to him one by one. When the last egg disappeared down his mulish gullet Helle and I were both filled with dread. We headed home with heavy feet to confess what we'd done. I remember both Rie and Robert were in the kitchen when we told them of the mournful mule and our good intentions. They laughed and weren't concerned about the lost bread. To prevent a repeated misadventure, Robert volunteered to walk to buy the replacement loaf. I tagged along with him and he had me point out the mule. Father agreed that he indeed seemed mournful with those dried tear tracks on his face.

Helle, my sister, attended first grade on the island. With her flaxen hair and sea-blue eyes it was obvious she was the only foreign student. Truth be told, later on she stood out equally in Providence classrooms looking like a Nordic doll next to the other students. Her teacher, Kyria Eleni, was fair but stern. For school supplies she had a soft little notebook with lined paper and a pencil. In lieu of gold stars, *aristos* – the highest mark of excellence – were drawn on the pages where Helle had done meritorious work. Each *aristos* was written across the whole page with a calligraphic flourish. We would go through her notebook wordlessly, our fingers tracing the intricate loops. She also had a hard-covered schoolbook from which she would teach me when we played school. I remember the day Helle came home and announced to Rie and me that roosters say *coo-coo-ri-coo, coo-coo-ri-coo*. I believe, though I may be making this up, that there was an illustration of a rooster in her schoolbook saying just that: *coo-coo-ri-coo, coo-coo-ri-coo*.

One fine day Helle bravely took me with her to school. I sat at the desk behind her in the classroom. One was expected to sit perfectly still and do one's work in silence. I was a wiggly mouse that had never had to sit still. The teacher warned me twice in a stern voice to behave. Somehow I fidgeted again. Helle was brought to the front of the class and given what looked to be a hard rap on her hand. The horror. The awful cringing horror of having caused that pain and embarrassment to Helle. I felt like the most awful creature. Poor, poor Helle. No wonder she had a scheme to sell me to the Gypsies to fund her life plan of running away to live with an Indian tribe. This had all been drawn out for me, literally: a panoramic drawing containing me, a small bundle being handed to a group of Gypsies, gold exchanging hands, Helle boarding a train and, at last, Helle arriving on the Plains, where her tribe waited by their tee-pees, bows and arrows in hand.

At lunch we went out into the school yard. The priest came to visit, his dark flowing robes flapping crow-like, heavy beard and beetled brows. He thrust his hands though the wrought iron gate. The children gathered and vied to kiss his ring. Then it came to me. I looked at those hairy fingers, closed my eyes and kissed.

Part of my days were spent at a little nursery school, the *nipio*. The priests would come there for kisses as well.

The stone houses of Hydra attract all manner of flying and crawling insects. Bugs plagued (perhaps too strong a word) our lives on Hydra. Once Rie saw a huge specimen of a centipede run across the floor and down between the stones on the kitchen floor. She took a bottle of nail polish remover (a precious luxury in those early days) and poured it down the hole in an attempt to kill it. Another time she saw a smiling me walking towards her with a tarantula dangling between two fingers. She slapped it out of my hand and then realised that it was no threat to me as it was already dead.

I had gathered the spider for one of Helle and my favourite games: Zoo. We would arrange twigs and rocks into partitioned "cages" on a dusty patch of earth, then we would encircle the whole shebang with flowers and leaves. Off we would go, the two great hunters, searching our jungle (garden) for specimens to stock the zoo. Most of the game involved re-catching the bugs that escaped and fortifying our shabby cages with thicker sticks. A dead spider makes no attempt at escape and so was quite the prize.

One bleak February Little Helle ingested poison. More exactly she ingested the venom that gets into your system from eating centipedes. Helle's gastronomic tastes included bugs of many sorts that Rie would find half-digested in her diaper but on this day she had chosen to eat a centipede. A dangerous choice of snack. Our flame-haired mother (channelling her own mother) took charge of the situation. She threw open the flybox and began to make a concoction of sweet, savoury and horrendous. She took her largest glass from the stack of mismatched glasses, mixed strawberry jam, baking soda and pickle juice (she made fantastic pickles, more on that later) topping it all off with a healthy dollop of mustard. She passed this devil's brew to her little golden girl and begged her drink it down. Helle needed to throw up the venomous tidbit she had swallowed, her mom explained. Helle picked up the glass and took a sip, and another and another and guzzled it until not a drop was left. She smacked her lips and slammed the glass to the table as a cowboy does on a polished bar and ordered in her husky voice, "MORE!" Rie knew that no poison was a match to her little girl's iron stomach.

Helle pointed out recently that she still favours "bugs of the sea," as she put it – lobsters, crabs and shrimp.

On Hydra and later in Providence, Rie would make large clear glass jars of mixed pickles. They were jewel-toned affairs with tiny onions, cauliflower, carrots, cucumbers, red pepper and always springy lengths of octopus. Our friends in America were intrigued (disgusted?) when instead of potato chips to go with our sandwiches at school lunch time we pulled out small containers of pickled octopus. (On Hydra our father had hunted octopus with a spear and Helle and I would stand on shore at the ready when he would toss one to us. Our job was to beat it on the rocks with frequent dips in the ocean to kill it and to tenderize the stiff flesh.) Finding exotic ingredients in white-bread Providence in the Seventies was not easy. Car-less, we three girls would walk to Fox Point: a poor neighbourhood known for its crime, easy to score drugs and brightly coloured houses, occupied by hard-working first-generation Portuguese immigrants. Well-meaning friends would warn Rie off from Fox Point but that was where we could find some of the exotic ingredients that we missed from Greece, including octopus. In its way it was an island of the Old World hidden in our stodgy university town. Where the wealthier neighbourhood resembled a ghost town even in summer, Fox point was alive with homeowners "making love to their houses," as Rie would say. Old men sat on their front steps smoking cigarettes and lazily dabbing paint on a railing, music played loudly from windows and laundry flapped from clothes lines, old women swept their porches with stiff straw brooms. My mom would point to the black-clad women and say, "They are guarding the street. With them here nothing bad can happen to us, they are like the old women on Hydra."

While we were in Fox Point we never failed to go to the bakery and buy two loafs of the soft, fragrant Portuguese sweetbread similar to Greek *tsoureki* but lacking the magical flavours of *masticha* and *mahlepi*. One we would eat on the way home, ripping off large chunks, feeling like a tribe of our own. They say all roads lead to Rome, but deep in our hearts and perhaps the heart of all who are captured in Hydra's snare, all roads lead to Hydra. The ache for our old life on Hydra followed us like the gap of a pulled tooth. Always your tongue finds the empty spot and probes the tender wound. This never fully healed for the three of us.

~

While Helle and I resented any moment away from the island in those all too short months we visited in summers there was one spot away from Kamini that called to us: Bisti. In those days Bisti was an uninhabited landscape of pine trees and scrubby oregano bushes with a pristine pebbled semicircle of shoreline. Once or twice a summer the adults (I use that term loosely) would plan a camping trip there.

In early morning, pink smudges still in the sky, we would meet at the port, secure our boats and the parents would scurry around gathering supplies. Into the boat went *karpuzi* (watermelon) a'plenty and *peponi*, a fragrant oblong melon with green mottled skin and a deep orange flesh. Moments before our boats left someone would run for the warm whole roasted chickens from down the alley right off the port. Those greasy mahogany birds wrapped in white butcher paper were redolent with herbs, salty and lemony, and we would tear them apart on our boat ride, and wipe hunks of fresh bread into the pale green marinade that stuck to the paper. Receiving the lion's share of the cargo room were the many bottles of alcohol. ("Children's parties," as they were called, were thrown regularly on the island and they were similar in most respects to other parties of the era, except they were held during the day. I remember once going to a "children's party" on the island and realising that no allowance had been made for children when it came to food or drink. The birthday child pitched a fit when she realised that there was not even a cake with candles to wish upon. I believe it was that same day that tensions boiled over with two warring tribes of children by the gully in Kamini, and a little girl threw a stone at a little boy during a verbal spat, causing a terrible gash on his cheek. Connecting the dots now, with an adult's perspective, between that boozy children's birthday party and the blood blooming on the boy's cheek later that afternoon, is easy. One final comment: it is telling that once the blow had been struck, and we realised the gravity of the situation, our little gang ran not for parents but for his au pair as this skirmish had occurred during siesta and we all knew better then to disturb our parents' sleep.)

Finally our boat as packed as it would ever be, the signal was given and our little caravan would leave the port. The "long" ride to Bisti through sea-glass water, arriving and setting up camp – all was relished by us kids. Sometimes when I tell a story from our times on the island it feels like a tall tale – like a wild exaggeration – and it is only when I confirm the facts with my family that I feel confident in my memory. One trip to Bisti is a case in point. The trip began as all our trips with the familiar rituals but ended quite differently.

There were the usual struggles with the adults. The kids wanted to add sweetened condensed milk to our morning (water-based) cocoa but the adults insisted we save the milk only for coffee. The compromise we reached was to make cocoa with water but with a regulated splash of milk in each cup as a topper, under the watchful eye of a self-designated milk inspector. One snarky adult kept saying, "Do you want some cocoa in your milk?" as we prepared our drinks. This was all usual banter in those days and we kids gave as good as we got.

At midday a yacht motored into the cove and the elegant white-clad people aboard (in those days it seemed most adults wore all white, from button downs to kurtas: the island uniform of the Eighties) invited the grown-ups to a party in the lone house on the tip of Bisti. How could they refuse? It is not like they were responsible for a troupe of children who would be left like castaways on the beach with the chance of drowning, fire … et cetera. Accidental parents they were.

An hour or so after the adults left, a group of Gypsies appeared, skulking through the tree line and moving towards our camp. By their hatchet-faced demeanors we just knew that they were not there to welcome us to the neighbourhood. A group of six or seven entered our camp and began riffling through our stuff as we stood watching them, mouths agape. Adrenaline surged though us and we each ran to grab what was most precious to our parents. Helle and I grabbed our dad's wallet and wristwatch and I remember one friend was later berated for safe-guarding her mother's purse instead of her mom's stash. All the children headed down the beach to a little cave half submerged in water. There we sat, our gang of expat children, prying periwinkles from the rocks with a kitchen knife and shushing the smaller children when they began to snuffle. (When I was pregnant with my son I had fierce cravings for those briny molluscs. I was like Rapunzel's mother longing for the greens of the witch's garden.)

Eventually the band of Gypsies left of their own accord and we headed back to camp. Toward sunset the parents arrived and we told them of our trials and they informed that the "Queen of Hydra" – the woman who graced the twenty-drachma bill – had been at the party they had just attended and would be joining us at our camp that night. The kids decided this would be the perfect time to perform the dance we had been perfecting all summer, the Hustle, preformed to the *Staying Alive* album playing on our banged up boombox. I cringe when I think of us dancing for our illustrious and genteel guest in the fire's glow to the high-pitched moans of the Bee Gees.

≈

In our parents' day the mail was passed out to the waiting horde by a young postmistress. Waiting until the day's mail that had arrived with the boat had been sorted, our mom would enter the post office in the late morning and stand at the back of the jostling crowd of expats desperate for a word from home. There she would stand, not entering the line until the postmistress would spot her and either call her forward with a welcoming gesture of the hand or signal her a negative with the oh-so-Greek gesture of raised shoulders, scrunching frown and *tsk* that meant no mail for her today. Later, in the Eighties, the post office was run by a "Madame Tipota" of the inhaled *tsk*, the raised eyebrows, the dismissive shrug, the almost voluble *"tipota"* (nothing). Those sweaty summer walks with Helle in the white Hydra light, daily begging for the mail, knowing just there behind the counter lay our letters. The lucky days when the dam would flood and she would hand a stack of bright letters and packages out, letters that had gathered over the week until her annoyance with keeping them hostage outweighed her pleasure in the magical word *tipota*.

Tightly gripping our hoard of mail we'd retreat to Tassos' and pool our few drachma to buy dewy bottles of *portokalada fresca*.

We'd sip our bright orange nectar through a straw, our thighs sticking to the seats as we each ripped open the first of our letters from our mom, always decorated with stickers and coloured markers. Bedstemor (our grandmother) would tape book-pressed wild flowers to the front of her tissue thin envelopes and we'd giggle over her dictionary-direct translations. Plain envelopes from Big Helle – our Danish aunt – opened to reveal thick pink paper written on with her typewriter's unique cursive script.

When Big Helle first visited us in Greece in 1966, she saw large slabs of bloody fly-covered meats laid out in the market by the port of Piraeus. She was disgusted. When she drew nearer she realised that they were actually black-seeded half watermelons. She bought one and brought it to Hydra, thinking that she was bringing Rie a present both exotic and rare. Of course, once on the island she realised that she had brought the proverbial coals to Newcastle. Hydra was overflowing with watermelons.

∿

When we were older children, and living in Providence, most summers my sister and I would fly to Greece to visit our dad. Never having bought a house on Hydra, unlike most of his friends, each visit meant exploring a new rented house. One summer my dad rented from a Greek family in Kamini who had divided their humble home into three apartments. One the family lived in, the other we stayed in and the third was rented by two British girls. The Greek family was made up of a father, mother, older daughter and son. The father was a brute and would beat the mother as we listened to her screams through the paper-thin walls. Later we would see or hear the mother berating and sometimes smacking the teenaged daughter for some infraction, almost immediately the daughter would shriek at the brother to feed the chickens in the yard or do some other chore. The end of this chain of sorrow was when the son would go into the yard and kick one of the animals, chicken, goat or dog. He would give the animal a good trouncing and peace would reign. That summer I learned what a pecking order was. In case anyone is wondering, renters ranked below land-owner in the pecking order. We realised this one afternoon when we heard screams emanating from the front of the house. One of the British girls was having words with the landlord when the brute jumped on her and ripped the key to the apartment from her hands, leaving a bloody palm. The British girl ran sobbing from the house and her roommate later smuggled her possessions to the quay, where the shaken-up girl was waiting to board the next ferry to head back to civilisation.

Greek boys were infamously hard on animals, often sadistically so. They thought nothing of beating a dog, or encouraging a donkey with a piece of lumber studded with nails, or drowning a bag of kittens in the sea to liven up a Saturday night. The girls were expected to be tiny adults from the moment they turned four or five. While their brothers were like marauding armies running all over the island, getting into scraps, the girls dressed in their buttoned-up, dark dresses and shiny shoes and helped their mothers or sat quietly in a chair, gazing wistfully out the windows at their brothers playing ball in the alleys.

There were those who remained aloof from the Greeks, looking down on them from their lofty hung-over thrones, and those who threw themselves fully into village life. My mother counted among her long-term friends more Greeks than expats. She was herself a village girl who had grown up on a chicken farm on the Danish–German border. She well understood the Greeks' antipathy towards the German tourists (both Greece and Denmark having been invaded by the Germans) and lived more the life of a Greek woman than most foreigners. Her days (her nights were another matter entirely) were spent tending to her children, shopping in the *agora*, hand-washing our clothes and leaving them to dry on the terrace, cooking huge vats of lentils and lining up with the village woman at the bakery with a pan of chicken and potatoes which for a few drachma would be roasted in the residual heat of the ovens after the morning loaves had been baked. Another fine trick Rie learned from the Greek women was bringing odds and ends like eggs and cheese and leftovers from the flybox to be enfolded in dough and baked into a savoury loaf at the bakers. I used this trick as I travelled in later years through Turkey.

~

Hydra is where we went to scatter our father's ashes in the old places off the cliff where he loved to swim. It is where we return to pour libations in the foaming sea, standing on the craggy grey rocks. Last year it was a can of the beer that slaked his third on dusty Sirocco days. Where I passed the first anniversary of my Mother's death holding tightly to Alison with one hand while with the other I shovelled in spoonfuls of childhood comfort food, room-temperature *gigantes plaki.*

There were four places I longed for when my world was crumbling. Four comforts. My mom's embrace, my aunt's voice, my dad's understanding and Hydra. Hydra still waits for me.

A Tiny Piece of Bread

Helle V. Goldman

> Isn't it strange how your childhood dogs you and
> tracks you and will not let you be?
>
> – Charmian Clift[1]

With your gossamer curls and sparkling, slanting-upwards eyes, you were their fairy child. Like a fairy, you were also weightless, or at least as light as any normal, healthy little girl could be. It was as if you had the hollow bones of a bird. And you could fold up and occupy almost no space at all.

Rie called you her collapsible child. She carried you in one of those sturdy Greek baskets. She bore one basket for little collapsible you and in the other hand she carried a basket for groceries. The bagless produce went straight into the basket. The shopkeeper nestled the eggs on top of the other purchases.

It was a good thing that you fit into a basket because you didn't much care for walking. I insisted on conveying myself everywhere on my own legs. But little *Maimou* – Monkey, as the Greeks called you – loved to be carried. Maimou was not a name you were fond of, and for a while you insisted on being addressed as Johanne–Jennifer. This was after Donovan wooed you with his song "Jennifer Juniper" at a party. You had other nicknames too. I didn't have any that I can recall.

---

[1] "Winter Solstice," Charmian Clift, *POL* magazine, Sydney, 1969 (posthumously). Reprinted in *The World of Charmian Clift* (George Johnston, ed.), Ure Smith, Sydney, 1970, pp. 57-61.

"*Please* carry me," you would say to Rie or Father in your sweet little voice, your almond-shaped blue eyes squinting in the sunlight, your head cocked to one side as you looked up at our parents.

They did carry you. You were, after all, virtually weightless, and collapsible. And carrying you was quicker anyway because when you walked you had to greet and then bid farewell to every living thing encountered along the way.

"*Yassou, loulouthia*," you would say – "Hello, flowers … Goodbye, flowers."

It took ages to get anywhere. I would be waiting impatiently, far down the stone-stepped lane. Rie stayed with you as you befriended and then took tender leave of each blooming weed.

Eventually little pixie-like you would tire: "Carry me, Mor!" (How old were we when we stopped calling her that? People had found it charming that the two little girls called her "Mother" in her native tongue and were disconcerted when we switched to the name she was generally known by: the Danish abbreviation of Ane Marie, which only Danes could pronounce properly. Yet it felt perfectly natural to us. And Father was for us always Father and never Dad or Pappa or something similar. More incongruities, more small mysteries.)

Rie would pick you up and make her way down the smooth grey stone steps to catch up with me. If I'd had to wait a long time, I'd likely found some way of entertaining myself, perhaps watching ants lay waste to a tarantula carcass. Around the time I became your big sister, I'd become an observer of bugs rather than a consumer, a habit that culminated in the occasion when Rie turned around just in time to see me stuff the last glossy red-brown segments of a centipede into my mouth. She tried to bring up the creature with a home-made emetic thrown together in a panic. After guzzling it all down I only wanted more of the mustardy potion. "More!" I demanded, in my characteristic gruff voice.

On our way to the port, we might stop in on Jimmy. The dapper old man made a meagre living selling the clothing of people who had died. The story went that as a young man he had worked in America at menial jobs, saving up. Returning to Hydra with what was by local standards a small fortune, he treated old and new friends to food and wine. When the money was gone he became a peddler of second-hand clothes. He invariably invited us in if he saw us passing his hovel. Rie always accepted graciously. We would sit there in Jimmy's tiny garden, chatting and sharing his offerings – a bit of bread and tomato, perhaps a boiled egg.

At the port, as Rie sat at Tassos' café with friends, waiting for the mail to arrive on the boat and be sorted at the post office, she'd let us pull out soft white chunks from the fresh loaf in her basket. We'd stretch out on our stomachs at the water's edge – the stones faintly powdery from dried splashes of seawater – and drop chickpea-sized balls of doughy bread to the little fish that darted among the boat lines. We called this "catching fish." Occasionally there was a net involved.

Rie was an indulgent mother, but the drachmas Father doled out to her for shopping were few. "No more bread for the fish," she said (at least that one time), or we would only have the hollow crust to take home.

Inside the post office, where the expats gathered in the hope of receiving a cheque from a publisher or an agent or a parent that would sustain them on the island for another six months, Rie waited by the door. The postmaster would lift his gaze over the crowd, catch her eye and with a small, neat upward thrust of his chin, his eyebrows lifting and eyelids closing, signalled *tipota* – nothing, no letters or telegrams for her today. She left without having to wait in the line.

To finish her shopping, Rie took us into a store, but you hadn't given up on the prospect of more fishing.

Holding out your hand, you asked in your sweetly plaintive baby voice (so unlike mine), "Please, can I have a tiny piece of bread? Just a tiny piece of bread?"

Rie refused.

You trailed after her in the shop with outstretched palm, "Oh, *please!* Just a *tiny* piece of bread?"

The other shoppers shot disapproving glances. What mother would deny her angelic tot a piece of bread? A *tiny* piece of bread?

Silently shamed into relinquishing the last of the loaf, she watched us dash off to the edge of the port and the hungry little fish that were always waiting for us there. She finished her shopping. Eggs last.

~

You were probably too young to remember any of that. I wonder if I was also too little to remember it. Maybe I only *think* I remember it because Rie told us about it so often.

"Tell us a story from when we were little!" we would demand of her years later, on the other side of the world.

And she would tell The Story of the Tiny Piece of Bread, mimicking you begging for bread and laughing at her own embarrassment. Or she would recount When Helle Ate an Enormous Centipede, or some other story. In this way our tattered scraps of actual memory – some as fractional as the smell of boat paint or yeasty bread, the taste of seasalt on hot flat stones, the flicker of small black fish in murky green water – were forged together with Rie's more complete recollections into the narrative that we now remember as our early childhood. Parents do this, inscribing the blank spaces of infantile amnesia with the origin stories their children will one day use to make sense of what they become.

~

Another story she told was the one we knew as The Get Up and Make Me Some Spaghetti Story. This is jumping forward a few years. When I was perhaps six years old and you about four, Rie fell desperately ill. Father was not around. We stood by Rie's bed.

You said shrilly, not the least bit angelically, "Why don't you get up and make me some spaghetti?"

There was fear in your voice. You just wanted everything to be normal again. If your mother got up and made dinner then all would be well. But Rie couldn't get out of bed. I was just old enough to realise this, though it was only many years later that I came to know more details and understood that she'd been on the brink of death.

An ice cream was the only remedy within my grasp. I ran down to the port to buy her one. (If I'd tumbled it would have been awful, at that speed. But we never did fall, did we? I'm sure it still inhabits your feet too, that feeling of hurtling headlong down those lanes, naked feet barely slapping the stones that the women of each household used to wash clean daily.) I raced back up the hill: if I could deliver the ice cream to Rie before it melted then everything would be alright.

Lily came to the rescue with an injection. Magnificent Russian Lily Mack had come to Hydra in the early Fifties with her first husband Christian Heidsieck (of the champagne Heidsiecks). Along with the Australian writers George Johnston and Charmian Clift, Lily and Christian were the first foreigners to settle on Hydra, buying property and raising children there. A couple of years later, Marianne Ihlen and soon-to-be-husband Axel Jensen, another writer, migrated south from Oslo. Charmian and George helped them find a house and engage workmen, and Christian taught Marianne how to work with ceramics. Timidly Marianne spread her wings in a place very different than the conventional one she'd left behind. She was at first afraid of Lily's intensity and eccentricity.[2] I don't think Rie, a Scandinavian like Marianne, was ever put off by Lily.

The contents of the shot that Lily was about to give Rie, and where and how Lily obtained it, are mysteries now. This was another thing you and I never asked through all Rie's recountings of this tale, which she told to illustrate Lily's valour and mine (the ice cream delivered before melting) and the notable condition of life on Hydra that there were never any doctors when you needed them. Yet these magical life-saving injections always seemed to pop up at the crucial moments, administered by eccentric Russians and other unlikely heroes. There was that ex-Korean War medic whose name I can only remember as Red-Cross-Chris-Cross, who gave you an injection when you were fading fast with dysentery-like symptoms. You were only about two. He nearly lost his nerve: it was one thing to jab a soldier, quite another the innocent flesh of a baby. But Rie, gripped by that primal fear of her child dying, made him give you the shot. I can picture her blue eyes looking into his, willing him to do it. You were saved.

Back to Rie on the bed and Lily poised with her syringe, and Rie rolling over onto her stomach and Lily pulling up the sheet.

We watched. Lily paused and turned to us.

---

[2] *So Long, Marianne*, Kari Hesthamar, ECW Press, Toronto, 2014.

"Which cheek?" she asked.

We conferred and solemnly indicated our choice.

When Rie finally mustered the nerve to return to Hydra more than forty years later, she and I stopped in on Lily's grave. As Rie lay a posy of late spring wildflowers on the marble slab, I thought of The Get Up and Make Me Some Spaghetti Story and Rie's subtitle for it, The Time Lily Saved My Life. Four months after that visit to Lily's grave, Rie died, out of the blue. There were no valiant Russians to save her that time, no miraculous injections.

But let's go back to the start, when the fairytale began.

~

Father set off on the *S.S. American Packer*, a merchant cargo ship, early in 1965 on his first trip abroad. Before that the furthest he'd been from his home in Massachusetts was Florida, where he received his naval training. The war ended before he could serve in combat. Discharged, good-looking and charming, Father and a Navy buddy led groups of appreciative retirees in calisthenics on the beach. The tips were generous. The two footloose teenagers made some money and had a good time.

Twenty years later, as the *American Packer* began her passage to Liverpool, Father penned his first diary entry in a small volume in red covers, which fell into my hands after his death.

"Left N.Y.C. at 6:45 p.m. Two other passengers aboard: a man and wife. They may prove to be interesting – I played a game of chess and I won, only because he played so badly. I have such a sad feeling about leaving … I feel that I'm headed nowhere."

In subsequent pages Father describes his fellow passengers, the crew, the weather, the sea, the ship's speed, his dreams. He complains of boredom, inertia and sadness. A line squeezed in at the very bottom of a page reads: "This trip will alter my life as I've known it." He was wrong about going nowhere and right in predicting that the trip would change his life (as he knew it).

His journey across Europe kicked off with several weeks in England. He got the feel of zipping around on his new green Vespa to see the sights and recorded detailed observations of his first exposure to what was, after all, a foreign culture.

After this gentle toe-wetting, he crossed from Harwich to Esbjerg and began his tour of Europe proper. There he was gibed about how uncultivated Americans were. (If these remarks struck Father as ironic, in light of the barbarism from which Europeans had been saved by Americans of his generation, this is not recorded in his diary.) He formed opinions about the national characters of the countries he travelled through and lay awake worrying about the future. He wondered whether he should hurry home to marry a woman named Edna, alluded to having lied about something and was anxious about facing people back home. I don't know who Edna was. Do you?

He made his way northward along the coast of Norway and crossed the Arctic Circle. At Narvik (a couple of hundred kilometres south of where I live) he was turned back by the cold. The scooter offered no protection from the elements. Retreating to the milder southern reaches of Scandinavia, he discovered that he hated Oslo ("This horrible, goddamn wet city with its rude people"), met Rie in Copenhagen, fell for her and her country ("I'm in love with Denmark as nowhere else") and left Rie to see the Mediterranean.

The detailed, exuberant, peevish, self-conscious, angst-ridden entries that document his tour up to that point dry up. Was he thinking of the young red-headed beauty he'd left in Copenhagen? Was he thinking of the woman named Edna? Was he thinking about how he was going to extricate himself from the mess – whatever it was – that lay in wait for him in America? There are weeks', months', worth of blank pages, then a two- or three-word notation recording the bare minimum, followed by another long diary silence. He went to Israel on a Turkish ship. He headed to Greece from Haifa, stopping in at Cyprus. There is a comparatively verbose – for this part of the diary – entry for Rhodes: "We missed our ship and had to stay overnight." Who is we?

Then: "Heading to Piraeus."

"At last!" you're thinking, "He's going to get on a boat to Hydra. Now we're getting somewhere!"

But no, there is no mention of Hydra in the diary. I was disappointed too.

He was in Athens for a week, took a boat to Corfu, crossed to

Brindisi, spent a day in Rome, travelled by rail to Hamburg and onward to Copenhagen.

There the diary ends.

The end of the diary but not the story. Near the conclusion of the year, Rie gave birth to me in her childhood home in a village in southern Denmark, in the very same bed on which she had entered the world twenty-two years before. She wrote to Father immediately to report that the labour had been long and exhausting but we were well. In this same recently discovered letter, Rie told him she'd saddled me with her sister's first name and her mother's middle name and hoped he wouldn't mind. She apologised that the baby looked just like her. This was a joke because Rie was very beautiful, with patrician features and hints of Jeanne Moreau in *Jules et Jim* and Anouk Aimée in *La Dolce Vita*.

He came back from America (from Edna?) for Rie and me. And whisked us off to Hydra.

~

In March 1966, Father, Rie and I arrived on Hydra. He'd probably heard about it from Jane Motley, a painter – and former girlfriend – in his bohemian circle in Providence. You remember her. She had already discovered the island. Father's tour of Europe the previous year had given him a taste of the expat life, the next stage of his reinvention. His own father – our Grampa Abe – had travelled in the other direction to make himself, sailing on his own as a boy from pre-war Europe. He worked hard, first in the garment district of New York, where he learned to cut and sew, and then in Worcester, Massachusetts, making men's trousers from discounted ends-of-bolts bought in New York. He had a talent for fitting his patterns onto the cloth so scarcely a scrap was left over. His car packed with his home-sewn trousers, Abe drove all over New England selling his goods to retailers. He married the daughter of eastern European immigrants much like himself, fathered three strapping sons, viewed from afar the genocide of his people in Poland, watched his first son head off to join the war, established a sedentary garment business and – never ceasing to toil until he retired – made a secure, comfortable life for his family.

Grampa's two younger sons – our uncles – consolidated the American dream their father had achieved and led lives that were extensions of their father's trajectory. Abe's eldest son – Father – would not. He moved to Providence, befriended painters and sculptors and potters, cultivated a beard and sometimes sported an eye-patch, took up pipe tobacco, immersed himself in literature, subjected himself to years of Freudian analysis, abandoned America for Europe, married a non-Jewish woman seventeen years younger than himself, let his children run around like wild things, speared fish for dinner, smoked hash from a hookah bought in Istanbul, had ambitions of writing and occasionally led people to believe that he was a CIA agent.

Going from America to Europe – finally to Hydra – Father shed the accoutrements of the life that Abe, migrating in the other direction about fifty years earlier, had toiled a lifetime to acquire. Wall-to-wall carpeting, 25-inch television embedded in a polished wooden console, richly upholstered furniture protected by plastic except for special occasions, a string of Cadillacs – these were absent from Hydra, where the good life came in entirely different packages: in one hand a basket containing a refillable bottle of wine, bread, tomatoes and feta – quite likely purchased on credit at the Katsikas family's shop – and in the other hand, the other basket, filled with you.

There's a picture of Father, Rie and me – the very first family photograph and our first photo of Hydra – at a table at the port. I'm four months old, feet in Father's lap, sprawled across the table, examining something obscured by my arms (the ashtray, perhaps). His large, strong hands bracing me firmly, Father looks into the camera, a light smile on his face. He's going on forty but – as he always did – looks younger, dark-haired, handsome, wearing a faded green polo shirt. Or maybe it's just the picture that's faded.

It was one of his short beard-less intervals. He would soon re-cultivate the beard that imprinted itself on me those first years of my life. When Father shaved it off a few years later I was dumbfounded, having no memory of the clean-shaven face he'd briefly worn during my infancy. *What is this face? Who does this man think he is?* Shaken and disoriented, I refused to walk near him when we went to the beach or the port. Then he let me cover his repugnant naked cheeks and chin with watercolours. Having painted Father's face in swirls of pinks, purples and greens, I walked beside him again down to the port, holding his hand.

His beard grew in quickly.

In that first picture Rie's red hair is cut in neat bangs and drawn up in a bun at the back (just like my own hair now). When she'd dyed her hair as a teenager it had caused a stir in the village back in Denmark. Children taunted her with cries of "Albino!" This didn't rank among Rie's many warm memories of the village of farmers and simple tradesmen where she grew up. You and I demanded stories of her childhood on the farm almost as often as we asked for stories of our own childhood in Greece, and she yielded them with relish. The lovely, tame Danish countryside would remain in her bones forever. But the village was too small for her. She went to Copenhagen as soon as she was old enough to leave home. She worked at a hotel in what was then a dodgy part of town, made friends, fell pregnant, went home to her parents to give birth, was fetched by her American and taken to Hydra, joining the other misfits.

Here on Hydra in the spring of 1966, she is young and pretty in her plain purple shift dress. Gazing at Father and me, rather than at the camera, she smiles a little shyly.

They look happy.

∼

Juliet Nicolson has written that "With the flimsiest scraps of information – a photograph here, a letter there … it is possible, with thought and time, to discover what a mother and father were once like."[3] Is it? Scrutinising this early photograph I look for clues to our parents' earlier selves and proof of their joint happiness, just as I dissect the later pictures for evidence of the dissolution of those selves and that happiness. Do you remember Rie and Father being happy together? I don't. A woman who was a girl when we arrived on the island told us that she remembers Rie and Father billing

---

[3] *A House Full of Daughters: A Memoir of Seven Generations*, Juliet Nicolson, Farrar, Straus & Giroux, New York, 2016, p. 7.

and cooing like two lovebirds, in the beginning. It had made such an impression on the romantic teenager that as a grandmother she could easily recall it. So, I tell myself (and you), they *did* love each other. They *were* happy.

Sitting there at that café in the spring of 1966, what idea did they have of the future? Could Rie have imagined that she would spend most of the next six years on Hydra? That in 1972 she would leave for good, always looking back on that time on Hydra as the defining moment of her life, always yearning for the island yet convinced that return was impossible? Could Father have imagined that after those first six years of more or less continuous island residence he would return to Hydra every year of the remainder of his life, until he could no longer travel? Did they imagine, on their first day on Hydra, that the island would have such a hold on them, or on the baby in Father's lap and the baby yet to come?

The plan must have been that they would stay a while. After all, Rie and Father hadn't stumbled upon the island as tourists, as some had. People alit on the Rock (as we came to call it) in different ways. Some came, like Father, because friends told them about it. Others were doing the Greek island hop when they disembarked at Hydra for a day visit that stretched into years, decades. It was like the myth of the island of Lotus Eaters. When Odysseus' men tasted their narcotic plant they were overcome by a blissful fugue. All thoughts of journeying home were forgotten.

Peel Me a Lotus is the title of Charmian Clift's account of her family's years on Hydra. (Don't be fooled by the photo of the port of Mykonos on the jacket of one posthumous edition.) Charmian described the island as "a long, bare rock shaped rather like a set of well-curved moustachios and cruelly fanged with sharp mountains: an island completely lacking in fertile soil, and, except for a few springs and wells, waterless."[4]

Does this sound like the kind of place from which one could not tear oneself away? Twenty years earlier, Henry Miller, who can be blamed for starting it all, had described Hydra as "a rock which

---

[4] *Peel Me a Lotus*, Charmian Clift, Collins, Sydney, 1969, p. 24. (First published by Hutchinson, 1959.)

rises out of the sea like a huge loaf of petrified bread," which was not exactly flattering either. Yet Miller was besotted, rapturous about "this purity, this wild and naked perfection of Hydra."[5] (I read this chapter of *The Colossus of Maroussi* aloud to Father as we sat in the garden, the summer before he died. It had been one of the most influential books in his life.)

Having peeled herself a lotus, Charmian described the town as rising

> "in tiers around the small, brilliant, horse-shoe-shaped harbour – old stone mansions harmoniously apricot-coloured against the gold and bronze cliffs, or washed pure white and shuttered in palest grey: houses austere but exquisitely proportioned, whose great walls and heavy arched doors enclose tiled courtyards and terraced gardens. The irregular tiers are broken everywhere by steep, crooked flights of stone steps, and above the tilted roof-tops of uniform red tiles the octagonal domes of the churches … Above the town the mountains shoot up sheer, their gaunt surfaces unbroken except for an odd white mill or two, a field of grain standing on end, a dark patch of fir-trees, and three monasteries, the highest of them so close to heaven that at night its lights are looped among the stars."[6]

Charmian and George bought their house in the mid-Fifties for the equivalent of less than five hundred British pounds. (When we came, about ten years later, it was still very cheap to buy a house there, or a ruin that could be rebuilt.) They moved in just in time for Charmian to be delivered of their third child in the house. As babies, you and I were subjected to much affection from the Greek ladies, but this baby of Charmian and George's

[5] *The Colossus of Maroussi*, Henry Miller, New Directions Books, New York, 2010, p. 49. (First published by Colt Press, San Francisco, 1941.)

[6] *Lotus*, pp. 25-26.

was the first foreign child to be born on the island and his arrival caused a sensation. The neighbours, Charmian wrote,

> "run in and out all day, chattering and laughing, bringing little bowls of soup and sticky sweets and bunches of flowers and ikons and amulets. Each of them spits three times as she crosses the threshold to ward off the Evil Eye from my room … [T]he baby comes in for a lot of spray, and his basket and blanket are encrusted with ikons and amulets and protective medallions."[7]

The neighbourhood women didn't approve of Charmian's then-modern method of child care. This entailed leaving an infant to cry alone, except when it was being fed according to a strict schedule, until it fell into a stupor. One after another, the neighbour women materialised uninvited in the house, informing Charmian, as if she couldn't hear the hoarse screeching coming from upstairs, "The baby cries."

"Never mind," Charmian replied sternly, "It won't hurt him."

The gentle reproaches continued until finally one of the women took the liberty of retrieving the howling infant.

> " 'I saw you had company, so I picked him up for you,' Kyria Spirathoula says blandly, looking me straight in the eye. 'I thought you might not have heard him crying'."[8]

In portraying herself as a neighbourhood laughingstock – out of touch with the natural callings of motherhood and stubbornly adhering to prescripts that simple village folk could see were patently unsound – Charmian hints at the cultural chasm that divided Greek from expat in those days. There were many misunderstandings. For example, it was commonly believed among foreigners that the Greeks were perpetually casting the evil eye

---

[7] *Lotus*, p. 59.

[8] *Lotus*, p. 81.

on one another out of envy and spite. But Rie explained to us that in the local culture, misfortune attributed to the "eye" usually stemmed from appreciation and admiration, which caused the jealous gods to take revenge. The custom of symbolically spitting on a child and never openly extolling it was mostly to protect it from petulant higher powers, not from one's fellow man.

Language formed part of the barrier. Like most foreigners, George and Charmian learned little more than the essential phrases. In one perhaps apocryphal tale, George requested that a shopkeeper provide him with a "hairy cunt" rather than the white-wash brush he needed.

The foreign children were another matter. The three Johnston offspring learned Greek fluently and attended the local school. When I was old enough, so did I. (An early memory: queuing up with the other children after school to kiss the beringed hand of a passing priest.) You were too young for school but you absorbed the language too, as children do. Leonard Cohen treated Rie and her two little girls to lunch for the pleasure – Rie said – of hearing you and me chat with the waiter and order dish after dish in flawless Greek. (This must have been one of those times when Father had taken himself off to Turkey, or someplace.) I suspect Leonard's enjoyment lay less in the linguistic prowess of the children and more in the mother's flinty intelligence, dark humour and movie-star looks, but I could be wrong. You and I would forget our Greek, but the Johnston children – at least the two eldest – never lost it. If their lives hadn't ended so terribly early, I would have said that I envy them – their long stay on the island before it became heavily commercialised, their retention of the language.

The language question aside, how much did the expats understand the Greeks, and were they (we) even interested, apart from exchanging amusing observations of the most obvious and superficial aspects of island society and culture, as expats do everywhere over sundowners? The foreigners tended to treat Hydra like a playground, where they could rebel against the strictures of their home societies, or as a blank canvas on which they could re-draw themselves according to their whims. But for Hydriots, who formed the background scenery in expat fantasies, the island was none of these things. Their children didn't frolic naked on the beach. Their women didn't wear revealing dresses, sunbathe nude in sight of passing caïques, drink heavily in public, stagger off with men who were not their husbands. Their men didn't flaunt homosexual preferences in broad daylight. The cultural divide widened as the tiny clutch of earnest, impecunious foreign writers and painters became outnumbered by decadent jet-setters. Charmian lamented, "We are watching the island in [the] process of becoming *chic*."[9] She was aware that her own presence – the arrival of the "creative poor"[10] – had set the process in motion.

One night at Gregori's taverna, Arndt von Bohlen und Halbach, flamboyant heir to the Krupp fortune, invited Rie and many others to a shindig on his yacht, anchored off the island. She declined icily: von Bohlen's *dolce vita* was built on the backs of slave labour during the Holocaust and she abhorred him on principle. It was, moreover, her rule never to attend a party on a boat not moored in the harbour. She wanted to be able to slip away when it was time to go home to you and me. (Even as a drinker, she was practical, maternal, responsible.) As it turned out, von Bohlen's was a party Rie was glad to have missed. There had been despicable goings-on, she heard afterwards. It was the Seventies. Keith Richards, who had run into von Bohlen in Morocco in the same period, recalled that he was "a degenerate even by my standards,"[11] which was saying something.

Australian journalist Jorge Sotirios, whose kin are Hydriots, has written about the non-integration of expats – who remained "deliberate outsiders" – into local society.[12] Between the two populations lay hurdles of language and lifestyle. Native islanders felt like country bumpkins in comparison to the cosmopolitan foreigners, yet they also looked down on them. In the view of Hydriots, according to Sotirios, "the interlopers brought over 'unmentionable foreign habits'."[13] Greek writer Margarita Karapanou put it in even more darkly in a novel set on Hydra: "They

---

[9] *Lotus*, p. 148.

[10] *Lotus*, p. 148.

[11] *Life*, Keith Richards & James Fox, Little, Brown & Company, New York, 2010, p. 231.

[12] "Who Cares for Cohen?" Jorge Sotirios, *Griffith Review* edn. 29, 2010 (no pagination)

[13] "Who Cares for Cohen?"

polluted the island with foreign thoughts that the island couldn't stand, weighed the island down with an unbearable burden that it tried in vain to cast off."[14]

Most expats were probably only peripherally aware of any geniune ill-will. They probably preferred to assume that their presence was an economic blessing for islanders and that their liberated ways modelled a lifestyle that the conservative Greeks envied, deep down, and would soon adopt themselves, shedding the shackles of their antiquated mores and religious orthodoxy. Sotirios suggests that the Greeks didn't look at it in quite this way. Charmian may have boasted of being the first woman to drink at a taverna (not uncommonly becoming loud and quarrelsome); for the islanders this was nothing of which to be proud.[15]

The expats' conceit was aided by the forbearance shown by Hydriots, on the whole, in the face of our disrespect for – or at least ignorance of – many of their values and norms. When Charmian failed to care properly for her newborn, the neighbour women corrected her in the kindest possible way. I was handled with similar kid gloves when, as a young anthropologist, I lived in a village on an island off the coast of mainland Tanzania. Especially at the beginning of my stay, I committed countless *faux pas* as well as serious breaches, such as being friendly to the thin, shy dogs of the village, which I later found out – through the most polite hints imaginable – had led the villagers to suspect that I was a witch.

With few exceptions, the Greeks were kind to us, and supremely tolerant. Do you remember The Story of the Scarves?

≈

One evening Rie and Father tucked us into bed, kissed us goodnight and went down to the port. During the night, we awoke and decided to find them. Before setting out, I raided Rie's sparse wardrobe and tied her few scarves to our ankles and wrists. In

---

[14] *The Sleepwalker*, Margarita Karapanou (Karen Emmerich trans.), Clockroot Books, Northampton, Massachusetts, 2011, p. 109.

[15] "Who Cares for Cohen?"

the warm gloom, we made our way through the lanes, down the mountain toward the port, without a thread on us apart from the diaphanous scarves wafting from our extremities.

In one version of this story – Rie's – the chief of police happened to come across us. Taking us in hand, he led us to the police station, where we were covered up and given something to drink. The police chief found our parents – probably at Lulu's taverna, or Douskos – and informed them discreetly that they could fetch their children at their earliest convenience. In Father's telling – our Hydra stories divided like meiotic cells, subsequently evolving in different directions, when our parents went their separate ways – you and I made our way to Tassos' cafe, where we were covered up and given refreshments until Father and Rie were fetched. In both versions, the Greeks were extremely nice to Father and Rie about the whole thing. I do wonder how they would have treated a local Greek couple who had left their children unattended at night to go out and drink and dance. As if such a thing could ever have happened.

Sotirios offers a glimpse into how Hydriots may have seen expats like us or, a decade earlier, the Johnstons, Lily, Christian, Marianne and Axel, followed soon by Leonard. But nothing is clear-cut; everything occupies a grey area or you aren't looking carefully enough. Some Greeks may have been aggrieved at the incursion – perceiving (accurately) the threat to their culture – yet were glad to receive foreigners' money. (Remember how Father used to joke, when he later lived on Nantucket, that what the Nantucket islanders really wished was for the summer residents and day-trippers to send their money and stay away?) One may show tolerance, generosity and compassion to aliens in one's midst and yet find their ways mystifying, deplorable. When Manoli – the gentle fisherman whom you remember as the man missing half a middle finger (torn off by a net winch in his youth) – and his brothers took Rie and us children out for excursions on the family boat, what did their parents make of it?

Could the Hydriots have been entertained by the drunken arguments, blatant infidelities and other carryings-on at the cafés, tavernas and swimming spots? There wasn't much else in the way of public entertainment. The only movie house recycled the same handful of films over and over again. (Throughout our teenage years, *Midnight Express* – probably the most hated film in Turkey – had several weekly screenings at that little outdoor cinema, where the soundtrack could not be heard over the audience's incessant ruckus; they were reading the subtitles, and had already memorized the story anyway.) The diaries of New Zealander writer Bim Wallis chronicle the fractious relationship of the Johnstons ("George and Charm are at the point of killing each other again"), the rise in drug use and other aspects of the evolution of Hydra's expat life through the 1960s.[16] All this must have seemed like a circus show to the island's natives.

Whether it was the foreigners who kept themselves apart or it was the Hydriots who never fully let them in, the differences between the Greeks and the expats used to be plain. This Otherness was surely part of the attraction for the foreigners. It was rooted in our long tradition of romanticising the Primitive, whose way of life seemed simpler and more authentic than our own, timeless and lyrical. Leonard wrote to his mother, "I live on a hill and life has been going on here exactly the same for hundreds of years. All through the day you hear the calls of the street vendors and they are really rather musical."[17] When I lived in Africa, there was a similar savouring of Eternal Primitive Otherness among the expats.

But things were changing for Hydriots too. The foreigners and their "unmentionable" habits – and their infusions of cash into the local economy – were having an impact. At the end of one of her visits in the Sixties, our aunt "Big" Helle noticed one of the conservatively clad Hydriot girls on the same boat sailing from Hydra to Pireaus. The girl was the younger sister of Manoli and his brothers, the fishermen. As the ship neared the metropolis, the young lady slipped into the WC, emerging in a stylish outfit that in London or Copenhagen would have blended right in but which would have earned her harsh reprove on Hydra. Years later, as you

---

[16] "New Zealand's First Man of Letters? Rediscovering Redmond Frankton 'Bim' Wallis", Paul Genoni & Tanya Dalziell, *Antipodes* vol. 29, 2015, pp. 293-308, p. 305.

[17] *Various Positions: A Life of Leonard Cohen*, Ira B. Nadel, Pantheon Books, New York, 1996, p. 85.

and I sat at our usual corner table at Tassos' café, I realised with a jolt that I could no longer distinguish Hydriots from foreigners at a glance. On the island, as elsewhere, the homogenising force of globalisation has been inexorable. As an anthropologist I'm not supposed to say this, let alone be saddened by it. Where the layman's superficial gaze – deceived by such bagatelles as clothing and hair styles – sees boring sameness, my trained eyes are supposed to perceive the deeper differences that persist or are newly emerging. But Hydra is too close to me. My education fails me.

It is easy to romanticize the primitive life when you can leave it any time you like and go back to hot and cold running water in endless quantities, a toilet that flushes without the aid of a basinful of old dishwater tossed into it, doctors and so on. For foreigners, there was something redemptive about living on Hydra in those days, when there were still significant privations. Charmian admitted that they derived "some peculiar satisfaction from our discomforts as we become more aware that we are learning again the true values of light and warmth and food and shelter, which for so many years we have taken for granted."[18]

Kept afloat by irregular royalty cheques, the Johnstons lived a simple life, ate simple meals, drank simply (though copiously) and formed the hub of the small community of expats that was headquartered at "six deal tables at the back of Antony and Nick Katsikas' grocery store at the end of the cobbled waterfront … [where] we usually gather at midday among the flour-sacks and oil-jars and painted tin water-tanks and strings of onions and soft white festoons of cotton-waste."[19] (Could they have imagined the swanky cocktail bars, French restaurants and discoteques that would proliferate on the island in twenty years?)

"At least," Charmian wrote, "our way of life is of our own choosing."[20] And:

> "Everyone of one of us, in his particular way, is
> a protestant against the rat-race of modern com-

---

[18] *Lotus*, pp. 44-45.

[19] *Lotus*, p. 15.

[20] *Lotus*, p. 44.

mercialism, against the faster and faster scuttling through an endless succession of sterile days that begin without hope and end without joy. Each of us has somehow managed to stumble off that treadmill, determined to do his own work in his own way."[21]

So it was for our parents. The travel journals of Rie's mother offer a clue to this. Here's my translation of one of Bedstemor's entries, which relates that Rie

"told me about her and Robert's hard work and thrift to realise their dream of an art-hippie existence here in one of the inexpensive parts of the world, far from the USA. Better to do without much money than to spend their whole lives on housework and an office job – both equally uninteresting for them … I was alarmed at first – but I am more and more convinced that they are right."

It didn't take much to get by. It was probably cheaper for us to live on Hydra than to live in Providence, even factoring in the cost of travelling across the Atlantic once in a while. We did this cheaply too, buying passage on freighters, one of which exploded and sank after we docked in Piraeus. You've seen the newspaper clipping that Rie saved to prove it.

To eke out the money on Hydra, Rie sewed our pretty matching dresses herself and made food go a long way. She picked figs and filled jars of brandied fig jam. She collected almonds at Barbara's house so we had these too. She'd received a sound training in home economics from her mother on the farm. Bedstemor had handled the family poultry business, doing the books, tending the Rhode Island Reds – a breed new to Denmark – and bicycling the boxes of live chicks to the train station. In the early years, little Rie was strapped to the back of her mother's bike too. A believer in vitamins before anyone else in the village had

---

[21] *Lotus*, p. 19.

even heard of them, Bedstemor preserved fruits and vegetables in great quantities, keeping her family and the hired hands well fed on nutritious, economical meals. She led her adoring children on expeditions to catch butterflies and pick mushrooms and she caught snakes for them. The villagers thought they were all peculiar, with their built-in bookshelves taking up a wall of the living room – no one had ever seen such a thing nor could imagine the need for so many books – and the cat that was permitted to sleep in the children's beds and the snakes in the bathtub and the tame rooster named King Christian the Fourth, who performed crowing solos standing on the back of a throne-like dining room chair.

Later, as an older woman, Bedstemor periodically visited us on Hydra and also travelled in West Africa and the Middle East. If the Danish village had been too small for Rie, it had also been too small for Bedstemor, in spite of her ordinary elderly Danish appearance, her prim dresses. Bedstemor had in her youth chosen the farmer's life – her parents had been a train conductor and a midwife – but born in our time she might have been a scientist or an explorer.

This is how she described her arrival to Hydra in 1966, the first time she came, in her journal for that trip:

> "A few minutes past five we rounded a point of the Peloponnese and Hydra emerged, rising practically perpendicular to the sea. And then the town itself appears around a lovely natural harbour. She is there – standing next to the gangway, shouting, and a long moment later I have her. Robert also gives me a hug and together we walk along the quay past the pack asses to their regular café. When the mail has been collected we ascend the famous Donkey Shit Lane, with its 180 sloping steps, until we are up at the house with little Helle, who is absolutely enchanting – and, on top of that, absolutely healthy and vigorous."

Enthralled by Hydra, over the years Bedstemor filled her thick travel journals with descriptions of

– Rie's meals: "She made dinner: fish and potatoes, with red wine, but first watermelon."

– her solitary treks up the mountain: "I pulled myself together for a mountain walk. And it was wonderful. It is beautiful here like nowhere else in the world."

– the local customs: "A woman pulled out a two-drachma coin and led me by the arm to the chapel, where, following her instructions, I deposited the coin and took a candle, bowed before an icon of the Madonna and lit the candle, which I placed in the offering tray."

– the picnics and boat excursions: "Everyone went around with a glass in hand, sat on the side of the boat and dangled their legs overboard, chatting and enjoying life … Helle caught bees and flies and thoroughly enjoyed herself."

– the nuns at the cloister on the mountain: "I just meant to peek into the garden but was captured by a nun, who dragged me into the sitting room, where a couple of housewives with children were sitting, conversing. I received a glass of lovely cold water and a convent cake."

– the sunsets: "The sun set, slightly blurred by the heat, behind the Peloponnese. The sky red and the sea silvery blonde when the golden sunshine disappeared. The stars gradually appeared and everything was absolutely quiet. Only voices once in a while and the regular beating of the waves against the shore. We sat outside. And in the Greek way we shared two shallow plates of salad and for me octopus. Ouzo and red wine. Watermelon. The children gorged themselves."

– her grandchildren's wholesome existence: "The children and I are just home from a bug hunt. They sit up on the uppermost step of the stairs and enjoy the catch."

– the slow rhythm of life: "Rie and I were at the port this morning and George [Lialios] took this picture of us. Now she is on the daybed knitting, with the doors open out to the terrace, where Robert has stretched a canvas for shade and moved the furniture out. He and the girls are at the beach."

Bedstemor was not the first mother to come to the island to check on the welfare of a wayward daughter and to nibble on the lotus herself. She was smitten. Standing up to the Germans during the Occupation of Denmark (but not so much as to endanger her three young children), and often not knowing if her "travelling salesman" husband, our Bedstefar, was dead or under arrest for his work as a Resistance courier, had stretched Bedstemor's nerves until they hummed. As indomitable as she was, she never truly got over it. Her trips to Hydra, extravagances (like her other travels) funded by extreme frugality at home, were a balm. The importance for Rie of her mother as a witness to this chapter in her life – the chapter against which all subsequent chapters would be compared – was immense. When we grew up Rie would likewise scrape together her resources so she could travel to us, wherever we were, to witness you and me in settings and circumstances that held significance for us. In this way she participated in these experiences, animating them with brighter colours and deeper emotional resonance. It was not that we sought her approval. We always knew we had that. After she died you said to me, "It was like nothing really happened for us unless she was there to see it." Who will do this for us now?

Father's parents never considered visiting us on Hydra when they found out there was no air-conditioning, no cars. The closest Grampa Abe came was meeting us in Athens when he stopped there on his way home from a holiday in Israel. Pregnant with you, Rie devoured a series of banana splits at the restaurant of the Hilton, where Grampa was staying. Father was embarrassed by Rie's unseemly appetite and removed himself to another table, temporarily disowning us from behind his *International Herald Tribune*. Grampa happily treated his rapidly expanding daughter-in-law to as much ice cream as she could consume, letting Father sulk by himself. The two Old-Worlders against the American.

Fortified by the Hilton's first-class banana splits, you came along a few months later.

∾

Nannies became common as the Sixties turned into the Seventies but we never had one. Not that we could have afforded a nanny anyway, but Rie was a very hands-on mother. Her contemporaries remember her as a woman who could be counted upon to prepare a warm meal for her children every evening and who kept herself together while all around people were, well, not keeping themselves together. Yes, she drank too much (until a few years later, in Providence, she gave it up for good), but she kept herself together. I'm aware that old friends may be putting a positive slant on it for our sake, and for hers, but I'm inclined to believe it's the truth. Or mostly true. I would be happy with mostly true. Wouldn't you?

Rie surely put a favourable slant on things herself as she told us our stories of Hydra, as you and I do in passing them on to our children. Yet what mother nowadays would gladly tell of leaving her small children alone at home and going out to drink and dance? Among the expats on Hydra at that time this was well within the bounds of responsible maternal conduct, and Rie wasn't going to pretend it never happened just because it would now be frowned upon (or get one's children taken away), especially since it made such an amusing anecdote.

We will never know what she kept back. She must have kept something for herself. I hope she did. Nonetheless, the impropriety of her revelations set us apart from other children as we grew up. If you or I had mentioned to our friends in Providence that Rie had told us that she kept her stash secreted in crannies in old stone walls, well away from whatever house we were living in, they would have gaped as if we'd informed them that our mother was a bank robber. They would have been scandalised, but for us it lent credibility to the entire body of stories and made us feel privileged. *We* had a pretty good idea of what our parents had been up to in the Sixties. Could our friends say the same? Or had their parents been as drab and square in their youths as they were in middle age?

Other people on Hydra hid their narcotics around their homes, but Rie couldn't risk being arrested and separated from us, even though in those years of the dictatorship the police largely left foreigners alone if they didn't brazenly flout the law. She didn't always play it so safe. Father warned her to stop visiting George Lialios, a Greek (not Hydriot) friend who threw grand parties in his mansion. Father was worried that George was being watched by the police, who came down much harder on Greeks than foreigners: Rie might get swept up in the trouble. She shrugged this off as Father's paranoia or jealousy and didn't drop George. It was at George's that Rie took LSD for the first time – another story an ordinary mother might choose not to share with her children. She lay on George's terrace, her back warmed by the heat the stones had stored up during the day, and basked in the glittering night sky. As she watched the shooting stars, she became convinced she was causing them to fall with her mind. For those few hours, she felt exalted, powerful.

But Father was right. George was arrested for possession, taken away to the mainland and hurt badly. It was a long while before he came back to Hydra.

For that time, for that place, Rie was a paragon of motherhood and our house an oasis of normalcy. People who had come to Hydra ostensibly to escape normalcy found themselves drawn to our house, to us. Visitors dropping by at the right time would share a solid meal. Now and again after a night out, Alison Gold couldn't make it all the way to the house she rented, on the far side of Kamini. She'd bang on our door. If Rie couldn't be bothered to let her in – she had her limits, after all, and she might have been out late herself – you or I would slip out of bed, open the door for Alison and share our covers with her. In the morning there was strong coffee and fresh bread. This was when we lived in that house opposite a bakery long since replaced by a hotel, near Four Corners. Rie would dispatch us across the lane to buy a loaf, which the baker would suspend from a string so we wouldn't burn our fingers. Later, for a few coins, the baker would slide Rie's roasting pan full of potatoes, tomatoes and chicken into his oven, still hot from the morning. She would pick it up in time for dinner.

Meanwhile, Father and his friends had decided that they'd stumbled across a significant archaeological site in the hills between Kamini and Vlychos. Day after day, bringing sandwiches and beer, they climbed up there and dug. They made a deep hole. In secret, Rie and the other wives and girlfriends dropped in broken bits of clay pots, which their menfolk were thrilled to find. You were too young to visit Father's excavation, but there are photographs of me on that hilltop with Father and the other men, my face squinching against the bright sun, brown beer bottles balanced on the rocks, the sea and the Peloponnese in the background. To the end of his life, Father believed that important archaeological artefacts came out of that pit.

Rie wasn't the only prankster in the family. Bedstemor wrote in one of her Hydra journals: "Robert loves to come home with surprises and is a master of inventing them." That was true.

Here is The Story of the Rabbits.

~

During a brief stint in Providence, we acquired two rabbits. Rie returned to Hydra with you and me, ahead of Father, who would follow soon after. We'd made him promise to bring the rabbits to Hydra when he came. This was completely unfeasible but he was compelled to agree. The combined will of two little girls is a force of nature.

When some weeks later we met him at the port as he came off the boat, he was bearing two little birds in a cage.

"Where are the rabbits?" we asked anxiously.

He explained. He had taken the rabbits with him on the plane, just as he'd promised. They were safely in a box on his lap. Suddenly there was a commotion inside the box. He described the clattering and squealing and squawking in captivating detail. When the racket had quieted down, he steeled himself and lifted the flap to peek inside. He could hardly believe his eyes: the rabbits had turned into two yellow birds.

Picture us standing there on the port, with our golden hair and our blue eyes wide with amazement. Our rabbits had turned into birds! The birds were of the type sold at every pet shop in Athens but we didn't make the connection: we were the two luckiest children in the world and our lives were laced with magic.

Father fastened mosquito netting against the deeply recessed kitchen window – the old stone houses had thick walls – to make an aviary. You and I were heartbroken when we came home one day and were told by a sad-faced parent that our little yellow rabbit-birds had, alas, escaped. (You are a parent yourself now so this may bring the hint of a smirk to your lips. Did the birds escape or was that another fairytale? Quite a few of our family stories took on a different cast, an extra dimension, once you and I had children.)

They were both good story-tellers. When Father first met his sister-in-law – Big Helle – he told her that he'd been raised a Catholic. She believed him. It wasn't until later that she put two and two together – not least his two Jewish parents – and realised that something didn't add up. It amused him to foment a cloud of mystery around himself. His sudden caginess, the red herrings casually dropped in his fine deep-timbered voice, left people guessing. Not a few naïve people, especially of the fairer sex, were beguiled. As teenagers, you and I rolled our eyes at all of them – Father and his acolytes. As I slid into middle age myself I began to contemplate Father's mischievous cloak-and-dagger act in the context of his life-long self-reinvention. He was by no means the only foreigner on Hydra engaged in this project.

≈

Charmian wrote of being on the island just after the birth of her third child there:

> "I almost have to pinch myself to believe in my own existence, when I walk along the waterfront with my body my own again … floating just above the cobbles through a myriad small radiant explosions of sunlight and an intoxicating geometry of café tables, ship's prows, doors, windows, houses, roof-tops, rigging, that sing their coloured scraps of arcs and cubes and angles so piercingly as to almost burst my heart. As though it is me who has just been born."[22]

For the expats, the island offered redemption and rebirth. People reinvented themselves among strangers who were (mostly) equally strangers to one another. Marianne recalled a scene in which the resident foreigners were gathered around a table at the

---

[22] *Lotus*, p. 64.

port, introducing themselves to a new arrival.[23] One man presented himself as a painter, the next was a poet, the next a sculptor
and so on. Marianne struggled internally, and in vain, to find
a label for herself, a worthy excuse for being on the island – for
being at all – apart from the fact that her boyfriend, Axel, was
working on the next great Norwegian novel.

One could live out one's fantasy of oneself in this remote place,
among people who only knew what – if anything – one chose to
disclose of one's former life. Like Athena and Odysseus in *The
Odyssey*, many of the foreigners on Hydra were masters of pre-
tence and disguise. It was another world, far away from briefcases,
bosses, starched collars, rush-hour traffic, vacuum cleaners and
parent–teacher meetings. The island offered an escape from the
conventional aspirations of parents and home-town peers. It was
a heady feeling, eschewing those yardsticks, side-stepping that rat
race, erasing chapters of the past and starting fresh.

"We invent our own lives," concluded the Welsh painter and
writer Brenda Chamberlain in her book based on her years on
Hydra in the 1960s.[24] It was wonderful, this prospect of reinvention, this chance to fulfill the ambition to write or paint, or to
find some satisfaction in going through the motions of writing or
painting. It was also risky.

"This island is full of writers," Karapanou has a character in her
novel set on Hydra say: "They all come here and drive themselves
crazy; this one can't write, that one can't stop, they all go nuts in
the end."[25]

A figure in Chamberlain's book describes how the expats were
"cooped up here between the sea and the mountains, trying to be
artists, or pretending to be artists."[26] In Karapanou's novel they
"drank and cried and used art to disguise their hopelessness; for
them art was the last stop, their final excuse to live a little longer."
For some this was literally true. Chamberlain left Hydra in 1967

---

[23] *So Long, Marianne,* p. 67.

[24] *A Rope of Vines: Journal from a Greek Island*, Brenda Chamberlain, Parthian, Cardigan,
p. 148.

[25] *Sleepwalker,* p. 89.

[26] *Rope,* p. 129.

and took her life a few years later. The tragedy of the Johnstons was on a larger scale.

Watching her three children, Charmian thought:

> "How sweetly the children sleep with thin, naked brown arms flung wide and sun-bleached heads gleaming silver in the starlight. Already they have almost forgotten that there was another life before this, when they did not have breakfast by the sea, when they did not sleep under the sky … Through them we are committed wholly to life."[27]

It was not to be. A couple of years after returning to Australia, Charmian gave up that commitment to life and ended it. A year later, her husband George succumbed to tuberculosis, his constitution weakened by a lifetime of hard living. Two of their three children – the tanned, gilded children who thrived on Hydra just as you and I did – died very early of suicide and substance abuse.

The little Johnston – the one born on the island and protected by the neighbour women's spit and charms – is, I hope, alive and well somewhere. He's about twelve years older than you.

≈

"Everyone on this island is hiding something," wrote Karapanou.[28] But secrets eventually come out, don't they? Even you and I, who were children and therefore partially screened from the normal gossip, came to know some ugly truths about the grown-ups – not just our parents – that forty or fifty years later they would flatly deny if confronted with them. They might even have genuinely forgotten they were true. People are always white-washing their pasts. (I do it too.) And other people who remember what really happened are usually kind and let them get away with it.

For the small assortment of foreigners who pushed their spindly roots down into the dry soil of this island, it was paradise. For

---

[27] *Lotus*, p. 144.

[28] *Sleepwalker*, p. 160.

some – not just the Johnstons and Brenda Chamberlain but many others whom you and I know – it also proved to be paradise lost. There was freedom, but especially in the later years there were no sanctions, no balls-and-chains to keep one within limits. When someone began to spin out of control, everybody knew it. It was such a small group, in such a confined space ("cooped up here between the sea and the mountains"). They were all witnesses to one another's indiscretions, marital brawls, bruises, child neglect, slides into addiction, descents into mental hell. There were few diversions from watching this.

One's private life was played out on an open stage for everyone – like the chorus in an ancient Greek play – to comment upon. This intensified the tragedies (not to mention the comedies), which back in the other world would have remained safely concealed. This was an aspect of life on Hydra that the expats complained about. Laid bare to public scrutiny, the torment of personal crises was exacerbated. It was humiliating, claustrophobic. In one of John le Carré's thrillers, the characters "leave for Hydra, but Hydra is too cramped, too ominous, there is suddenly nowhere to go but Spetsai."[29]

In later years, after we were settled in Providence but spent the occasional summer with Father on Hydra, he was sometimes tangled up in that gossipy web and would pack in a huff. He was never coming back to Hydra, he announced. He was finished with it. He would find another island. *Did we think that there were not plenty of equally beautiful places in Greece?*

You and I would be thrown into a panic, tears and snot streaming, stomachs knotting. Not because of his anger, but because if Father was not coming back to Hydra then neither were we. (At ten or eleven could you imagine that in a few years you'd be travelling vast distances under your own steam?) Never coming back to Hydra? Other places in Greece? No, there were no other places for us.

He would simmer down and the following year would return to Hydra. He couldn't stay away. And, if we were lucky, we spent another summer with him on the island.

---

[29] *A Perfect Spy*, John le Carré, Knopf, New York, 1986, p. 114

The betrayals, the violence, the despair, the secrets – none of it touched you and me, did it?

~

For us, as children, Hydra was paradise. Yet it was not without its jeopardies even for us. In addition to the centipedes, there were bold octopuses, as I found out when I was about six years old. This was a story that Father told: The Time Helle Was Almost Strangled by an Octopus.

Father used to go spear-fishing in his mask, snorkel and flippers off Kastello Beach. This was the gentle beach where the Hydriot women brought their youngsters to swim and the old ladies came too, wading in on strong pale legs and splashing water on their bosoms. Out of respect for them, there was an unspoken rule among the foreigners that adults kept on their swimming clothes at this beach. This was not where the chic expats bathed, mind you. Even now – with that new bar rearing up behind it, its lounge chairs encroaching onto Hydra's tiny remaining swatch of public beach, its loudspeakers blaring music in all directions – Kastello is still our favourite beach.

If Father got an octopus, which were abundant back then, he would swim close to the shore and flip the live creature off the end of his spear and onto the beach. There I would be ready to receive the octopus, which I would kill and smash against a rock to tenderise it. That was the routine.

One day the octopus that Father flung onto the beach for me was bigger than usual. Or braver. Or I was sluggish that day. In any case, after I picked it up, but before I could start whacking it, the octopus began to make its way up my arm. I stood frozen in fear as the wretched animal clambered toward my head. There was no one around. It wasn't summer and there were no bathers.

Out in the water, Father paused from his hunt to see how I was doing back on land. Seconds later he was on the beach, ripping the octopus off me. Its suckers left round marks all over my arm. In spite of experiences like this, when asked at around this age what I wanted to be when I grew up, I answered that I was going to be a diver by day and a writer by night, like Father.

You discovered another hazard to children on Hydra: falling into cisterns. These were cavernous rainwater storage chambers built into the ground levels of all the old houses. Usually cistern openings were surrounded by a low wall and were securely covered. On one occasion, during renovations, some friends left their cistern open and unwalled. Paying them a visit, Rie sat with our hosts while you and I wandered around the terrace holding hands. Suddenly you disappeared down a hole and I was left hanging onto your arm for all I was worth. I shouted for help and you were hauled to safety.

The island's donkeys and mules posed a potential danger too. For a while we had a donkey called Gamla Gubben. This means something like Old Geezer in Swedish. I think he came to us with that name; perhaps we'd inherited him from Swedes. Gamla Gubben was mainly employed to carry heavy loads up and down the hill, things like stove gas canisters, which were virtually impossible for even a fit man like Father to carry on his own back for a distance. Gamla Gubben had a grudge against women and Rie could not handle him, so Father was in charge of him. There's a photograph of you and me on that donkey, with Father walking beside him down stone steps. This was on the sea road to Kamini, just above the little harbour. It's spring and the red poppies are in bloom. We are in new dresses. Father is grinning. Gamla Gubben is behaving himself. It might have been Easter.

When I happen upon a certain corner in the lanes of Hydra a wisp of a memory comes to me of Gamla Gubben getting very stroppy just there. A scary moment, even with Father, so strong and capable, looking out for us. I've experienced this unsettling flash of a half-memory every time I've been back to Hydra. I can hear the donkey's hooves clattering chaotically on the stones, the sharp sounds amplified and repeated by the high stone walls. I can see – from a child's low perspective – the donkey and his heavily loaded wooden saddle lurching unpredictably in the narrow lane. Had Gamla Gubben been provoked by a passing female, human or equine? Or was it one of those mysterious spots on Hydra where donkeys sometimes come to a standstill and refuse to take a step forward? According to local belief, it's a sign of ghosts.

Years later, when you and I were perhaps eleven and thirteen and Father was staying in Lindsey Callicoatt's house, he borrowed Lily's donkey for us. You remember Oswald. When he came to us there were oozing sores on his long face where the metal nose-piece of his halter had scraped through the skin stretched over his bones. The wounds healed under our ministrations, but his blindness in one eye we could not cure.

I had to brace my nerves to ride Oswald on the sea road. He had the habit of veering off to the outer edge of the road. That was back when there wasn't a thigh-high wall running continuously along that stretch of mountainside. Oswald's half-blindness tricked his brain into thinking that he was plodding along safely in the middle of the track when he was actually only a whisker's breadth from plunging down the rocks to the sea. I rode Oswald anyway and always side-saddle, in accordance with local practice. (Only tourists ride astraddle.) I knew the basic commands and carried a short length of rubber hose to encourage the donkey over ghosty spots. The muleteers – donkey men, we called them – greeted me as they passed and expressed approval at my handling of the animal. I was suffused with pride. Even now I blush when I think of it.

Every so often, in spite of our pampering, Oswald would escape from Lindsey's garden. We'd run through the lanes, anxiously looking for him. High drama, for us children. We felt a little betrayed every time. *Don't we take good care of you, Oswald?*

After we left at the end of that summer, Father returned Oswald to Lily. We were later told that the donkey had been struck by lightning while grazing in the little field behind Lily's house. We were heartsore. And suspicious.

Then there was The Time We Were Set Upon by Gypsies.

≈

Before Bisti was ruined forever by imported sand, umbrellas, beach beds and a restaurant, the expats used to make excursions there. Arrangements would be made with a caïque man. On the morning of our departure, the group of friends would gather at the port with baskets and bags of food and drink, rolled-up blankets and towels and a camping stove. The grown-ups would dash around at the last minute buying another watermelon, a few more loaves of bread and litres of wine and rounding up the youngsters. Everyone piled into the little open boat.

We putt-putted westward, along the rugged coast, the islands of Dokos and Spetsai up ahead of us. (In those days, the boats went *putt-putt*. They've been replaced by motorboats with engines that rip through the air like chainsaws.) The trip took a long time. We children were bursting with anticipation.

The pebble beach at Bisti was C-shaped, bracketed by a steep mountain on one side and a smaller rocky hill on the other. There was a cave in the mountainside, at sea level. Gaining entry entailed running a gauntlet of sea urchins and sharp rocks. Behind the beach was a pine forest, which reached up the mountain. The beach was spangled with casts of white heart urchins and green and purple sea urchins, along with pearlescent ormer shells and other treasures. Under the clear water it was similarly pristine and rich with life. The bottom was covered with jagged rocks, bristling with silky black sea urchins whose spines moved gently if one paused long enough to observe it. Inevitably someone ended up with fragments of spines in his feet, sparking off a familiar debate about the best way to remove them.

We'd set up our "camp" – a haphazard spread of towels, blankets, bags, bottles and clothing – just above the shingle beach, in the shade of the pines. Whenever I hear pines whispering, I think immediately of sitting on a carpet of red-brown pine needles in the shade at Bisti and wolfing down a slab of watermelon or a chunk of bread before running down the beach again – quite an art on those stones, but that's what our feet were used to – and plunging into the water. You and I and the other children were in the water and on the beach all day, apart from refuelling breaks, while the grown-ups swam a bit and mostly lazed in the half-shade, enjoying the idyll in their own way.

During one of these outings to Bisti, all the adults went off to dine at the invitation of a party that arrived on a yacht moored in the next cove. Off they trooped that afternoon, leaving us children on the beach. We played and swam, until someone saw strangers approaching. This was odd: it was very rare to encounter people at Bisti. We weren't alarmed until we noticed how the newcomers seemed to be carefully observing us while sidling up to our camp. They weren't tourists or expats like us. And their demeanor was not like Greeks, who would have been friendly and courteous, not sneaky.

Gypsies! (Well, that's what we understood them to be then.) We quickly snatched up our parents' wallets, watches and jewellery. I picked up the watermelon knife and one of the other bigger children grabbed the bread knife. We abandoned the camp and ran in the late afternoon sunshine down the beach. The smaller children began to cry as they were herded into the water and into the cave. Our parents' valuables were kept dry over our heads.

From our spiky perches inside the cave, we watched as the footpads ransacked the bags and baskets left under the pines. The little children shivered. I tried to work out what we were going to do if the Gypsies came after us. Wouldn't they be furious that we hadn't left any money or jewellery for them? Did I have it in me to stab my knife into a person, even in self-defence? *Where the hell were our parents when we needed them?*

The Gypsies (or whatever they were) eventually vanished into the forest. After waiting a while, we cautiously ventured back onto the beach and to our camp. The grown-ups showed up later, evidently having enjoyed their dinner on the yacht. They were duly sheepish when they heard about our adventure, but one of the children was scolded for not having grabbed her mother's dope.

During one of those excursions the boat man didn't come back for us on the appointed day. The adults discussed the feasibility of locating the rough path that was supposed to lead up the mountainous length of the island, back to civilisation. They speculated about how long it would take, how much water would be needed and whether it wasn't wiser to wait and flag down a passing boat. In the meantime, I tried to help by collecting wild food. I enlisted you and the other children to prise limpets off the rocks along the shore. I made these into a soup with the mushy half tomato we had left and wild oregano harvested from the hillside.

"Mmmm, it's good," I said. The other children were skeptical. In a show of sororal solidarity – one of many during our lives – you ate that soup with me and pretended to like it.

As our supplies dwindled, the mood grew grim and the smaller children became whiny and weepy. Back in town, the caïque man remembered that he was late to fetch a party of foreigners at Bisti.

Perhaps the boat was only one day late. Maybe it was two. It felt like a week. Do you remember that boat ride back to town? How cold and thirsty and sunburnt we were?

~

In spite of the murderous sea creatures, jagged rocks, off-kilter donkeys, treacherous cisterns and bands of thieves, you and I never felt safer than when we were on Hydra. The island's perils had a fairytale quality that we seem to have perceived even then. Walking down the gangplank and setting my feet onto the port was like being swaddled in a soft blanket.

If the adults enjoyed greater freedom on Hydra, so did we children and this contributed to the feeling we had of living in a fable. Alison would send Thor, who was then about five (like me), across the valley to our house, or Rie would send you and me to Alison's. They'd pin notes to our shirts or dresses: "Send the girls home by 6." "Come have dinner with us. Bring bread if you have any." We were a little too young to be entrusted with delivering notes carried in our hands or pockets, which ended up bulging with withering flower heads, beach glass, dead scarabs and gecko tails. Going across the village was perhaps a long walk for such small children but it was perfectly safe and we knew our way through the maze of crooked lanes. Rie never worried. The Hydriots could be counted upon to stop and help a child in distress and there was not a square inch of public space that wasn't monitored around the clock by some old crone from some window.

Occasionally we had to go to Athens and *that* felt dangerous. For Rie and Father, Athens offered amenities unavailable on Hydra so their feelings about it were mixed. For you and me it was mostly misery. The automobile exhaust gave me a headache that lasted for the duration of our stay in the city. Rie kept a white-knuckled grip on our hands lest we step into oncoming traffic. Such were the disadvantages of raising children on an island with no cars. But it was in Athens that you and I saw our very first film: *Yellow Submarine*, which entranced me. You were just a baby.

Another time, a few years later, on our way to the Kingsmills' wedding in Athens, you, Rie and I got stuck in an elevator. Rie was sorry to have missed the ceremony. She and Christina were good friends. The two of them would sit at the port and enjoy animated conversations in pretend French. Christina and Anthony were so in love when they married but their first encounter, at Lulu's taverna, had not boded well. We were sitting at a couple of pushed-together tables when Anthony, who was a painter (and once Charmian Clift's lover), joined us. Unamused, Christina turned to Big Helle, who was visiting, and deadpanned, "What's Gertrude Stein doing here?" (There *was* a resemblance.) Later, he recited a sonnet and she saw his paintings and she was hooked.

The elevator unstuck, we made it to the wedding festivities, where Rie and Alison, assisted by us girls, decorated the bride with flowers as she lay naked on the bed, as a surprise for Anthony.

As teenagers, we were taken from Hydra to the Acropolis, Thira, Epidauros and other places. Father had made it his mission to expand our knowledge of Greece. Tromping through magnificent archaeological sites I was filled with a sullen longing for Hydra. Alright, I was at an age when one is prone to sullenness, and to tromping, but I have always had this heartsick feeling, akin to grief, upon leaving the island.

When the four of us left Hydra in 1972, headed for permanent residence in the US, you and I no idea when, or if, we would ecome back. We stood on the deck of the boat and watched the island pull away from us. As Big Helle related the incident, I said, in my grave, gravelly voice, "Goodbye, everything that is good in my life." I was six and given to laconic pronouncements.

∼

While we were on Hydra, the rest of the world shot forward. On 20 July 1969, when you were just a year old and I was three, Rie (who was twenty-five) took us down to the port. It was abuzz with the news of the moon landing. A shopkeeper – Sourelis – had put up a television and people had gathered to watch the replay. Rie bypassed the tv and the crowd and sat us down at Tassos' for a slice of chocolate cake.

Tassos' was then one of the main cafés patronised by the foreigners. (This was pre-Pirate Bar.) Tassos, a large man, was one of the Katsikas. Their store – then still, as in Charmian's time, the general emporium of "flour-sacks and oil-jars and painted tin water-tanks and strings of onions" – was just across the lane from Tassos' cafe. Katsikas' shop often extended credit to foreigners and the proprietors were known for their many kindnesses to both Greeks and aliens.

When Rie left Hydra in 1972, she and Tassos said goodbye. He predicted gloomily that she would forget him and they would never see one another again. She promised that she would never forget him and that they would meet again. He died about a year before Rie finally returned to Hydra, forty years later. It pained her that she had not been able to keep half of her promise to Tassos. The other half – that she would always remember the man – she did keep.

Domna was another Greek friend that Rie didn't make it back in time to see again. She and her partner Ada had owned one of Hydra's first tourist shops, a few doors over from Tassos'. We once spent Christmas in the apartment above the shop. We had been staying in a house owned by the von Helands – he was a Swedish diplomat. Father was away and Big Helle was visiting. When the von Helands came back, unannounced, to celebrate Christmas on the island, Domna and Ada offered us the flat. Rie tossed the bare necessities into a pair of baskets and we moved in for the holiday.

She had promised us a Christmas tree that year so she cut branches from a fig tree and stuck these in a ceramic jug on the living room floor. She added sprigs of evergreen that she filched from a cypress tree in the cemetery, tying these to the bare fig branches. A string attached to a hook in the ceiling kept the tree more or less upright. She and Big Helle plaited small heart-shaped nut baskets, sixteen-pointed stars and other traditional Danish paper ornaments. Big Helle sacrificed her necklace so the beads could be hung on the tree among the paper hearts and stars.

After dinner, we held hands and danced in a ring around the tree as we sang Danish Christmas songs. The way Rie told this story later, our joy carried us out the door, singing and dancing and still holding hands, onto the port and up Donkey Shit Lane.

Some American tourists joined our dancing chain as it snaked down to the port again. Was there ever a better Christmas?

The house of the von Helands was by far the grandest we ever lived in and there we had the uncommon luxury of a telephone. The flat roof offered a good view of the harbour. If we spotted a cruise ship approaching the island at an odd hour, Rie would ring Domna, who would refresh the kohl rimming her dark eyes, pull a brush through the waves of her thick black hair and dash down from her house in a slim skirt and high-heeled boots to throw open the door and shutters of her shop.

One day a tourist questioned Domna about one of the icons she had for sale. His tone hinted that he doubted the age and authenticity of the piece. Domna drew herself up and said haughtily, "I will have you know, sir, that this icon is more than two thousand years old!"

~

Tassos, Domna, Jimmy, Manoli, the priests, the baker, the donkey men, the boat men and the old women at their windows saw Rie and Father and the others foreigners come and go like a parade. Some of the expats had humble origins or had survived heart-breaking events during or after the war. Some came from aristocratic families that had (or once had) money. Not a few had shady pasts. Many were creative. Many were eccentric, or more than eccentric. Some were seeking. Some were fleeing. A common element in those who would thrive on the island as well as those who would ruin themselves on it was a streak of abandon. That other reality back in New York or Oslo or Sydney faded instantly to insignificance. The only important thing became to find a way to stay. It was better to live as a pauper on Hydra than to play out that comfortable bourgeois existence back where one came from. The primitive life on Hydra was infinitely more sumptuous. People who didn't see this flitted away to other islands, other countries.

In this microcosm, people became friends who would otherwise never have even crossed paths. They drank the same cheap Greek wine at the same wobbly tables, tearing hunks from the same loaf and swabbing the same plate of yellow-green oil. They danced together to the same Greek music, conversing passionately (at least volubly) until late into the night and then dragging themselves up the hill to stone houses and beds that were all about the same in terms of their comfort, or discomfort. Rie – only recently a farm girl – found herself holding Philip van Rensselaer (we called him Skids), scion of New York royalty, after his failed attempt to do himself in. She rang the police and comforted her friend as they waited for the helicopter that would take him to the hospital in Athens. There were many such improbable connections and implausible scenes.

There was an ethos, in the early days especially – as there is in any small expat community – of helping one another out and shoring one another up during rough patches (gossip notwithstanding). Greenhorns were taken under the wings of foreigners who were well-established – people like the Johnstons, who had knew how to rent or buy a house, get repairs done and so on. This process of learning the ropes and being incorporated into the group was exhilarating for the newcomers and gratifying for the expats who guided them. Father and Rie experienced this too, as fresh arrivals and later as old hands.

The material scarcity was equalising and liberating in the old days too. Marianne and Axel's first home on Hydra was furnished with the car seats they ransacked from the Volkswagen they'd driven from Oslo and left parked on the Peloponnese. This would have been inconceivable in Norway. When we rented Kalliope's house, Father furnished it with cheap plastic blow-up furniture in orange and sky blue. On the white-washed terrace, there was something *Clockwork Orange* about it. Meals were often cooked together, with friends contributing whatever they had to impromptu feasts. Clothing, children's gear and household furnishings were circulated until they fell to pieces. Marianne's little son wore the Johnston children's hand-me-downs. Rie ended up with a purple crocheted dress that had been Marianne's.

Just about every corner of Hydra was beautiful, in all seasons, at any hour, and this beauty could be had for a pittance. It cost very little to rent a house, buy food and spend evenings at the taverna laughing and dancing. It was free to swim in the warm sea.

When Rie dived into the black water one night shortly after her arrival and discovered the glowing trail behind her, it seemed like magic. It was free to walk barefoot on the smooth stones and be caressed by the lustrous air as one lay down for a rest by the side of the road and looked up at the stars. The beauty of the place shone back on people and made them beautiful too. There was, as Leonard once put it, a kind of gold dust on everyone: they were all young and beautiful and everything they did seemed significant and full of promise.[30]

For the artistically inclined Hydra seemed like the perfect place to work. The simple daily routine in this luminous, tranquil setting cleared and focussed the mind. If one was not already an artist upon arrival, it wasn't long before one began experimenting with different media. Shall I paint? Sketch? Sculpt? Write? Photograph? Make things out of driftwood and beach glass? The island seemed to pull this out of people. Or perhaps it was merely a matter of going with the flow, bending to the subtle form of peer pressure that bore down on Marianne, the odd one out at a table of artists. In any case, the island's "wild and naked perfection," which had pole-axed Miller just before the war, was a source of boundless inspiration.

However, if a person also bore within himself the seeds of self-destruction, living on Hydra fostered dissolution. If there were cracks, they deepened and widened, as they did for the Johnstons, our parents and others. For all its slow, soft rhythms, Hydra was perhaps less a restorative place for some people than a crucible that tested one's mettle. Creativity was intensified, character defects aggravated, weaknesses amplified. The sunshine and blinding white-washed walls could never completely obliterate the turbid shadows of the past. This was the chiaroscuro of Hydra. Some people made lasting successes of it. Others floundered, sank.

They would eventually limp away, sometimes to recover, sometimes not. It was one or the other, it seemed: health and happiness or disaster and defeat. "There can be no half-measures on this rock, no poetic dreams," wrote Brenda Chamberlain. The expats saw this process of destruction play itself out, time and

---

[30] *So Long, Marianne*, p. 99.

time again. We were there as small children and it was there for you and me to see too. But a child doesn't really see what she can't understand. This kind of blindness is a very good thing. It was only later that you and I could comprehend this darker side and ponder how it had touched our own lives.

Though forsaking Hydra failed to heal the cracks in our family, my conception and yours of Hydra as our own Eden stayed constant, even when the scales fell from our older eyes and our minds grew capable of understanding ugly adult dramas and we came to see that the island was not a paradise for everyone who had lived there, not even for Rie and Father, whose love of Hydra outlasted their love for one another or for any other person, apart from you and me.

Hydra cast a spell on our parents and for you and me there was no existence before it. It got inside us. We carried Hydra within us everywhere. Or rather, we left a piece of ourselves behind. Throughout our travels it would forever tug at us like a magnet, reminding us of the direction and distance between ourselves and that waterless rock. We would never feel utterly at ease or wholly ourselves until we were back there, "most marvellously and mysteriously renewed and made whole again,"[31] as Charmian put it. You and I leaped out into the world on our own, exploring it and becoming attached to other places, yet something has always been amiss, a niggling sense that something is not right, that we are not in the place we are supposed to be.

This was why Father kept going back year after year, in spite of being so vexed by the gossip that he swore he would turn his back to Hydra forever, promising that there were other enchanting places in Greece that he would patronize. You know as well as I do that there were no such places for him.

This was why, when Rie returned to Hydra after her self-imposed banishment and she felt the smooth, warm, grey stones under her bare feet, the coil that had been wrapped around her slackened and fell away. The burden of four decades of exile suddenly lifted and she was made whole again, restored with parts of herself that she had left behind for dead and with mysteries that

---

[31] *Lotus*, p. 133.

she had kept even from you and me. This was the port where she had arrived with her American, in love and about to embark on a great adventure. Down these steps she carried you, her fairy daughter, in her basket. Here was where we fed her loaf of bread to the fish. There was the café doorway where Tassos stood, and over there Domna opened the shutters of her shop and sold icons that were older than Christ himself. There was the beach where you and I learned to swim, and in there used to be the baker who baked our dinner – all the stories she had been telling us for all those years, as much for her own sake as for ours. It was if she were suddenly weightless – as you had once been – ever young and beautiful and hopeful and shimmering with gold dust, suspended between the bioluminescent whorls in the sea and the shooting stars overhead, skidding past the highest monastery lights.

There Are Rocks

Lindsey Callicoatt

I once lived on Hydra. Now I live on Hawaii, the "Big Island," the one with active volcanoes. The two have little in common besides "H" heading their names and, of course, being islands. Hawaii is one of the youngest geological places on Earth, with almost no architecture to speak of, nine of the world's climate zones, one of them being a very wet, mossy Garden of Eden-like setting, in which I can be found. Contemplation of plants has become my primary activity. Whereas Hydra is old; who knows when it was pushed up from the sea? An architectural wonder of gorgeous buildings dating back centuries, preserved and adored. Small and shaped like a serpent, mostly dry, but with surprising seasonal plant magic, and vistas that would enthrall you. I am growing old on this tropical island, but I was once young in that old enchanting place.

≈

I was eight years old when I vowed I would go to Greece, after seeing a picture of the Parthenon in a school textbook. At twenty-three I arrived in the middle of the night on a boat from Brindisi to Patras. I kissed the ground, despite its harbour griminess, as Isadora Duncan and her brother had done, on their first arrival in that land they deemed sacred.

Greece did not disappoint them, nor me. Places in Europe had surely charmed me, but here, here it was *foreign!* Centuries of invaders, settlers, had left aspects of their cultures to form this marvellous world of East meets West. Athens in the Seventies was glorious, tawdry, bustling, old buildings mixed with new, and glimpses of the ancient wonders. There was no closing time in Greece, *bouzouki* to all hours, one could (then) climb on every part of the Acropolis. On the full moon it was open late and you could view its glory from the centre of the Parthenon, the columns framing it, all the way to the Aegean, shimmering on the water, like the cover of a pack of Hellas Special cigarettes.

~

It was a good time to come of age, the Sixties and Seventies. The Reagan Era hadn't started, the one percent weren't able to hoard all the money, there was work, even for teenagers and college students. I was from the lower middle class, yet had recently graduated from a state university, with no student debt, and I was in Europe!

First time on Hydra I had no sense that it would become … what? … pretty much *everything* to me. I loved the Greek islands without a discriminating eye, but this one, while beautiful, did not seem to want me, no women came to meet the boat offering inexpensive rooms, no *souvlaki* stands or beaches. It did not cater to the casual tourist! I went to the "swimming rocks," something I came to much prefer over beaches: no sand getting into things, easy jump into the sapphire of a sea. Pretty girl mistook me for the Danish au pair to a baby named Thor. I didn't correct her, nor did I know I'd become lifelong friends with that baby and his mother, (the writer Alison Gold) – I was just pleased my ancestral Danish DNA was apparent. Walking by the sea that night I kissed a girl whose look would be very fashionable thirty years later, then I slept behind a ruin – they were very plentiful on Hydra at that time – on a towel given to me years earlier by a boy I was in love with, but never knew carnally. I still know him, and he's still hot. Next morning I beat a retreat to the neighbouring island of Poros, a place more accommodating to the likes of me.

Went to a disco on Poros with a couple travel buddies, met sisters, Greek, sophisticated, younger one spoke English, the sultry one French. I knew a little French. (Stay with me, my Hydra destiny is involved.) I liked her a lot and when I later lost a coin toss (more destiny) for a ticket to England, where my cousin could offer some security, I told lovely Maro Ipiotis I wanted to stay in Greece, needed a job. "Try the American–Hellenic Union, they might know of English teaching positions," only she said it in French.

As I walked through the glass doors, an elegant man, made me think of a camel (I like camels), was coming out. Inside they said, "That man was looking for a teacher of English. It's on an island but they'll pay more for that." Island! Pay more!

I was to become the *Kathegetes Anglika* at the historic Merchant Marine Academy of Hydra, where captains of Greece's great merchant fleets were trained. I think it paid about $180 a month – not bad.

So Hydra was to become my home. While I'm on the boat there maybe I should clear up some of the sex stuff. At that time I don't think *I* knew what my orientation was: the acronym LGBT had yet to become common in the media or the western world's conscience. I was sometimes referred to as "L" when I was living with my son's mother, otherwise not (but I *do* adore many lesbians). "G" seemed to be the preferred direction of my dick. "B" probably describes me most accurately, but doesn't really cover it. "T", well, I'm pretty content with the gender I was assigned. Being male has its advantages, plus I tend to find women infinitely more interesting than men, but I don't have it in me to be the mystery they can be. I think now of myself as polyamorous. (Polly Amorous, a drag name?) I'm even aroused by well-crafted furniture, not to mention plants, especially tropical ones. Anyway, it's October, 1970, I'm twenty-three, going to a new place to do a job I'm untrained to do. Was I scared and lonely? Probably, I don't remember. But I was going to the island of Leonard Cohen, there was a comfort in that. I will spare you my story of discovering his music/poetry, but will say that when I got a one-way ticket to Europe the previous June my one bag contained record albums by him.

The naval school was in a mansion on the port, windows behind my students gave a view of the harbour, yachts and buildings holding port-side shops with the colonnaded School of Fine Art (once headed by Pavlos Pantelakis, who started the movement to preserve Hydra's unique character). The boys I taught were eighteen or nineteen years of age. I felt sheepish when they stood at attention as I entered the room. Roll call sounded so exotic – Eustace, Demetri, Sotiri. I made up for my lack of teaching experience by bringing in records with good vocabulary (Judy Collins' "Turn, Turn, Turn"), beautiful girls – Anne Ramis being one – to converse with them (got in trouble for that one: *You brought a woman into the classroom?!?"* said the shocked commander of the school), and having a reasonable command of English grammar, thanks to my mother. I only had to work about eight hours a week, but was jealous of the other foreigners who could apparently spend all their day at Bill's Bar.

There's another little harbour about half a mile from the main one, the area seems sweeter, more peasant-like. I got a house there. It had a big terrace, off that I had a little room with windows on three sides, they viewed small islands that looked like whales. A plaster bird on the ceiling no longer held a chandelier. I learned that what I had considered necessities were actually luxuries. No running water or appliances, save a little propane stove on which I heated cistern water to bathe. That Spartan life taught me much; I'm not a slave to comforts, the "necessities" of First World life.

Hydra. To the unschooled eye (mine) Hydra was just another of the many lovely islands of Greece at first, simple, gentle, they all floated on that luminous pale blue evening sea, giving you the feeling that you want nothing more. Hydra had that, yet more. In time I sensed an elegance unique to her, one that would grow in my perception. In the Seventies her population wavered around three thousand people, yet it was once a *city*, of more than thirty thousand, in the late 18th, early 19th centuries. Yes a city, a wealthy one in fact, of ship-building, sea captains and far-flung trade. Essentially its own country, Hydra had treaties with other nations. And for the most part its Genoese-style mansions, ship-building halls, public buildings, churches, were still here, despite the intervening decades of decline. Years of poverty, and a topography not conducive to automobiles, kept these magnificent structures from being modernised, desecrated, into the state in which we find much of the earlier (and usually superior) creations of mankind. I had the great fortune to be living in a place looking as if it were still 1790. Yes, there were many sites in varying states of decay, but when nature has had the time to do her magic on a building that's when I find it the most beautiful (the three houses I have owned in my life can attest to that – and the attending problems of livability).

Seventies Hydra life retained much of the early 20th century, thanks to no cars. Merchandise was transported by donkey, shops had a lot of their stuff hanging from the ceiling, customers brought their own containers to refill olive oil or wine, vegetables and fruit were misshapen, but more tasty. In the marketplace, things were weighed on suspended balances like the Scales of Justice, or like the one in Marigoula's market (the best): two platforms outfitted with brass bird heads, half kilo weight on one side, add the potatoes on the other until the beaks align. Only one tv on the island (at Sourelis' cigarette store); long-distance phone calls were made at the telephone office across from the police station. I had no watch so listened for the boat whistle at eleven and five, or checked the clock tower when in the port. I loved it.

Many of us passed our evenings at Lulu's taverna. The jukebox had Carole King and Santana and a great selection of Greek music. Greeks danced for themselves then. They did it often. And they were all good. Three were exceptional, Demetri, a tall, talented god, Terry, thin and technically perfect, and Nikos Antonatos, my favourite. He was one of my students, beyond handsome, his nose came straight from his forehead giving him the appearance of an ancient Greek warrior carved in bas relief on a temple wall. His dancing had a natural grace; he danced with pathos, joy, humour. He danced who he was.

Not so much that year in which I was a teacher, but in subsequent times I'd go months without putting on shoes (frowned on in Greece as a sign of poverty and lack of civility) because it was such a sensual experience – those stones! Years of wear polished the streets and steps into something of which I had to have contact, especially in the evening when they retained some of the day's heat, and they glowed in the pink light with an acid trip effect. Old women, always in black, would sit before Marigoula's market on the high road. In passing I'd hear them say (in Greek, of course), "Good boy he is, but why no shoes?"

≈

Hydra is the nearest to an aesthetically perfect place I have ever known, both panoramically and in detail. I mean where human-kind has been. Unmolested nature is always perfect (less and less of that as time goes by, no?). I can find beauty anywhere I go, especially as a bit of corroded metal will thrill me, or the way light falls on even the most mundane of things; but on Hydra that light always fell on something sublime: the sea, a wheat field at dusk, a small terracotta face of Ares set among roof tiles, an aged wall, churches, their bell towers, it is endless. In a world that has had to accommodate serious overpopulation (with the inevi-table, unfortunate structures that it brings), Hydra was this place where pretty much everything was a pleasure to look upon. And the ruins! Both the simple and the grand. Fig trees growing from crumbling stone walls, years of white-wash applied in varying col-ours flaking off to make delicious abstract paintings; wondering what had gone on in these elegant rooms that had falling beams and scattered roof tiles. I never tired of exploring them. That first year I learned the value of passing time doing nothing productive, just looking, thinking, absorbing; a gift I have perhaps taken too much to heart. It's been with me everywhere since.

The affair with Maro went on sweetly through most of that winter, but eventually she said, *"Je crois que je t'aime, mais j'ai peur que tu n'es pas responsible."* Last time I saw her she had finished medical school, gone back to the lover before me, and had a dar-ling (aren't they all?) baby.

~

I met Anne and Harold Ramis on a cloudy November day, in some obscure lane. He was tall, curly-haired and hot. She was hard to peg, with her amusing, original thought patterns, and had a fascinating way of speaking (to this day I can't properly describe it, but still love it). She'd be famous for it if she were an actress. She also wore a big hat so she wouldn't have to say hello to people unless she wanted to. He wasn't a famous filmmaker yet, had been a joke editor for *Playboy* and I imagine had done his stint writing for *SCTV* (but I didn't know what that was). Later they brought me to a rehearsal of the tv show *Saturday Night Live*, where I met

Gilda Radner and Jane Curtin called me Mister Sincere, which I don't think was a compliment. Anne and Harold, they were the first of many important friendships that began on Hydra. Many of these people were life altering (in the best of ways), almost everyone I care about I met there, or through people I met there. It was a place that attracted minds, hearts, talents, beauty (physical and in the soul). I fell in love regularly. Besides attracting these people, Hydra put you together with them: no cars! You met them in the lane, at the post office, on the swimming rocks, in tavernas, on the boat from Athens. One only had to go out the door, there they would be.

One afternoon, passing through the port, I sat down with Anne and Harold at Tassos' cafe.

"Come to celebrity watch?" Harold said, moving his eyes to the left.

Draped in a nearby chair was Jackie O, white pants suit, signature sunglasses. She'd helicoptered in to look at one of Hydra's mansions, possibly buy (how did I know this? Harold?). She gracefully tapped the arm of the chair next her and said, "Furniture." Why after more than fifty years would I remember a banal utterance by a moderately attractive, though stylish, woman? Because she had been the queen of our empire, her Chanel suit had been covered in her husband's blood, the dear woman had carried on best she could, and now she was considering how to make a house *comfy*. I think that's why.

≈

I went often to Athens in those days. Sometimes twice a week, as passage on the boat was free for Marine Academy staff. I headed for Boîte Mykonos (written on a tiny sign), a nightclub in Plaka, on a lane that ended at the ancient Tower of the Winds. Nikos Giottis, a painter who loved me for an innocence I didn't know I had, must have told me of it. On Adrianou Street, in a crumbling Neoclassical building, he had a one-room apartment filled with icons he restored for a living and wonderful Cubist-style paintings from his own imagination. I lost an aspect of my virginity in that room. The building has since been torn down, replaced by apartments with a souvenir shop beneath: I sometimes enter it and gaze upon the shelf of Venus de Milo statuettes now occupying that space in my history. One enters Boîte Mykonos through a garden passage, down some steps. It's a charming music-filled shed full of people from everywhere. The bar was run by Nora, an Alexandrian Greek, gruff, but adored. I once gave her a turquoise ring I'd found in a *souk* in Saudi Arabia – she never took it off (except when it really didn't go with her outfit). There was a darling Argentinian piano player, Roberto Tagliabue Rossi, entertaining the clients. I asked him to play "Windmills of Your Mind" (he took requests), and afterward whenever I would enter he'd begin playing that. I'd sit by the piano and drink the drinks people sent to him. I think he liked me for my looks rather than my fleeing innocence, photographed me a lot. Later I heard he'd won contests in an Argentinian photo magazine with pictures of me, which would say more about his skill than my pulchritude. Harold referred to these forays into the gay world as my "shadow life."

The school year would be ending, time I thought about going home and sorting out draft dodging stuff. The FBI was harassing my mother, they made her cry. Like many of the young men of the time I had thought military service was inevitable, I'd even taken the test for the Air Force and was offered officer training as I'd done so well.

When I told my pacifist ceramics teacher of this plan she said, "Why ever would you want to do that?" It got me thinking. Then I went to a friend's graduation from boot camp and I saw men marching around, doing push-ups and being yelled at by awful men. I thought, "I can't subject myself to *that*." Going to Vietnam and possibly getting killed hadn't even entered my consciousness. Being totally controlled by maniacs was what scared me. Anyway I still had to deal with that.

Not long before shipping out of Hydra, knowing in my heart I'd be back, my friend Meri Lobel said that she'd met an older English woman whom she thought I would enjoy – a recommendation that would have great consequences. Her name was Mary G. U. Aitkenhead B.A. (that's how she wrote it on the backs of letters) and she happened to be on the same boat as the one I was departing on. I helped her with her luggage. I should point out here that I *really* wanted to have a house on Hydra, and in the early Seventies houses on that paradise were were so inexpensive, especially the semi-ruined ones. She and I chatted, about ourselves and Hydra, all the way to Athens. She said my last name meant "good house." I told her of my desire to have one on Hydra. She said maybe she could help and gave me her address.

≈

In California I saw an FBI agent, told him my "failure to report" was because I was travelling. He asked if Greek girls were sexy. We didn't accomplish much. My mother had moved in with her recent, and fourth, husband, a Canadian bartender. I painted their rental, made a little money, she added a little. I went back to Europe, it was winter, I went to Mary's. Mary lived in a tall brick manse called Hollin Hall. She had nursed her parents and aunt until they died. Her father had owned a factory making harrows. We'd ride around the countryside going to stately homes (Chatsworth from *Pride and Prejudice* was one), dining in wonderful old establishments, had goose one night before a huge fireplace – well, I did; she was a vegetarian. She'd tell the driver to "put it on the old mill bill, Gordon." I seriously liked her. She was about the age I am now (late sixties), pretty, cared about the fate of animals and was generous. Promised me a thousand pounds towards my house if I found one.

Went to Hydra, couldn't find anything affordable, went to the island of Tinos, slept in a ruin again (it had a masthead wired to a tree in the garden, beautiful stone dovecots on the side of the hill). It snowed that night, but I could tell Hydra was the only island for me.

Went back to Hydra, stayed with various people, had stories too numerous to tell and found a house. Derelict, too perfect to describe here, but I can say that I feel a pang to this day when I think of it, and it had "For Sale" roughly painted in Greek on the side. I went to Demetra, one of two real estate agents around, to inquire. Demetra was a beautiful lesbian married to a Frenchman. They had tastes in common, I thought they were so sophisticated. Demetra's clean looks, the way she spoke, moved, fascinated me.

When I see anyone that at all reminds me of her, I think, "I'm probably going to like this one."

The house was $7,500 – out of my price range, alas, alas. However she found me a jewel. A little place built high, in Kiafa, where the original city began. The house hadn't been inhabited for decades. One entered through a simple door in a high wall into the sweetest courtyard, shaded by a gnarled apricot tree. An outside staircase went to the upper floor with a high-ceiling bedroom that had tall deep-set windows and a terrace (falling in) from which you could see the whole world, which included the mountain and monasteries above, the Peloponnese, the sea and both of the town's harbours. Downstairs was the kitchen (more on that later) and a large room with a packed manure floor where the animals had been kept. It had a ceiling made of cypress beams crossed by branches, and it opened to a disused garden with an old almond tree and wildflowers. I had to have this house or die.

It was $5000, double what Mary had promised. I had to call her.

She said OK. She'd bring cash.

Found the house, money was coming and I was broke. Was staying in a charming place; I was white-washing it in exchange for rent. At first when I brushed this water–plaster mixture on to the walls it made them look strange and more decrepit, which I liked but thought, "This can't be right." Then it dried and became a blinding white, an Easter Miracle. I also carried bags of broken stone down a hillside to a building site, feeling like a slave in a Biblical movie; I adored those movies as a kid.

Demetra said to let her know when the money arrived and we'd arrange the deal, then she left for Paris. I imagined her going to those exotic "Paris is a Woman" bars where you'd see Marlene Dietrich types. She didn't come back, time passed, I went to the other agent, Magda, a formidable woman, Eastern European, who was reputed to have once been a great beauty (I found that believable). I never really liked her, but appreciated her colourful presence, something I can say about several of the players that made up Hydra's foreign community. Mary came with a bag of money. I put it in the bank (once a hall to build ships) on the port. Magda had been stringing me along, always intending to get the house for another client, George Slater. He'd been on the island for some time, I don't know for how long. Had the reputation of being a rascal. He was handsome in a pirate/Dodge City gunslinger sort of way.

I was devastated.

Demetra came back. Told her the story, she was *not* pleased with me. *But* she came through! Told me to draw out half of the money, in thousand drachma notes, and put it in an envelope: we would be going to Pireaus.

It was evening, we went to a tiny street level apartment. Inside I was introduced to a sweet old lady (owner of the house), her grown granddaughter – also sweet (reminded me of Minnie Mouse, my favourite cartoon character) – and her nephew, maybe in his fifties, weaselly face, skinny, well dressed. Apparently he had the greatest interest in the money from this possible sale. We sat in the parlour; I held the little dish of preserved fruit with a spoon, commonly offered in Greek hospitality. Everything was conducted in Greek. I was clueless and Demetra translated when we left.

Sitting comfortably in the most comfortable chair, my Saint Demetra had said, "Well, we have here an honourable man, who wants to buy your house, an upstanding man, he was a professor at the Marine Academy." She then opened the envelope and fanned herself with the stack of money. Eyes widened.

"Do you want to sell your house to a roustabout, a gigolo, or to this boy? And you better decide soon or that house will fall down and nobody will have anything!"

They signed.

Outside, while relating this to me, she handed me the deed, very old and *handwritten*.

George recently told me Demetra had called him a murderer, but I don't think she had gone that far.

The papers documenting the sale were filed at the monastery (the one on the port that has the clock tower) in little offices that I believe were once the chambers for monks. The birth of my first son was also recorded there fifteen years later.

Somewhat ironically, George and I ended up on the same plane to England: me because I needed to get more money from Mary to make the house livable, and he because he *didn't* get the house.

We ordered drinks from the stewardess and toasted fate. There were slender, very smooth, tree trunks on each side of a door in my newly acquired house, their top branches held up ceiling beams in a way that was reminiscent of classical Japanese architecture. I told George how fond I was of them. He said they reminded him of crutches and would have removed them immediately. Apparently we had different approaches to interior design.

For the record: I paid back Mary all she had so generously given me, though much later, and she and I were not lovers, despite it being widely assumed that we were. Anne and Harold were amused by the concept of things going on one's *permanent record*.

Got repairs done to the terrace, which also served as the roof to the kitchen. The builder used an old mast from a caïque to further support the ceiling beams. He hadn't asked me, but it made me so happy; the scars from the ropes were still evident. Nikos Giottis had good connections at the Athens flea market. Got a wardrobe, Victorian iron bed frame, dining table, all sorts of stuff, all old, all beautiful, all costing so little. The stuff came on a caïque, then up the 379 steps on the backs of hard-working donkeys. Under the kitchen was the cistern, fed from the terrace. First drops from the rain would echo like the beginning of a Pink Floyd song. Access to the water was afforded by a beautiful, ancient-seeming, cut stone wellhead rising into the room. Two centuries of coloured washings made it a masterpiece, looking of old maps. (Renters painted over it with brown *oil paint*. I scraped it off, then another did it again. Did I have to leave *signs?*) I wanted to retrieve some lost buckets, had a friend there to call for help in case I were to get trapped, and lowered myself into it. The entire room arched like a chapel, the water, the sounds … I better understood the meaning of "sacred." I'd sing into it, my not particularly good voice sounded ethereal. Once I had guests over to hear Terry Oldfield play his wonderful flute compositions into it.

Just beyond the house the lane was walled, and had arches that once held up what must have been something palatial. I know because I have explored that piece of land and all that remains is what must have been the cellar, with a vaulted ceiling made of precisely cut stone, as in a cathedral. This area of the original town had many of its buildings arching over the passageways, judging by the intriguing remains, but much has fallen into ruin and the stones carried off to build the equally (perhaps) exquisite structures below.

∽

On the hillside across from my terrace stood a dilapidated stately home. Every evening a tiny figure – I could barely make her out – emerged and began to wail. Her powerful voice echoed through the valley, lending a chill to the atmosphere. What is she crying? And why? I don't remember who finally told me, or the accuracy of that account, which was that she was once an Hydra beauty who married a man not from the island, an act frowned upon. Eventually he left her, destitute, with three small boys. (When they grew up, Georgo was hard working, Dino a poetic Adonis, and Philemon an entertaining reprobate.) Men came round thinking her poverty would weaken her virtue. She rebuffed them. They destroyed her reputation on the island with lies. No wonder that decades later she was still screaming from her balcony: "All the women of Hydra are whores!"

I think it should have been: "Some of the men of Hydra are real assholes," but it was probably the island women who gave her the most attitude.

∽

Hydra seemed the navel of the world. California, though much in itself, was far from everywhere. Hawaii is practically as far as you can be from anywhere. Hydra was a boat to Athens, and then so much was near. Went with Roberto to Egypt the first year. I was still so unworldly, for a moment I wondered why so many people in the airport were wearing pajamas. Europe, the Middle East, even India were not so far. I brought back things to adorn my little palace. Portobello Road in London, Clignancourt in Paris, the Grand Bazaar in Istanbul, *souk* in Saudi Arabia, all had worn treasures, therefore affordable and (to me) all the more precious. Still have many of those things, bartered others, gave away most.

Letters could get to me from anywhere with a three-word address: Lindsey, Hydra, Greece.

I never needed to have ID papers, even at the bank. If a waiter was too busy, I left and returned the next day to pay; *I* would have to tell *him* what I'd eaten. When travelling in other parts of Greece I could run out of money so long as I had enough to get back to Hydra, where I was known and trusted. This foreign place, a place where I knew only a few words of the language, had become my home, more so than anywhere I'd ever been. Or would ever be.

The first spring my household was comprised of four lovely women, and me. I shared my bed with Hedva, Israeli; she had a ring on every finger, gave me the best one.

I have many friends who are men, loved some. I especially like the artists, the painters, they are like trees. But women interest me so much more, they keep me fascinated, the smart ones most of all. I never understand them completely (part of what I like), but I think I understand them more than most men do, or can, or try to. I like women the way I like colour: infinite, making life worthwhile. Also they tend to be much more fun. (I doubt I'd be so obsessed with movies if it weren't for the actresses.) I am useless at giving advice on hair or fashion – I'm not that kind of friend. Whereas I can so appreciate the looks, often original, that my women friends put together, it is their brains, personalities, way of looking at things, that win me.

I see Hydra as feminine: the endless lanes of discovery, the way the harbour envelopes one on arrival. The island beckons women, it's civilised, they are not harassed, they bloom in that backdrop. And I was able to reap many of them, some lovers, all friends, they nourish my spirit to this day.

Antony Kingsmill, the painter and island icon, came home with me after a night of drinking. It was late. I made soup for him. Looking around at the peasant perfection of the room, he said, "Lindsey, you have found grace in this kitchen, don't ever sell it."

No doubt he was right, but sell it I did, years later. While still looking much as I had had it (including furniture) it was featured on the cover of *Maison et Jardin* magazine and in a book on

Greek architecture. The man who bought the house eventually transformed it into sort of a "villa." The simple door to the street became this elaborate panelled thing with large brass unusable knobs. He subsequently sold it for almost a million dollars. As I wander nostalgically, when I pass that house there is never anybody home.

There are rocks that rise from the sea and at that point, rounding a promontory of the Peloponnese, one gets the first view of Hydra, far off, shrouded by mists. Those rocks resemble reptilian monsters. To me they seem to be guarding a dream. Every time I return I wonder if it was, is. Seriously, I do.

Sliding Gangplanks
(or simply an excuse for having an extra "large one")

David Fagan

This is far from a boast, more of a selfie-roast, but I have yet to meet someone else who did what I thought to be the most natural thing in the world: investigate further than the allotted one hour a place that was totally captivating. To *klepsy* from another travelling fellow, I came, I saw (loved it) and stayed. (J. Caesar would have too, being that conquering was never going to be part of the equation.) Even after four hundred years the surrounding Ottoman Empire had failed to breach the island's defences. But I did, lost and in the process gained more than any fellow in a funny plume-feathered helmet could have.

≈

The first stop on the three-island tour, Aegina, was grand and quaint; it had an old Cadillac stuck in a narrow roadway, which I photographed. Poros, the next stop, was equally up to the cruise; I remember a puppy catching the monkey's fist (a knotted rope) tossed ashore by a deckhand as the boat was mooring. Then came the Rock, Hydra, a place where nobody, neither army nor fleet, had over centuries managed to plant their flag. Yet I thought I could, not with gunpowder but with simple charm – a rather large miscalculation. Hydra was and remains invincible: if you wanted to stay, you had to be prepared to start from scratch, several times. The mix would include a life of fluctuations of the roulette wheel, fortunes from near starvation to jet-setting guest status.

The fact that one was on a prepaid return three-islands-in-a-day cruise ticket wasn't an issue. One could simply phone the hotel in Athens and explain that we had inadvertently found ourselves "marooned" on an island and please would some kind soul pack up our belongings and keep them in storage. Of course I figured they would appreciate the courtesy of having the room vacant to rent, and naturally, for the safekeeping of our baggage, reimbursement for the favour would be settled upon return.

Then all I would have to do was inform the purser of our cruise ship that his guest list would be shy two return passengers. Easy, logical and quite within what should happen in the tourist/hotel order of business. I was about to see why a simple plan to satisfy my curiosity about this place that had grabbed my attention at gut level was not so simple to implement. It should have been a forewarning, a clue, that an un-simple life on a vehicleless Rock in the Saronic Gulf was to become the rest of my existence to date.

First one had to find a phone to make that call to inform the hotel of the change of plans. Seemed a simple thing, except for that telephones were a rare commodity back in 1983. Finally I found a taverna right where the cruise ship docked that sported a large red swivel dialling device, for Greece only, that could connect to Athens when a two-drachma coin was slotted. Had I known then that it would take me nearly five years to get a phone number of my own, would I have stayed? Yes, because time was about to become a dimension only other folk took seriously.

The *Hermes*, our day three-island-cruise ship, honked an "all aboard" and as fellow passengers legged it up the gangplank, I ordered another pint, much to the consternation of my travelling companion and girlfriend, not yet quite accustomed to Irish spontaneity.

"But," she blurted, "that's our boarding call!"

"No worries, Luv. It's all taken care of, a welcoming pension with a friendly garden tortoise and sea view has given us lodging. Plus I found a pharmacy and basic tourist clothing shop while you were pottering around touristic trinket vendors. Toothbrushes, toothpaste, shampoo and even some spare underwear have all been taken care of (we had only brought our swimming togs and beach paraphernalia). The hotel very obligingly is packing our suitcases and keeping them safe until we get back to Athens."

While not exactly ecstatic with my unilateral decision, the tranquillity, and absolute inability to flee said island at that point, she had no other choice but concede to the wisdom of finding out more about Hydra; the day was won.

That same evening I wandered into an innocuous little place just off the harbour front modestly called Bill's Bar. There I got involved with a couple of long-time patrons. My idea of opening a pub on the Rock was applauded as a splendid plot. And that was it: hook, line and sunk – firmly set, caught, trapped, landed. Like the Eagles once said, you can check out anytime you like, but you can never leave.

~

It took a total of six, maybe seven hours to convert – to leave normal life and become something other than a projected ladder-climbing corporate clone; to give up worldly things, dump golf clubs and gold card expense account dinners for a place where Rolodexes and Rolexes were superfluous to punctual business lunches. Here lunchtime was fluid in every respect and was the business of the day, where only the sturdy could progress to evening conferences at sunset and beyond. I was strong, of green blood and up to the task. I could be as perpendicularly ambulant and conversant as the best of them, or so I thought.

I later heard that the island in those times was sometimes called the largest open-air asylum in the world, and I like to think the affectionate adjectives that adhered, like Irish lunatic, fun-loving, eccentric, genius (or is that Guinness) inmate I was to become were not insults.

Now there is and always will remain the romantic side to the island's lore – you know, the fame and flame side to its exotic reputation; I could name-drop and tell a funny anecdotes about those folks but this was not my forum or reason for residency. They, it and I all happened in situations that only Hydra could produce. The list is even far more extensive than most realise, beyond the more bandied Leonard, Melina, Joan, Sophia, Princess Diana, her other half, Charlie lad (separately) – in fact, more royalty and heads of state (Bush I only; W would probably not been served fresh *kalamari* at the time) than have waffled away at the UN podium have wafted through our little isle. In 2004, during the Olympics, for instance, more than 22 heads of states were hosted on Hydra. For the most, it's a rather vapid paparazzi list in fact: "Did you see Paris Hilton at the Up 'n High last night?" Damn, bugger, blast! Missed that one.

Imagine the devastation of not spotting a Kardashian these days. I do not mean to sound condescending at all; it's just that sort of stuff was supposed to stay in places where red carpets and limos existed without the chance of donkey shit smearing a designer stiletto heel. We were supposed to be safe. True to form I digress ...

Instead I would like to take the glorified shine off what real existence was like on our Rock before televisions were the norm in any public place. As my mate, a long-standing Aussie skipper and fellow survivor, put it, we expats were the *Dallas* and *Dynasty* of the day. Hence the locals tolerated us with interest and looked upon as their theatre, not, as we assumed, the other way around.

So while give-or-take three decades does not qualify me for real oldie stories, I feel I've served enough time, winter in, summer out. Hydra has been a constant place of survival, home and family through thick and thin. So instead this piece is about life, not people, and how our beloved little Rock has changed beyond recognition, about the transformation from the days when requesting a donkey by cell phone was the stuff of *Star Trek*.

≈

I must say this now, in case lint-pickers and self-appointed custodians of Hydra lore decide to set light to my pyre: I love my home; in fact I am an invited, permanent, honourary citizen and do not tolerate derogatory quips about our way of life. Only we can do that, with love and humour.

For instance, you may call me a *malaka*, a word that can be overheard in conversation frequently in colloquial lingo, but be sure you have been welcomed at a table of me and mates. It is a funny, intimate word not to be bandied about by smart-aleck tourist louts. Similarly, counting five on fingers is palm in, not out, that latter being probably the equivalent of flipping one the bird.

Let's start with the most fundamental matter to life: water – not just the stuff visitors take as a natural thing to obtain by opening a tap, but the substance encountered by those of us who stayed a week or month in midsummer three and some decades ago. In those years our only freshwater came across daily on a small ship, the *YΔPA I*. Some who owned houses that collected winter rainwater in underground cisterns had that available for sparingly use.

This not a story of tough times, just what life was like in the days before the water source on the mainland had to be changed, and of course these days improved pumps and piping systems have been laid, and we now have a water-generating desalination plant.

Back then water was precious as gold. Urbanites dwelling above Four Corners, about a third of the way up from the port, lived in drought-like conditions in the high season. Thirsty green pot plants changed to autumn shades in June and drooped in sadness no matter how long one stood coaxing some extra drops of moisture from the hose.

One summer I decided that taking on a plant-watering job for some midsummer weeks would be an uncomplicated, easy gig, extra pocket money. But I quickly worked out that obtaining fluid at ideal watering time, the evening, coincided with holiday-makers' return-from-beach showers, meaning I got nothing but drip, drip from the outside faucet, maybe.

My best chance to keep plants alive was if those holiday-makers had showered and were out and about, wining and dining. In other words one watered gardens after midnight, and even that was hit and miss. Leaving a party to go and water a garden up the hill, only to be greeted by a cough, splutter and hiss from the hose, damped one's festive mood somewhat.

All summer long, I was fighting a sad, losing battle keeping the elephant ears and basil plants in my charge alive on the mountain top. And when my employers returned, they found said garden hardly ... happy. While they couldn't come right out and accuse me, I knew they assumed I had been neglectful in my gardening/watering duties. But a world-famous-in-Holland Dutch journalist and Rock resident came to my rescue the next day.

After a year or two of tolerating water more likely to kill plants than nourish them, a world-famous-in-Holland Dutch journalist and Rock resident did what she did best: opened an investigation. After complaining to the ex-ex-ex-mayor, she refused to take his *"Ochi problima"* – No problem – for an answer. She took a random sample of our tap water to a laboratory in Athens. Not only was it ascertained that the water being brought to our system was too salinated for plant life but it was also unfit for human use, even douching. (Drinking it we had all given up on years prior.)

Our Joan of van der Ark steamed into the ex-ex-ex-mayor's office brandishing said official report, overwhelming evidence that she had an infallible case. Fluent in a bunch of languages, she demanded, "What about ladies, us woman and our private ablutions?"

Any of us who have spent some time here and dealt with matters of local infrastructure know that the Hydriots have a quick-witted answer to any question. For instance, one expat resident complained to Demetri, owner of the Four Corners no-room-for-baskets-never-mind-a-trolley supermarket, about the wasps buzzing over the fresh fruit on the cobbled street outside. She advised him to cover the goods for health and protection.

"Ah!" he answered instantly, "and how do I keep the insects from landing on fruit while they are on the trees?" Stumped his patron was, and to hammer the point home, he added, "You know, here in Greece we wash our fruits before eating, even if they come from a big indoor market in Athens." Anyway back to the water board.

So to the journalist waving the evidentiary piece of paper, our mayor, completely unflustered, came back with an immediate Hellenic answer. He shrugged, *"Ti na kanoume?* (What can we do?) If it bothers you so much, wash with bottled water."

Think about that for a second. So we admit a bit of a problem with our water supply; plants are also unhappy, perishing for the most. But we have a deal with a church mandate, a political, documented commitment or something, and the contract did not foresee rising salination in their freshwater. Etcetera, etcetera, rhubarb, waffle, cough, splutter, ahem. Bottled water: there is your easy solution. Thank you for bringing the issue to our attention. We were aware and working on it. Next please!

And in walked a *yiayia* (grandmother) with a complaint about a new street light shining directly into her bedroom.

That's the tip of the water iceberg from back then; things are easier these days. Someone invented desalination and after a decade of debate our plant went into operation. Now plants thrive, ladies can shower in safety and husbands needn't worry about dingle-dangles falling off after a delightful Greek island vacation.

≈

The next and probably equally important commodity to any little town would be electricity – the stuff that was a huge opulent addition to any household in the Fifties not long after it was installed generally.

Of course it is apparent that the more appliances invented, the more juice and outlets in the home were needed. But here is one little snippet that probably could only have occurred on Hydra at that time. In the rest of the world, news, television, magazines – you know the media – kept the populace in touch with happenings, including the commercial side of life, or entertainment. New movies were promoted long in advance; ground-breaking products were known about long before they hit the shop shelves.

Imagine for a moment, because you are not in touch via the usual media, that something completely unbelievable happens when a newly arrived guest unpacks his suitcase. This would be around 1987 or 1988, and yer man produced this very flat, shiny, small, round, mirror-like thing that he stuck into a strange-looking device, and suddenly it blurted out incredible high-fidelity music. Astounding stuff to a chap who thought his fancy yellow walk-about-man cassette player was the limit of portable sound technology and had no warning about the future and changes in the real world.

"It's called a CD, or compact disc," explained the fellow. Well blow me down, the future had arrived without my knowing it.

I have written elsewhere about many incidents involving voltage and near-death excitement as Rock inhabitants learned about using 220-plus volts to keep beverages and other consumable commodities chilled or to cook without gas or wood. The advent of universal three-phase electricity also eventually invited televisions, till then virtually unseen, into every taverna. Captivating soccer and basketball, live-televised games, quickly replaced the gentle clack of dice on a backgammon board. Card players and chess competitors also lost concentration and the will to continue old rivalries in the face of the new entertainment and boisterousness of goals finding the net. We didn't quite grasp the full impact at first, but it was without doubt the end of an era.

So we adjusted and came to live with the new centre of social interaction. We simply opted not to face the goggle box and sat in the most distant corner. But even we got sucked in, to the point of competing with other clientele for the remote control. This variety of TV required silence at table, no chatting. *Baywatch* and *The Bold and the Beautiful* became particular post-lunch favourites, even before the actor who played Rich stopped by for a cocktail or coffee on the Rock. Some even claimed to have exchanged a hello with the soap star. I have to admit, I never really got caught up in this telly lark, probably because it would take me another decade to afford an idiot box of my own.

Electricity was a learning curve too for many an overseas guest who had been assured their accommodation was electrified – perhaps a little too much. A number of travelling devices did not cater to our higher amperage, being designed for 110 volts back home. There was much disappointment back then when a small blue explosion and a semi-melted hair drier put a dent early in a summer holiday. It took a season or two for visitors to get to grips with bringing step-up transformers and three-pronged plug adaptors – a far cry from most universal extras and universal power supplies employed today.

When the first freed Albanians arrived on the island, this electrical business had to be explained too. I was renting a small room in a building owned by another ex-mayor and mate, who kindly accepted some drachmas, a few dollars and a couple of pounds to make up the approximate monthly let, whatever tips and or wages I had earned odd-jobbing. Apart from myself and a retired Canadian doctor above me, the seven bedroom house was empty. Then somebody pulled down the Berlin Wall and the contagion spread throughout Europe within months. Next thing we knew our domicile had one Canadian doctor, an Irish what-do-you-need-help-with fellow and an estimated two dozen of our newly liberated brethren from the northwest border. (To this day, the island nickname for the joint is the Albanian Embassy.) Poor guys had little and shared six to a room, but also they used up electricity, more than the place could handle.

One midnight I awoke to the smell of smoulder, the distinctive electrical type. Our new roommates kept tripping the fuse box and discovered a way around this was to tape off the offending fuse with a drachma coin. I hauled their leader unceremoniously out of bed and showed him the blackened box and too-hot-to-touch surrounding wall. I might have escaped a conflagration, being on the ground floor, but a fully involved fire would surely have cremated the lot of them in their beds. Despite the braille-like translation from Irish to Albanian, Pax Alvania understood. That's enough of that subject.

≈

Food, an equal part of survival, too has changed the menu monu-mentally. I suppose one example was when I popped into our local and largest grocery market below the post office and was utterly surprised to find that, for the first time, I could hardly get in the door, which was blocked by more *yiayias* in black than a penguin colony and making about as much noise. There was a run on some-thing, obviously not fish but a product called Nounou, canned evaporated milk. A place in our hemisphere called Chernobyl had had a nuclear accident or meltdown and milk in Europe, it was said, was about to run out as cows would be dispensing only radi-oactive dairy for the next 10,000 years. My point to this? Well, the island didn't get fresh milk in those days. Nounou was our only type. Nor did we get bananas (except the rare and minute Cretian variety), and an avocado rumour could cause a run on the veggie market.

Don't get me wrong, apart from this new Nounou rush, we were never short of supplies, just variety. Visiting friends and guests, when asked if there was anything they could bring, would inevitably be told that a curry, chutney or Marmite would be most gratefully accepted. Having less to choose from did, however, make shopping a simple chore. The bakeries produced wonderful goodies, and local produce was tops; it was just limiting after a while to long-term expat palates. After another delicious dish smothered in traditional red oil, someone at the table would say, "That was grand, as usual, but I could really do with a rare fillet and sour-cream baked potato." Somebody else would add, "Hell, even an old fashioned hamburger." And so followed an hour-long debate about who had the best memory of a meal Mum used to make. But we ate like kings, economically, and one never felt pressured to hurry it along. If your lunch lasted until the sun had set, so be it.

≈

Life before small digital screens and wi-fi (which is free just about everywhere these days on Hydra) became the main attraction was a lot different. Back in the olden days everyone who was part of the port-front cafe community had his or her own "Wish I had that on video" story. One of my favourites happened out of the blue on a normal, tranquil, late-breakfast morning. Absolute chaos erupted in a most unexpected fashion. Along the quay, at the water's edge, are sporadically spaced, square, metal rainwater drainage grills – heavy, sturdy, sort of like manhole covers. Ideal for tethering a mule.

One day, just after the three-island-cruise ship had disgorged its daily multinational two-legged cargo, *it* happened. It may have been something as simple as the nip of a horsefly to start a chain reaction, but the mule jerked and the grate came loose with the clang of Big Ben on the cobblestones.

With horror, the mule took off at a full gallop to escape the fearful noise, but being firmly attached, the clanging and banging "monster" kept pace right on its tail no matter the speed of acceleration, heading straight towards the just disembarked tourists. Since this was the most exciting chase event in living doggie memory, every port pooch joined the pursuit; a howling pack of hounds followed on the heels of the mule, so intent on escape that his large ears were flattened. Behind slower would-be captors, a gang of moustaches, one of them no doubt the driver of the escapee, yelled and hollered in a futile attempt to stop the stampede. The Keystone Cops couldn't have staged it better.

This mixed brigade charged straight at the camera-wielding tourists, who scattered to port and starboard, too fearful to take that memorable holiday shot of a lifetime. The spontaneous conglomerate cavalry raged on through the waterfront and eventually disappeared around the bend headed towards Mandraki. No injuries were later reported.

There was always something going on in the theatre of life downtown. Sometimes a well intended rebuke turned into a most unforeseen situation. Before I get into this, there are two things to explain. Firstly, the daughter of the central character said I was welcome to retell the tale. I worried because it was quite controversial at the time.

Secondly, we had recently won an important battle to save the island. A bulldozer had mysteriously appeared in Vlychos, a smaller seaside village west of Hydra town, and began cutting a real road along the coast where our panoramic donkey path had existed forever. Some lame excuse was tendered about a fire break, but we knew there was a contingent of islanders who thought the idea of a little bus to commute the forty-five minute hike would be a progressive step.

The long and short is that there was outrage and, almost to a man, every influential home-owning foreigner – and I am including Athenians – plus a lot of locals with political clout literally stopped the mechanised beast in its tracks. We argued that one moped, one bicycle path would ruin the Rock in a way that some could not yet foresee. It would take away Hydra's uniqueness, and then the Rock would be just like any other Saronic island. A road for one small bus was but the thin edge of an awful wedge.

So when we were all loitering one sunny afternoon at the Pirate Bar, still a favourite watering-hole for all and sundry, a Mercedes Benz was seen to be parked audaciously in the middle of the port.

One of our leaders, in defence of our strict and hard-won regulations against motorised vehicles, decided she would have her say.

She was one of the most beloved and charismatic people to grace our small population. Petit and of – I kid you not – Jamaican, Irish, Chinese and Swiss ancestry, she was never, ever known to mince her words or pull her punches, no matter the wallet size or rank. In fact, nobody could argue that this diminutive lady was not a force to be reckoned with. One wanted her as an ally and never to be on the other side of a debate.

It had been a long lunch, and Herself decided, true to form, to declare her disapproval. She stuck a napkin on windshield, bearing a strong note announcing that cars were not welcome on Hydra, and somewhere in there the M-word was incorporated to express displeasure at this breach of island etiquette. Most of us backed her brave stance with the usual "Bravo!" until some bloke in a cloak came over and enquired as to who had written the note.

Turns out the vehicle had a special permit and had transported an Orthodox archbishop visiting on serious ecclesiastical business. On top of that, he had only come with a car because he was on crutches with broken ankle or such. You can only imagine how mortified our culprit was. There was a touching moment when she waited until he emerged from the cathedral, went across and apologised most profusely, and, as is custom, kissed the ring. He was very jolly about the whole matter and blessed her, saying it was lovely to see a foreigner so passionate about protecting Greek rights and law. So all ended well, but for those who know this society, using the M-word in association with a senior man of the cloth was not going to score well at the Pearly Gates.

~

As a community we all rubbed along and tried our best to respect different beliefs and cultures. One example of such interaction and fun happened back in the winter of 1985. It was a sporting event, and if it had been officially sanctioned it would still hold several records in the Guinness Book. It all began in my bar, the Bahia – a debate that led to a soccer match unprecedented. The expat world against an Hydriot squad of sporting enthusiasts.

I am going to call the sport soccer, as opposed to football, which a bunch of fans call it. It should in fact be called football, as it entails booting the leather ball around a pitch, and the use of hands is strictly not permitted. Football, on the other hand, for some obscure reason is a North American sport which uses hands to get the ball about a field, and only rarely is it kicked. Even then a specialist is brought on to punt a field goal through a set of posts that resemble rugby posts but with only one supporting grounded pole in the middle.

Again, to clear up any confusion, while the shape of the ball, ovalish, and the goal posts both require a player to kick the ball twixt posts at a level some metres above ground, the similarity ends there. The American sport has indeed nothing in common with the more internationally recognised sport called rugby. Americans are allowed to wear Kevlar body armour and crash helmets and may take frequent breaks to catch their breath so that sponsors may ply their wares, whilst pretty, leggy girls wave pompoms and high kick in mini-skirts to keep the fans occupied, just in case spectator interest wanes.

Our sport has rules too, in case one may be under the misapprehension that this side of the puddle we play a game for wussies. For attempting to garrotte an enemy player, one earns the ignoble decision of ten minutes in the sin bin. If a player is bleeding too profusely, he is entitled to ten minutes' stitching in the blood bin. If it looks like he cannot be patched up in ten minutes to rejoin the fray, the team may call in a blood substitute, which doesn't count against the team's limited use of a normal substitution.

I digress; let's get back to our infamous international match, which, by the way, did accumulate blood bins due to the coarse nature of the gravel pitch and the lack of perpendicular participation by contestants, aided no doubt by the regular alcohol-laced refreshments against dehydration.

The meet had made headline news of the week on the island's tom-toms, and just about everybody attended the much anticipated event. No popcorn or peanuts were seen in the stand, but even the less sporting enthusiastic inhabitants turned up armed with hip flasks and inquisitiveness.

Pan was the senior man on the other side, employed to recruit a team of Hydriots brave enough to take on the rest of the planet. With the exception of Pan and Gianni Drakopoulos, the average Hydra team member age was nineteen; ours, about forty or thirty or sixty.

One nice quirk about the island was that nicknames were given to differentiate and establish who was who or when a person had no known/pronounceable name otherwise. German Willy was Bavarian, as opposed to Little Willy, whose nickname had nothing to do with anything anatomical and arose purely because at seventeen he was the youngest to turn up and stay. There was the Plastic Man, whose store stocked in loose piles every plastic household utensil or chair under the sun. The Frozen Man's shop sold all things, surprisingly, frozen; the Gunpowder & Video Man offered, again you got it, ammo and rented videos.

So, Ouzo Jimmy was the ref and doubled as refreshment dispenser, which meant he situated himself behind the goal line, next to the porta-fridge, and conducted the match behind a dangling fag of smoke and a whistle.

Somewhere during the game, the expat girls on our team (a genderly mixed side would have been another Guinness record first) decided that they couldn't kick as far as the gents and allowed themselves to throw the ball (I believe that is how rugby was invented).

As the match progressed, a further new rule was introduced: every time we were losing too much, Pan switched sides and became an American, generally right in front of the goal, and evened the game up for us aliens. Pan, bless him, was a dual citizen and therefore quite entitled to switch on a whim. He was supposedly caught jumping ship in New York and offered deportation or US citizenship, if he went on a vacation to Vietnam. Which he did with distinction.

The outcome of the tournament, as to how many goals were scored, could not be determined, so we headed down to the "office," the Liako taverna on the port front, for a post-game debate. It was agreed that the score was an even 22–22 draw, in itself another *Guinness Book* record.

∽

It was a life almost unfathomable today, even on Hydra. The age of the cell phone altered our existence for better and worse. Waiting to meet a client off a Flying Dolphin could be a long tedious affair before the mobile age. One knew the date of arrival, but it was almost impossible to communicate exactly which hydrofoil to meet, which meant diligently waiting in one's favourite waterhole, a.k.a. the arrival lounge, to meet and escort folk to their holiday home and possibly arrange a donkey for suitcases. However, one must admit, for convenience and health, knowing via text or e-mail the exact arrival time is a whole lot easier on the legs and liver.

Hydra had another obvious character who would be a dinosaur in these times. It's almost hard to remember a lunatic photographer called Thomas. For boat arrivals he would stand at the bottom of the gangplank, three or four cameras hanging around his neck, and madly snap away at everyone stepping onto the island. He got them to smile with a constantly repeated, "Fotoe exxppresss, yes pleeze, welcome to Idra." Then he would rush back to his developing lab and be back with still dripping prints, slotting the snaps onto an elasticised multilayered board. Surprisingly he enticed enough reboarding visitors with a photo keepsake of their brief visit to keep it up for years.

How antiquated does that sound today, when everyone has a palm-sized video camera as a standard part of their phone. This removed privacy everywhere and turned us into a generation of selfie paparazzi. Again, our world today, even on this little island, is the stuff of science fiction in comparison to three decades ago.

≈

So as I mull these musings, I suspect some will interpret this as a lamentation of the past, and in some ways it is. Of a time when we communicated with hand-written notes left at a local tavern, bar or shop. In some cases we even used semaphore: it was not unusual to send a message across the valley via towel or mat, each colour designating an individual on the opposite side of the valley, that one was home and the door was open if they wished to hang.

Once, while I was dog-sitting and looking after a house on the top of the west side of Kamini in January, we had an unusually warm sunny day. I took the opportunity to do a little laundry. Within the hour half a dozen mates turned up expecting a brunch party. I had hung a bunch of damp towels and mats out to dry.

So yes, I miss those days, but I also consider myself equally fortunate to live in an age when we have at our fingertips the ability to contact and keep in touch with just about any person, loved family member or distant friend. This technology has reconnected me with a lot of old friends and family who would otherwise probably have been lost forever.

Still, there was something special about waiting for snail-mail (I would guess that expression will not even be understood in a few more years) in the post office and bumping into other inmates, catching up on local news, arranging a coffee together after a quick shop.

I was, back then, the youngest member of the so-called A-team, most of members of which have sadly now passed. I have never regretted not going up that sliding plank to a projected, more normal, lucrative life with kids, swimming pool and even fancier sports cars. Even when the chips were really down, I would stop whatever menial labour was at hand for a cigarette (also a thing of the past), look out across the gulf and think of all those poor sods stuck in traffic, twice a day, at least five days a week. I inherited so much hand-me-down clothing, some quite fancy, that all I ever had to buy for myself were socks and underpants.

~

If I had gone up that plank, I would not have met some of the most interesting and diverse people one could imagine – certainly not from behind a desk with a secretary and fax machine. I would never have had the freedom to sail and crew the seas or, at the drop of a hat, join a safari to the Caribbean, the Middle East or northern Europe. I even got to be the guest of some super jet-set on terms that were pure friendship and fun. I have had it all.

The island was also to reward me for my perseverance, with the most important factor of life itself: marriage for true love. I know it sounds trite, but it is what we all hope for. I could never have found it without being directly connected to the old island network, as Jennifer's father had become one of my first mates on landing on the Rock three decades ago.

So to sum, by now you will know I am mad. Not only do I talk to dogs, cats, donkeys, fish and birds, but I am a gent with no further aspirations. I don't need a bucket list. I am grateful, happy and healthy, with two dreadful dogs and a beautiful wife, content with what life will hopefully continue to offer. To ask for more is called greed.

Painting, Poetry and Music

Kevin McGrath

Imagine an island, bare except for a small town built upon the hillside about a port; an island of the old Levantine Mediterranean, of waterless stone and rock and some pines. This is an island without wells and where winter rainfall is collected from terracotta roofs and stored in cisterns built into the earth beneath each house. It is an island once populated by Albanian migrants – the Arbanites refugees and later colonists – who first established a town on the hillside and who were to found the original kinship system of the isle. Then, two hundred years ago almost the entire population was decimated by plague and the place became deserted; an isle where only decades ago during the Civil War many suffered and died from starvation and famine. This was once an isle prosperous from the commerce of shipping and marine conveyance; and more latterly it was an island of sponge-divers who ventured as far south as the coast of Egypt in their search for sea-harvest. Nowadays the magnificent architecture of the town – its old mansions and picturesque lanes, buildings constructed from the vast wealth accumulated from maritime trade – supplies the place with an overt prestige, visual sophistication and a tasteful patrician ostentation.

In the later decades of the 20th century the grey stone houses – many of them beautifully grand and built in an 18th century Italian style – were frequently in ruin and decayed and life was poor; families had migrated to Athens or elsewhere beyond Greece. Where thirty thousand souls had once flourished at the end of the 18th century now less than fifteen hundred struggled to live from the rough landscape or from fishing; many of the men served in the Greek commercial fleets like Hellenic Lines and were absent for years, returning on connubial leave for the begetting of children whilst yearning for the exotic prostitutes of Asia and the hashish and *rembetiko* dens of Piraeus. The poet Kavadias well portrays such a nautical living.

Then the island became – beginning in the Fifties – a station or refuge for painters and poets, for novelists, sculptors and musicians, for artists and those who aspired toward aesthetic venture and innovation. This was a community of cosmopolitan individuals who pursued a bohemian life of unconstrained idealism and artistry, of a mental and spirited trajectory towards an understanding of stability in the cosmos and the production of objects which could represent such conceptions.

What happens when a culturally diverse group of young and foreign people are assembled in one small location that is benignly separated from the rest of life by the sea and by the fact that a ferry perhaps only visits once a day if the weather is good? What happens if these persons do not really need to labour and work in order to live and survive and if they are all in pursuit of an aesthetic experience and there are no social nor even moral constraints upon their daily activity? Such ambition, for what might be construed as artistic truth – and such freedom from inhibition and responsibility borne within such a physical beauty of terrain and topography and encompassed by a coruscating and vivid marine world – all combined to effect a wonderful super-creativity which, without discipline and mental restraint, led to much emotional suffering and *agon* as well as to the production of magnificent works of art. This is the almost Dionysian mystery of human creativity, here made local and specific insofar as the scene was limited to just one harbour and town upon a singular and isolated rocky extrusion of fifty square kilometres.

≈

Hydra was an island without roads and where few ever departed from the town into the hills or wandered toward the other coast on the south side. On the other and unpopulated littoral there was still a vague lost world of the Eastern Mediterranean, with old paved threshing circles beside former terraced fields, small one-roomed shepherd crofts with their cisterns and thorny goat pens, and a flora of prickly pear and sage, of arbutus and wild olive and almond. One or two former signalling stations from the 18th century still remained on hill-tops looking out across the vacant and glittering Aegean.

An event of this nature is rare in human experience and time, if not unique. One thinks of 5th century Athens or of Renaissance Florence and Venice, or of Mathura in India in the mid-First Millennium B.C.E. There are many such locations in cultural history of intense universal fusion where objects of artistic beauty were fabricated; yet the isolation of Hydra as an island and the distinction of the town and its port – as there was no other communal habitation on the many miles of stony terrain – make this moment and these individuals most uncommon. Needless to say there were many suicides or young deaths and the incidence of extensive drug use and a passionate consumption of alcohol led to much malaise, often with long-term and generational effects: for not only did the parents often die or suffer from mental instability but so too did their offspring.

There was a strange admixture of extra-ordinary inspiration and ingenuity with what can be termed a concomitant self-destructiveness: for those who did not succeed in sustaining their vision of an absolute beauty were consumed in that effort. As the cleric John Donne remarked long ago, "Who sees Gods face … must dye." It is not so much the view of an absolute margin which leads to the production of fine art but the human tenacity to withstand and to conduce to the translation of that perilous conception into material reality that ultimately counts, at least in terms of social reception and benefit; otherwise there is calamity.

≈

Those decades were a brief and spectacular moment, a time of Utopian endeavour directed towards that which is generally disregarded in contemporary bourgeois European and American society: where consciousness is thoroughly and carefully attuned only toward the secular. Beauty and truth, those intensely flickering lamps of originality and causality which have charged personal experience for millennia with its primary indication of form and without which there can really be no human livelihood nor any signification, are typically not pre-occupations of modern Western society. Yet, in a sense, all meaning is founded upon such instants of epiphany – even if the instant is hypothetical – and all transcendental belief originates and derives from those occasions of untimed veracity. This is what artists do nowadays in their work: they reformulate a reception of such vision, that ideal moment from which all subsequent nomination and metaphor are generated.

The reason that paintings can nowadays secure vast prices at auction sales is because those depictions – images like the Rothko murals – represent a uniquely still instant when value – human value – can be said to first occur as an object and thus become fungible. Meaning itself does have an origin.

~

This is what Ghikas accomplished, or Marios Loizides, or Demetri Gassoumis, or the Mardens, and the dozens of other similar painters who have lived and dwelled on Hydra; this is what Leonard Cohen in his early songs of exposed *tristesse*, or what George Seferis and Maria Servaki in their poetry depicted, or George Johnston tried to capture and narrate in his novels. For each of these public successes however there were many tens of others who worked in similar fields of artistic production who did not acquire such material triumph. Among such artists were Jane Motley, Panagiotis Rappas, Marcella Maltais, Jane Porter, Angelika Lialios, Richard Vick, Ioannis Kardamatis, Felix Thoresen, Piers Kemp, Terry Oldfield, Guy Allain, Adam Shapiro and Anthony Kingsmill, to name but a few of those sparkling and gifted men and women who worked for years within the terms of their ability and imagination, quietly revealing the tenderness and sublime discretion of what they knew as neither mundane nor diurnal.

For a period of two or three decades a community of intellectual and aesthetically-minded young people were drawn to Hydra and its unorthodox foreign community and astonishing ferment of achievement, conversation and the social exchange which obtained on the isle. There were other and more famed visitors of course, the Audens, the Leigh Fermors, the Mercouris and their like, but such ones never really participated in the brilliant resonance of the island. Let us now attempt to give a summary portrait of what was happening during some of that time.

～

Firstly, cultures always possess a gathering of myth in which not only their formation and structure are metaphorically represented but also their ideals. The heroes of Hydriot society then were Cézanne or Byron, or Johann Sebastian Bach and Mozart, Augustus John, Sam Beckett or Braque and Brancusi; these were just a few of the models whose lives and enterprise towards the supreme and absolute were emulated and no one went gently. Such dead artists of the European past were the metonymical saints who had enjoyed aesthetic perfection and who could be imitated, revered and somehow attached.

Many of the young poets and painters, the musicians, lived freely in the ruins of the fallen and once-pillaged merchant houses: frugal, exoteric and profoundly romantic. There was a strong and vigorous ethos of vision and invention, of kind ingenuity that was curiously generous and non-judgemental. Hydra did not receive domestic electricity of running water until the latter decades of the 20th century and even now there are no motor vehicles on the isle, all transport being conducted by ponies, mules and donkeys. This pristine and naïf quality of life only honed and pared the days and minutes of those foreigners as they lived among the Hydriot – and originally Albanian – township. Less was certainly and doubtlessly more, plus it was cheaper.

～

Secondly, any social organisation possesses ideas of valence and worth concerning an object which human labour has produced, regardless of how an external market weighs such production.

During the period that I am describing capital was scarce on the isle and land was the salient medium of wealth amongst Hydriots, primarily composed of the landscape that was situated around the port. There were some fields in the hills that were sown for barley and there were flocks of goats somewhere up there which produced meat and cheese; the economies of ship-building, chandlery and navigation were long gone. The ideals of artistic production however – whether of painting, of poetry, of the performance of songs, or of novels and stories or sculpture – were the primary activity of these alien young men and women and what little wealth that existed amongst their groups was often shared, among friends and lovers; just as drugs and wine were similarly often taken in common. This was *not* a competitive society but nor was it in any way fixed for there was a great impermanence among these outside residents and they possessed little realia. The true residence was one of consciousness rather than of any mediate presence.

This was the philosophical medium, for these exiled individuals were aware of their particular insular conventions and aspirations; certainly, there were cliques and rivalries but there was simultaneously a great sense of personal esteem and mutual concord where resilient self-awareness thrived. People took photographs of each other, for instance, knowing what was really happening and how exceptional that time was in terms of the European tradition. It was this self-consciousness of the community – well illustrated by this present book – which really allowed the system to function so successfully, for it was an open-handed grouping of lives all in pursuit of a similar unearthly experience and its worldly reproduction.

≈

Then thirdly, all communities own patterns of kinship, how it is that men and women join and regenerate and how it is that sexual unions are agreeably arranged. On Hydra during this period of the late 20th century – during the post-war epoch that focussed about the Sixties with its habits of sexual promiscuity and mobility – sexual congress was various and diverse and genuinely transient. Few marriages were celebrated and yet children were born. In a sense it was the intimacy of work and of the engaged artistry which took priority over the emotional affect of kin; I know that this is a large generalisation but I think that it does bear a certain witness. Sorrow and jealousy existed yet there was a communal and idiorhythmic vision, an exertion which superceded all else.

Such practices of course were neither original nor innovative; there had been the Bohemia of Soho in London at turn of the last century or the mid-century Beat culture of New York and California and the *nouvelle vague* of Paris. The Twenties in London and Paris and Berlin were of a similar nature for artists, who developed the neo-Romantic antinomian manners of the previous century, where radicals and travellers typified by the genre of Wordsworth, Shelley or Turner, flourished so victoriously.

The domestic rituals of such a group centred about dining together and drinking together and often in impassioned dancing and musical recital; this would happen during the evenings at gatherings in the tavernas like Douskos or shops like Katsikas', or in the adjoining western hamlets of Kamini or Vlychos. These were secular occasions and not limited or circumscribed by any calendar of festivals. There were also the journeys to the ancient Hellenic sites like Epidauros or Mycenae, or to Delphi and Olympia, essential to the intellectual frame of the place; just as there was a cultivated awareness of the Orthodox feasts of the year, especially of Easter. It was a outlandish hybrid culture of the Hellenic past and the high style of Western modernism and it always nonplussed me how kindly and hospitable the Hydriot Greeks were to these eclectic foreigners, as if they respected and acknowledged the concentrated synthesis that these expatriates were attempting with their abstrusely refined and expressionistic work ethic. That was very much the nature of old Greece though, the pre-EU Greece whose cultural sophistication and dignity were remarkable in their easy munificence; alas, that old tradition has diminished now and become savagely frayed.

≈

So, imagine what potential this amazing likeness of Utopia can bring to the world, if the necessity of work and labour are reduced or removed and individual endeavour is in constant pursuit of an understanding and subsequent representation of absolute figures of the beautiful: literal, pictorial, sonorous or plastic. If there are no social constraints nor inhibitions – in fact where the opposite actually prevails and drugs and alcohol and sexual disposition are freely exchanged – what then are the consequences?

What happens when a group of attractive young men and women are geographically isolated upon a small island and where – in general – none of them have to work much in order to feed or to shelter themselves and where all of them possess an immoderate *pothos*, a terrific "longing" for universal or cosmic certainty and precision? As their community was physically apart from the world and even essentially separate from the rest of the barren topography of the isle, they were able to conduct themselves socially in a fashion that would elsewhere be thoroughly impermissible. Such was a rare condition and the stress of that equilibrium was often conducive to a near-perpetual disorder.

The Greek inhabitants of the place, the Hydriots, being culturally disposed towards hospitality and the respect due to artistic pursuit, tolerated all kinds of otherwise inadmissible behaviour, and this extremism actually became an acceptable paradigm of existence. That is, except for the bishop who always frowned – sternly if not mutely – upon the foreign community and their occasional compulsive antics; for even he acknowledged that something inimitable and valuable was occurring. This was a situation of Utopia, where anything was possible given the enthusiasm and there were few restraints. What happens in such a time then, if human beings are capable of responding and accomplishing the extra-ordinary; although many of them succumbed to self indulgent excess and narcissistic or remedial definition.

～

Paintings, poetry, musical performance, sculpture, prose were all dynamically generated during those decades of late-century Hydra. In years to come in European history, scholars will look upon this place and era as superlative, insofar as the human spirit exceeded all received convention. Despite the degenerative habits and the frequent suicides and psychic collapse when such complexities of influence became unbearable, much was achieved and produced. There exists a lucid balance between possibility and endeavour when they are combined with both social and private freedom, yet only where a certain discipline – the principle of hard-edged discrimination – is able to sustain and cohere so much dissolution, are masterpieces actually fabricated. To create the icons of human culture one must visit and court the Muses, but then, there is the return journey and the recapitulation, and it is this latter which is the most difficult and dangerous.

It is paradoxical, yet even in situations where such tremendous intellectual and emotional liberty are generally achieved there always remains that necessary requirement for constraint and inhibition; although these are not the conventions of typed society but are personally induced or self effected. Yet without that integration all is lost. Material culture is founded upon prohibition and exchange – whether social or individual – and if there is a steady effort and expectation of mysterious and epiphanic experience that too requires its own unique system of containment and circumscription. The source or font of that coherence is mysteriously imperative and is perhaps due to the theophanic stability of the conceptual Dionysos, that divine agency of masks and performance. Work will always require incalculable resources of living energy but simultaneously it necessitates formality and constitution; even the most free spirits have need of a certain self-imposition that it repressive and so there is never any complete escape from *dis*-content.

∼

Hydra today is an elite tourist venue, international and affluent, the destination of cruise ships and of wealthy Athenians and Berliners, of the new-prosperous entrepreneurs from London and Manhattan. The days of Bohemia – as finely recorded in the monochrome photographs of Bjørn Saastad – are now iconic tokens that supply the island with its glossy record of a distinguished past; there are even websites devoted to collecting images of those earlier and creative days where youth and beauty and aspiration laboured to apprehend and to represent what everyone knows as TRUTH, which few are ever able to envision and then equally to express.

Those moments are what supply corporeal culture with its visual, moral and acoustic items of paragon, and without these trials and exertions, these assays into an unknown body of knowledge and the successful conversion of such refined experience into convenient metaphor, our lives here on earth would indeed be poor, horribly callous and profoundly lifeless if not worthless.

The Muses – daughters of memory – are, for those who pay devoted attention to their presence and make the attempt to recall what it is that qualifies us here on earth as distinctly human, must first forget all the conventions that are merely founded upon informed truth; then they might proceed toward the original and unqualified and yet enigmatically discrete. Without that necessary act of oblivion there can be no recollection and without that recollection there is no prospect for human culture: the art lies not so much in the view itself but more in the technique of reminiscence and public expression. Rarely in human time do temporary and liberal societies appear that are so focussed and described about such a plan; those recent decades of life on Hydra were supremely unmatched in this respect.

If Utopia is a place or circumstance, a situation where the absolute might become apparent in a worldly fashion – as for instance during the mythical Generation of Gold which the Hesiodic poets once portrayed – then it would be the work of artistry which made manifest those perfected ideas. Nowadays, to experience access to those initial principles of nature and language requires a marvellous abandonment, yet a simultaneous firm discipline is equally mandatory if knowledge is to become consistent and communicable. Only then might we translate our atemporal and ingenious moments into the mundane and vernacular–social: mortal life as it is historically known and maintained. Our aim must always be true or else there is no aim.

∾

Let us now focus more precisely and allow our lens to zoom in and examine one particular body of work, not just for its specific excellence but more for its aesthetic presentation of Hydriot marine and seafaring culture. If Ghikas can be said to have captured the visual topography of the isle, its vegetation and Cubist architecture then the paintings of William Pownall arguably portray the nautical and marine traditions of island ethos. Unlike the realism of Porter or the stripped and often tantric work of Motley, or the opaque and dark visions of Kingsmill, Pownall's work has always remained firmly embedded in the earthly *matériel* of the island's rocky surfaces and within the immediate currency of the surrounding sea.

Pownall's modernist pursuit of abstraction has drawn him through a working life of more than half a century and, much like the polytropic hero Odysseus, that progress has enabled him to refine *noos*, consciousness, in a fashion that has culminated in his present late series of ink sketches where the single elements of the square, the circle and the triangle, have become intensely refined and integrated into depictions of what is virtually perfect yet active form. That kind of effort toward minimal representation is neither a lessening nor a diminution of imagery but an intensification of the figure into a model of complete order, a concentration of meaning and something that approximates absolution: *hora*, or thoroughly sensual and material equilibrium.

Yet at times the work of Pownall does not evade representation or even narrative, but these characteristics are so reduced, so purified and simultaneously enhanced that the result estimates what is sure visual form, both chromatically and in terms of arrangement. Sometimes qualities of collage enter into this process, supplying the work with a strongly and irreducible physical connection to the landscape and seascape, filling these canvases with material repletion as they silently emanate towards the viewer.

Pownall grew out of a non-expressionistic British tradition of abstract painting that included artists like Pasmore, Scott and Heron, where the visual sign was reduced to colour, depth and composition. On the Saronic island of Hydra where he has worked for several decades Pownall is among a group of peers:

Ghikas, Tetsis, Loizides, Gassoumis and Marden, have been his immediate and historical milieu.

Minimalism as an explicit medium of refined human communication is an activity that eliminates quality and so perfects its model, much as the sculptor Giacometti stripped down his depiction of the human shape to a bareness which magnified the unseen psyche that inhabits those objects. The minimalist plays with detail and precision, making minute adjustments that ultimately incorporate and express a far greater totality than can be delineated through the signs of any realistic genre, for he or she works with the truly vital, the hidden vigour of the image.

~

In this Pownall labours in a similar manner to Newman or Kelly, where all that remains on the canvas is a fully charged and tensile delineation of an hypostatic subject. It is as if time as a condition has been pared away and removed from such pictures and they become wholly iconic, imbued with a strangely yet profoundly satisfying cosmic stasis.

Pownall has always founded his work upon terrain, however – the hills and the sea about his studio – and this kind of abstraction – like the sculptural work of Moore or Hepworth or the painted canvases of Nicholson – finds in topography and marine order the fundamental visual and tactile components of human experience. He works at the frontier of non-representation and authenticity as if poised upon a membrane of what does not exist and yet which may be apprehended. As the poet Elytis observed about Pownall's understanding of worldly phenomena, "he has arrived directly at the limits: at the earth, at the sky, at the sea." Occasionally these limits include human anatomy as with his 2005 work, *She Dreams*. This kind of modelling, of course, finds its origins in the Kykladic depiction of the human figure where what is being signified is a torso and mortality that has gone beyond any temporal envelope or frame and which has become fixed solely as an object of perception, being removed from all timely efficacy and cause.

This kind of beauty is rare and fragile, it is vulnerable and transient, inherently ephemeral, and despite the substances of collage that the artist employs in many of his works – like marble dust – the tone or mood of many of Pownall's canvases is one of delicacy and humanity, of humankind that is only scarcely tangible. This is so unlike the similarly abstract collages of certain Italian and Spanish artists of the last half century, where the roughness of existence provides the paintings with a near carnal or tragic mood.

Such a kind of work and effort is actually representative not of a material world but of a single human life, one that has resolutely pursued in fact a modelling of truthfulness by the gentle and yet completely disciplined practice of observation and relation. Ultimately it is not the paintings which remain with the viewer but a received sensibility which Pownall has carefully and practically followed and tracked for a lifetime: an attempt at visual certainty and resolution that is absolutely grounded in the earthly and diurnal and yet the completely changeless. In this one can observe human triumph, something that does not decay but which is universally stable and is apart from any moral stance: the *kleos aphthiton* which only Achilles was aware of and to which he at last and most exclusively surrendered everything.

≈

At times the Immortals are said to descend upon the earth and to walk upon the ground, to dine and to converse with humankind and sometimes to make love with them, perhaps occasionally imparting some of their divine cognisance and foresight during those moments of reserved and intimate encounter.

A few of the older generation of Hydriots are still with me in my mind's eye and heart's core; they were the autochthons, those who arose from the earth itself, who lives were born from many generations of Hydriot marriages and households. There was Maria Goulas who ran a little shop high up on the hill in the Kiafa district; her family also looked after the church next door. She belonged to that old and faithful world of Orthodoxy, a generation who had known of the Dictator Metaxas and the ensuing Nazi Occupation and then, of the Civil War and the subsequent horribly cruel conflict between Communists and the Nationalists; she also, like so many, lived through the crude dictatorship of the Colonels. All that experience was visible in her features, so much suffering and yet such gentle fortitude and sure reverence. I well recall the afternoon when her son-in-law was found hanging from the balcony to their house and how Maria endured even that grief. Since the days of Andromakhe and of Briseis, lament has always been an inherent part of Greek musical genre; and in that view what we have lost and forsaken is more beautiful than what we might ever possess. That grief remains like the shadow of a fish in water, yet it is always to be conveyed.

~

There was also Kyria Sophia who was aged, faithful and lived above her taverna which was on the way up the hill towards Kala Pigadia; she sold wine and sometimes continued to entertain, at Easter especially. She lived in great pain from her legs and her later years were an ordeal; she was one of the last of the Hydra women to wear a head-scarf. There was also old Maria – the only woman muleteer on the isle – who lived beside the inland and paved path towards Kamini; she was unmarried and she too was one of the few to still wear the head-scarf. Her house was next door to the candle-maker who could be seen in those years pouring redolent bees-wax onto the suspended threads. Maria's mother must have had some terrible condition like syphilis for she often sat upon the marble threshold looking out upon the world as it passed along the path, her face terribly scarred and wounded.

There was Ioannis Kremos whose family had the last ship's chandlery down on the port, dating back to the century before when stone quays had not been built and ships were simply drawn up onto the sandy shore; he also lived above his shop but had a country house out beyond Vlychos. In the Seventies chandlery soon gave way to tourist items and that kind of quick commerce. In his youth he had been at sea, like most of the male Hydriots, and he loved to tell stories about brothels and prostitutes which he would illustrate with drawings.

There was also Gregorios, who was a gardener who carved figures in the wood which he brought home from his prunings. My wife and I still have a group of four heads as well as many wooden spoons that he once fashioned. Like most of his kind, Gregori's marriage had been arranged and his bride had come to the island from a small village to the south on the mainland Peloponnese; I actually know that Lakonian village well. The ground floor of his Hydra house was empty except for a great loom at which his three or four daughters were always working. Theirs was one of the happiest families that I knew on the isle, always lightly replete with goodness and lucid kindness and endeavour.

It makes me sad to think that these people – and they are but a few of many – are no longer in the world and that their Greece too has vanished, along with its virtuous generosity and dignified human kindness. The modern philhellenes are now the young middle class Greeks themselves who attempt to revision and to reconstruct a former pre-modern livelihood, a lost nature which has been so submerged by Europe. I always feel slightly melancholic now when I return to Hydra, for it is as if one does not actually exist any more, being unrecognised and unseen, which is a strangely transparent condition and not mortal.

≈

It is not simply that an economy – when ploughing was done with a yoke of mules, when harvests were taken in with sickles and the threshing and the winnowing that ensued were accomplished with rites of joy, nor that the occasion each October when the winy *musto* arrived aboard caïques and the port was noisy with a tap-tapping of coopers as they caulked their barrels with dry palm frond and rinsed the stale lees from the containers with sea-water – but it is that a most ancient sensibility for the natural and sentient tempo of this earth has been harshly forsaken. It is as if a steel blade of technology has severed the knowledge, awareness and traditions of what must amount to several thousand years of human experience and that these have been suddenly put away and forgotten. Kyria Sophia, Maria Goulas and their kind of humanity are no more, and that imagery of life – once so well recorded through the lens of Fred Boissonnas – has perished.

A former streamlined amity founded upon ritual cycles has suddenly given way to anonymous and timeless media; artistic entrepreneurs are now dominating the gallery scene and figures like Ghikas and Brice Marden and their vision of paradise are no longer considered among the avant-garde. The artistic resurgence which took place on Hydra from the mid-Fifties to the mid-Eighties has been thoroughly and drastically superceded by a novel manner of aesthetic business.

～

For me personally the most communicative and memorable hours and days that I knew on Hydra were when I left the port and the town and set off over the hills or along the coast and made my way towards the far side of the isle. It was there that I found the true life which so evaded me on the other and more human shore, there among the old grey stones and the perfect threshing circles, among the prickly pear and the pines and thyme: ilex, myrtle and wild fig. The solitude and the silence over there were beautiful and the open horizon to the south was always sustaining. Those days and afternoons were the happiest hours that I knew on Hydra, for their near-transcendental loveliness and tranquillity, moments of inspiration and of pleasure.

Walking for me has always been a moral and visionary activity, a medium for retrieving one's being within a context of slowness and observation; it is a condition of being *apart*, of being uncivil and outlaw. Only when away from the port and alone along those dusty paths – among the seething and susurrating resin-pines and the chrome-yellow bushy genista, in the company of hawks and small pink snakes – only then could I find the fidelity that inheres within poetry as its core and element. There within an acoustic atmosphere of raving cicadas in summer or the melodious and tuneful knocking of goat-bells in the cooler seasons did I encounter something rare and unbelievable.

Walking, with a pen and a notebook in my shirt pocket and a firm oak cane from Athos – given to me by my friend and fellow walker, the composer Terry Oldfield – I would ascend and descend toward another life, one of terrific and untarnished veracity. Leaving the town and the port behind and disappearing along those thin dry paths was like being stripped of care and diurnal thought, as if one's chains were falling away onto the ground. If it was January the wild pear and judas trees would be in blossom in great fragile clouds of candid whiteness.

~

I have walked in many other parts of Greece and in various other places in the world but never have I secured such experience of unqualified natural beauty and the ease with which one could pass out of time and temporal fashioning. I found both equilibrium and humility there on the far side of the isle, an elusive and immaterial stability which cannot really be perceived which was nevertheless indestructible; that is what Hydra gave me more than anything else, more than human amity and friendship itself. It was there on the other coast of the island that I received whatever grains of mastery that I now possess and that is why I continue to write about Hydra and in my professional life to teach about Homeric culture and to research its literature; those times were my primary source and truly original terrestrial residence. Much of my book *Windward* came from those long ago walks as have many of my later prose pieces and many of the short lyrics in my book *Eros* were actually made in that time.

There was the coastal path that ran along the littoral towards the West and the old Turkish farmstead at Palamidas; then the path turned inland and uphill towards the hamlet of Episkopi. There was also another path that ran from the precinct of Kala Pigadia with its double ancient wells up into the hills past the monastery of Agias Triados before turning southward toward the other coast. There was also the central route that led up over the top of the isle past the monastery dedicated to Profitis Elias and onward toward the rocky spine of the island.

Sometimes I would actually go and sleep up there on the heights of what we used to call Mount Eros, what was in fact the tallest hill on the island where there remained traces of a shelter once used centuries before by lookouts spying for the sails of marauding vessels and corsairs. At the time of the moon's plenitude the planet would be rising on one side of the island just as the great sun was setting towards the west, and one's sense of cosmic symmetry during those instants was remarkable: as if all of being was poised between these two giant and tediously moving spheres. In the low pre-dawn the islands to the south of Hydra would occasionally be visible in the misty light, conical and dark, as if hovering in space; an immeasurable airy volume that extended all the way down towards the western Cyclades.

～

During one winter I went and spent more than a week at the tiny cove of Kerali, a small bay deeply inset within steep rocky cliffs. I would walk up the hill through the pines each morning and go to where I knew a cistern held water and there refill my supply. I had brought a large bag of rice with me and that – infused with sage and thyme – was my staple. I used to collect driftwood and spent hours beside small fires in the cold air watching the sea and waves, free from all the usual anxieties of life beside that enormous solitary envelope of air, sky and water. I saw and witnessed so much there and those supernal experiences have continued to nourish me for decades. That was not only an old Greece but a profoundly archaic Greece where unidentifiable ships would pass at night and voices were audible from across the water; where immaterial gifts were made and unspeakably exchanged. It was as if one's psyche was being translated to another and much grander and imperishable station. It was the Levantine Hellas, the idyllic and pastoral world of the old Aegean and not the modernised European Greece, where life continued to be still deeply fitted into the earth and fully engaged with the aerial passage of light, clime and season. Edward Lear and John Craxton – in their paintings – have well recorded such views, drawn from the landscape of other districts in Greece.

My wife came from an old Anglo-Greek family and when I had married I had become Orthodox and had entered into that hallway of belief. I would often pause during my walks when I passed near one of the many island chapels; in those days the doors were never locked and there was often a cistern beneath the terrace from which one could drink. I loved the piety so overtly apparent in those small thickly-walled buildings, with their rows of icons and the scent of incense and of creamy candle-wax. At one particular chapel the shepherd of that hill used to store his fragrant cheeses in the coolness of the room. The sound of those remote interiors when the wind was blowing was beautiful and cosmic, for it was as if one was lost in aerial space with only the tonic buffeting of strong musical air upon the thick mineral walls and stone roof. They were good places to sit and rest for a while on super-hot days, as one adjusted to the gloom and darkness and the still expressionless gaze of the saints. That was my Greece, that world of Byzance and the nearbye Morea, which I could view with such ease and facility on that lone and farther shore of Hydra.

∾

I returned to Kerali often during the July of 2001 when I was preparing to swim the Hellespont in imitation of Philhellenic Byron. Up and down the coast I would swim for three hours in a wonderful isolation and exclusion and there it was that my swims became a work of art themselves, perfectible, mantic and otherworldly. Then I would lie bare on the pebbly shore of the beach and snooze for a while covered in thin powdery salt before returning uphill quite naked through the odorous pines. The radiant intensity of sunlight then was overwhelming and yet simultaneously intoxicating and it was as if one could not see any more, such was the charged brilliance of the white-heated air; it was sexual in itself with an unearthly concentration.

Often on winter afternoons I would be in that tiny bay, swimming and then unclothed as I warmed myself up beside a fire whose saline driftwood burned with dense yellow and blue flames; walking back up through the susurrating woods where anemone and cyclamen and later, poppies and marigolds would be blooming. There were capers to be gathered and small wild asparagus to be picked from beside the sharp flinty rocks and little grape hyacinth would be there in spring and the shy orchis and reclusive fritillary. Human nudity in a bare terrain contains within its footsteps a sensual yet certain metaphysical liberation.

Within such a magnitude and transparency of solitude one is never alone but imbued by and integral with all of life and it is difficult to describe how that *love of place* touches one perhaps even more closely and privately, more acutely than *love of person*; and how it is that what one receives during those internal moments of psychic passion can never be expressed nor mentioned thereafter.

Unlike human love, love of place is never unrequited. That territory remains indelible and indestructible within us as if some uncommon and unworldly fuel which provides further life, something that is more present in our brief time here on earth than anything else; that is, of course, if one's aim is true. If Greece gave me everything, then Hydra was the basis for that ground and its perspective, and from that hard island commune came my own personal *mythistorema*, the invisible heart's clear bell.

Michalis Oikonomou's House on Hydra[1]

Panagiotis Rappas

Michalis Oikonomou is a notable figure from the first decades of 20th century Greek painting and one who is, unjustly, little known among the general public. His work was highly personal and significant too, even though his life was very brief and came to a tragic end.

His end brings to mind another great artist – one from the world of literature – Georgios Vyzinos. Their two lives and two paths differed distinctly from each other but concluded in the same way, in the confines of the Dromokaitio Mental Hospital. One is awed by the mystery of a human existence that manages to penetrate boldly into the nature of things, observe them and reflect them in art with a clarity and definition that surprises and stirs, but that also disappears in the course of that attempt into the labyrinths of the heart and mind without ever finding the exit and the way back. To our eyes this terrible discordance makes them look like saints or, rather, martyrs to their own art.

The son of a middle class family from Piraeus, Oikonomou had painting lessons as a youngster from Konstantinos Volanakis. He then went study naval architecture in Paris, where he decided to devote himself to painting and to make his living from it. He spent twenty years studying, exhibiting his work and meeting fellow artists. (The early 20th century was a time of great changes and modernist movements in the visual arts, most of which had their beginnings in the City of Light but which influenced him only slightly.) He returned to Greece, where he married Eftychia

---

[1] Translated by Vivienne Nilan.

Argyriou, his faithful consort until the end. In the years that followed he lived, worked and exhibited in Athens and Piraeus. In 1932, physically and mentally ravaged by syphilis, he was confined to the Dromokaitio Mental Hospital, where he died in 1933.

House on Hydra (1929-1930), oil on cardboard 24×28 cm, Michalis Oikonomou, 1884-1932. E. Averoff Art Gallery, Metsovo.

House on Hydra, a work he painted between 1929 and 1930, belongs to the final phase of his creative activity, when his illness had become apparent and, historians say, he found tranquility and solace in escaping to Poros, but more frequently to Hydra. It being extremely difficult in the absence of adequate sources to record and date his output in that final phase of his life, historians call it his Hydra period. What is impressive in his work, including this particular painting, is his ability to convey a certain impression and the emotions it arouses so intensely as if to stop time, even to negate it. Looking at the simple, clear shapes, the limpidity of the light and distinctness of the compositions that shun anything superfluous, one has the feeling that time has stopped forever. Not at a specific moment, however, but at all the moments that have passed and all those that are to come. The house, which is his subject, becomes an archetypal house, enclosing within itself the history of all houses from all ages that have housed everyone in every era since time began. He makes it seem like a crystal ball that magically encompasses life and time.

But a relationship with a work of art, and with time too, for that matter, is essentially very subjective. It is a relationship that everyone constructs from material arising from an absolutely internal dialogue, where senses, memories, emotions and thoughts are raw material for something both personal and solitary.

As Aphrodite Kouria aptly notes in her book on Oikonomou and his work: "for the informed observer of these works, the jagged rocks of the island whose powerful shapes project threateningly into the uniform greyness of the sky and the sea could have symbolic meaning. That is, they could be read as a visual metaphor for the implacable destiny already bearing down upon the artist in the final years of his life."

But the artist–work relationship is only one of many dimensions one may discover in getting to grips with a significant work. As Zacharias Papantoniou rightly comments, "Oikonomou seems capable of rendering the most enduring element in objects."

For me, having also spent twenty years of my life outside Greece, this painting was often a window onto the world of my childhood, which I was lucky to spend on Hydra, and on what I then left behind. In a mysterious way, however, it was also a window onto everything that had existed before me and what might come after.

Indeed, I know the house in the painting. As a boy I went past it countless times in the summer on my way to swim at Mikro and Megalo Kamini (Little and Big Kiln), with my mother and my brothers and sisters. Since I suffered from seasonal conjunctivitis, which lasted all spring and well into summer, the only suitable time for me to swim was in the late afternoon when the sun was setting. Naturally the entire family was compelled to have their swim with me at the same time. And so, as I climbed the stairs to Megalo Kamini, compelled to keep my eyes half-shut against the relentless itch triggered by the sun, at dusk everything looked exactly as the artistic probings of Oikonomou have reflected them in the painting.

Every time I look at it, long-lost memories resurface with incredible intensity. The voices of my brothers and sisters as children, the melancholy I felt at being unable to join in their escapades, my mother's comments, the smell of fishing nets drying in the sun and of basil plants in the surrounding courtyards. The bulk of Mantrahoriza hill descending vertically over the sea and behind the house, dark and full of mystery. My godmother coming from Rahi to meet us. Goats' bells and the clatter of hooves as mules approached, making us step aside. The taste of the aubergines in tomato sauce, fried potatoes and meatballs that Mother used to make for us to eat after bathing. Lighting the candle in the church of the Holy Virgin and at the caskets containing the bones of our departed relatives. But also the picture of Grandfather, after whom I was named but never met, as he died only nine years after Oikonomou and quite a few before I was born.

In the early 1930s, while Oikonomou was "collecting elements of engagement with the hours and events of the external world,"[2] or, to put it more simply, making preliminary sketches for this painting, Grandfather used to anchor his little boat below the house in the picture to unload his catch. He was three years younger but looked older, weathered by the sun and the salt.

It is very likely that one fine summer evening their glances would have met, together with their concerns. One trying to "render the imposing contours of the island … which dictate the vertical articulation of the composition," the other trying to provide for an exceptionally large family. Perhaps they greeted each other. Perhaps.

I also wonder, whenever I look at this painting, whether that brushstroke of reddish ochre behind the house, just off Megalo Kamini, is Grandfather's boat. Perhaps it is …

What is certain is that this painting has granted many journeys to those who have happened to see it and have spent a bit of their time with it. It will continue to so do as long as it stands the test of time, there in beautiful Metsovo. We know this was something that troubled Michalis Oikonomou greatly about his paintings:

---

[2] *Μιχάλης Οικονόμου 1884-1933* (*Michalis Oikonomou 1884-1933*), Aphrodite Kouria, Adam Publishing, Athens, 2001.

"They won't last …," he was often heard to say anxiously, his wife reported.

He himself did not last. Two years later he was gone. As was Grandfather, just a few years later. Both of them, shortly before going to their last resting place – the common fate of humanity – hearing chanted for them the wonderful words: "Everything thinner than a shadow, everything more deceptive than a dream … "

On Time and Worry Beads[1]

Daniel Martin Klein

Seen from the sea, Hydra seems as flimsy as a hallucination. A lucent mist envelopes the island, and the incoming hydrofoil throws up a spray that further filters its landscape, softens it, makes it appear to float. But here on the island, even when the sky is as cloudy as it is today, every view is severe with detail. The shadow of a rock a mile off on the Peloponnesian shore appears as well defined as the lemon tree just outside my window. And because Hydra rises from its main port in a steep, horseshoe-shaped hill that is girded with houses, everyone is an innocent spectator to private scenes in remote courtyards and terraces.

At this moment I spy a middle-aged woman in a floral-patterned housecoat hanging out her laundry while carrying on a lively conversation with a brown-and-white cat perched on her garden wall; two terraces above her, I see a pair of grade school children sitting cross-legged under their garden door's awning, one pulling a picture book from his backpack, the other biting into a chunk of bread slathered with honey; and at the top of the hill, I can clearly make out a tall and portly Orthodox priest in black robe and chimney-pot hat sitting stoically on his garden bench while his diminutive wife, standing just behind him, lectures him, possibly about some item he failed to purchase on his morning trip to the port.

[1] From *Travels with Epicurus: A Journy to a Greek Island in Search of a Fulfilled Life*, Daniel Klein, Penguin, New York, 2012. Reprinted with permission of the author and Penguin Books USA.

This is the celebrated trick of Hydra light: it transforms daily life into intimate theatre.

In the white-washed nineteenth-century house where I am staying, all the windows are screened with two crossed iron bars. "To keep the Turks out," some islanders say. "To keep Albanian pirates out," say others. Clearly these iron bars work: neither Turk nor Albanian has clambered into my room. The bars do not obscure the view from my desk window; rather they frame it into four discrete images: a hill studded with houses in one frame, a grove of almond trees in another, the harbour, the sea.

My lodging is high on the hill. Through the harbour frame, I now view the terrace of Dimitri's taverna, and it is empty. The clouds threaten rain, so I imagine that Tasso and his tablemates are either inside the café or skipping today's symposium.

But rain or not, I am hungry. As the figs in the hanging mesh basket in my room are in that awkward stage between fresh and dried, I set off for Dimitri's taverna, passing Tasso's house along the way. I catch a glimpse of him, sitting alone on his third-story terrace, where he appears deep in thought.

The only people inside Dimitri's are Dimitri himself, sitting in the kitchen and listening to the BBC World Service news and, at the far end of the dining area, by the window, his eighty-year-old father, Ianos, who is reading yesterday's Athenian newspaper while playing with his *komboloi*, a loop of thirty-three amber beads that are known in English as worry beads.

Like many of the island's men, Dimitri was a sailor when he was younger. He worked his way up to ship's radio operator, a job at which he picked up fluent English and a smattering of other languages, both Western and Eastern. When he reached his midthirties, he returned permanently to Hydra, opened his taverna and married the local woman he had hired as his cook. The idea that life has natural, discrete stages comes intuitively to Dimitri.

I realise I have seen far fewer men fingering worry beads than when I first came to the island in the 1960s, and I ask Dimitri if that tradition is fading. Before responding, he signals for me to select my meal from the open metal trays at the front of the kitchen. As always I have a choice between *moussaka*, stuffed zucchinis, *pastitsio* (a Greek macaroni and cheese, with ground meat, which got its name from the Italian *pasticcio*, meaning "hodgepodge," a term that could describe most Greek dishes), and Dimitri's *pièce de résistance*, roasted lamb with potatoes. I spring for the lamb, despite the fact that a small party of flies is cavorting in its gravy. Dimitri turns off the radio, serves me up a generous platter of the lamb, pours two glasses of retsina and sits down across from me.

"To start with, 'worry beads' is an ignorant translation," he begins. "It says more about the way English people think than it does about the Greeks. *Komboloi* have nothing to do with worrying."

Whenever Dimitri and I have these conversations, he assumes a teacherly air with more than a hint of strained patience, but none-theless it is clear to me that he enjoys his role as my cultural interpreter. He is, in fact, an unusually astute and cosmopolitan man.

"*Komboloi* have to do with time, with spacing it out, making it last," he goes on.

Spacing time out? Making it last? Like many Greeks I know, Dimitri slips naturally into metaphysical pronouncements, although he certainly would not call them that. Dimitri is simply expressing his worldview, and that worldview sees time as a mal-leable thing, multidimensional, based not just on planetary move-ments and clocks but also on the way we personally apprehend it. So for him, time can shift depending on how a person experiences it, even by how he *chooses* to experience it.

Filmography and Bibliography of Hydra

Compiled by Valerie Lloyd Sidaway, Brian Sidaway,
Helle V. Goldman & Kevin McGrath

What follows is a partial list of fictional motion pictures filmed
on Hydra and books about, or set on, Hydra, in whole or in part.
To the extent possible, publication details for first editions are
presented.

Filmography

Το Κορίτσι με τα Μαύρα (A Girl in Black), Michael Kakogiannis
dir., Hermes Film, 1956

Boy on a Dolphin, Jean Negulesco dir., Twentieth Century Fox,
1957

Phaedra, Jules Dassin dir., Jorilie/Melinafilm, 1962

Island of Love, Morton DaCosta dir., Belgrave, 1963

Κορίτσια για Φίλημα (Kiss the Girls), Finos Film, Giannis Dalianidis dir., 1965

Γοργόνες και Μάγκες (Mermaids and Rascals), Giannis Dalianidis
dir., Finos Film, 1968

Incense for the Damned, Robert Hartford-Davies dir., Lucinda
Films/Titan International Productions, 1970

Έλα Να Γυμνωθούμε Ντάρλινγκ (Darling, Let's Get Naked), Giannis
Dalianidis dir., Giorgos Karagiannis & Co., 1984

The Blue Villa (Un Bruit Qui Rend Fou), Alain Robbe-Grillet dir.,
Nomad Films/Euripidi Productions/CAB Productions, 1995

Boat Trip, Mort Nathan dir., MPCA/IWP, 2002

Fugitive Pieces, Jeremy Podeswa dir., Cinegram, 2007
The Capsule, Athina Rachel Tsangari dir., Haos Film, 2012

Memoirs and biographies

Brown, Max, *Charmian and George: The Marriage of George Johnston and Charmian Clift*, Rosenberg Publishing, Dural, New South Wales, 2004

Clift, Charmian, *Peel Me a Lotus*, Hutchinson, London, 1959

Fagan, David, *Rhubarb! Tales of Survival on a Little Greek Island*, Hydra, 2013

Genoni, Paul & Tanya Dalziell, *Half the Perfect World: Writers, Dreamers and Drifters on Hydra, 1955-1964*, Monash University Publishing, Clayton, Victoria, 2018

Gold, Alison Leslie, *Love in the Second Act: True Stories of Romance, Midlife and Beyond*, Penguin, New York, 2006

— *Found and Lost: Mittens, Miep and Shovelfuls of Dirt*, Notting Hill Editions, London, 2017

Green, Roger, *Hydra and the Bananas of Leonard Cohen: A Search for Serenity in the Sun*, Basic Books, New York, 2003

Hesthamar, Kari, *So Long, Marianne: A Love Story*, ECW Press, Toronto, 2014

Jensen, Axel & Petter Mejlænder, *Livet Sett fra Nimbus (Life Seen from Nimbus)*, Spartacus, Oslo, 2002

Kinnane, Garry, *George Johnston: A Biography,* Thomas Nelson, Melbourne, 1986

Klein, Daniel, *Travels with Epicurus: A Journey to a Greek Island in Search of a Fulfilled Life*, Penguin, New York, 2012

Miller, Henry, *The Colossus of Maroussi*, Colt Press, San Francisco, 1941

Nadel, Ira, *Various Positions: A Life of Leonard Cohen*, Pantheon Books, New York, 1996

Piercy, Jill, *Brenda Chamberlain: Artist and Writer*, Cardigan, Parthian, 2013

Simmons, Sylvie, *I'm Your Man: The Life of Leonard Cohen*, Ecco/HarperCollins, New York, 2012

Thoresen, Knut Flovik, *Jernkors og Penn: Mysteriet Felix Thoresen (Iron Cross and Pen: the Mystery of Felix Thoresen)*, Forlaget Historie & Kultur, Oslo, 2013

van Rensselaer, Philip, *Rich Was Better: A Memoir*, Wynwood Press, New York, 1990

Wheatley, Nadia, *The Life and Myth of Charmian Clift*, Harper-Collins, Sydney, 2001

Fiction

Chamberlain, Brenda, *A Rope of Vines: Journal from a Greek Island*, Hodder & Stoughton, London, 1965

Hodes, Tamar, *The Water and the Wine*, Hookline Books, 2018

Howard, Elizabeth Jane, *The Sea Change*, Jonathan Cape, London, 1959

Isaia, Nana, *Η Ιστορία Τότε και Τώρα (History Then and Now)*, Delfini, Athens, 1997

Johnson, Susan, *The Broken Book*, Allen & Unwin, Crows Nest, New South Wales, 2006

Johnston, George, *Closer to the Sun*, Collins, London, 1960

— *Clean Straw for Nothing*, Collins, London, 1969

— & Charmian Clift, *Strong-man from Piraeus and Other Stories*, Thomas Nelson, Melbourne, 1983

Karapanou, Margarita, *The Sleepwalker*, Clockroot Books, Northampton, Massachusetts, 2011

MacLean, Robert, *Home from the Party*, 1995, Ronsdale Press, Vancouver (reissued as *Greek Island Murder*, Pretentious Pictures Publications, 2012)

Michaels, Anne, *Fugitive Pieces*, Alfred A. Knopf, New York, 1997

Osborne, Lawrence, *Beautiful Animals*, Hogarth, London, 2017

Vlachodimitris, Stamatis G., *Πολεμοσ και Ερωτασ στον Αργοσαρωνικο (War and Love in the Argosaronic Sea)*, Arteon, Athens, 2016

Winterson, Jeanette, *Lighthousekeeping*, Harcourt, New York, 2004

Winton, Tim, *The Riders*, Pan Macmillan, Sydney, 1994

Young, Charles, *Σύννεφα πάνω από την Ύδρα (Clouds over Hydra)*, Plaza, Athens, 1996

— *The Hydra Chronicle*, Cosmos Publishing, River Vale, New Jersey, 2011

Poetry

Cherkovski, Neeli, *Leaning against Time*, R.L. Crow Publications, Berkeley, 2004

Cohen, Leonard, *Stranger Music*, McClelland & Stewart, Toronto, 1993

Johnston, Martin, *Martin Johnston – Selected Poems and Prose*, University of Queensland Press, Brisbane, 1993

Layton, Irving, *Seventy-five Greek Poems 1951-1974*, Hermias Publications, Athens, 1974

Maelzel, Richard, *Poems to the Poet-Greece*, Merlin Books, Braunton, Devon, 1990

McGrath, Kevin, *Eros*, Saint Julian Press, Houston, 2016

Rivers, Ann, *Samos Wine*, Mammon Press, Bath, 1987

— *A World of Difference*, Whispering Pines, Athens, 1995

— *A Life of Its Own*, S.H.Y. Publications, 2011

— *Characters: New and Selected Poems*, S.H.Y. Publications, 2011

Slater, George Dillon & Sinclair Beiles, *Cathedral of Angels and Luna Park*, Anglo-Hellenic Publications, Athens, 1976

Travel, history, architecture, art, photography and style

Arnaoutoglou, Chrysavgi K., *Greek Traditional Architecture: Hydra*, Melissa Publishing House, Athens, 1986

Bradford, Ernle, *A Companion Guide to the Greek Isles*, Boydell & Brewer, Martlesham, Suffolk, 1963

Durrell, Lawrence, *The Greek Islands*, Viking Press, New York, 1978

Historical and Ethnological Society of Greece, *The Lazarus Koundouriotis Historic Residence*, Athens, 2002

Keeley, Edmund, *Inventing Paradise: The Greek Journey, 1937-47*, Farrar, Straus & Giroux, New York, 1999

Kouria, Aphrodite, *Μιχάλης Οικονόμου 1884-1933 (Michalis Oikonomou 1884-1933)*, Adam Editions, Athens, 2001

Maelzel, Richard, *Greek Island Landscape*, Merlin Books, Braunton, Devon, 1995

Michaelides, Constantine E., *Hydra: A Greek Island Town – Its Growth and Form*, University of Chicago Press, Chicago, 1967

Ministry of National Education and Religious Affairs, Historical Archives, Museum of Hydra, *Hydra through the Eyes of 20th Century Greek Artists*, Athens, 2002

Panchout, Catherine, *Hydra: Vues Privées (Hydra: Private Views)*, Gourcuff Gradenigo, Montreuil, 2015

Paraskeva, Phoebe, *Hydra, 1920-1970*, Militos Editions, Athens, 2007

Pownall, William, *A Letter from Hydra*, Studio, Ulm, 1981

— *William Pownall: Works on Paper*, Hydra Press, Ulm, 1998

— *Stillness in Paintings – 1997 to 2013*, Hydra Press, Ulm, 2014

Slesin, Suzanne, Stafford Cliff, Daniel Rozensztroch & Gilles de Chabaneix, *Greek Style*, Clarkson N. Potter, New York, 1988

Sofianos, Aristodimos, *Hydra*, C. Christou, Athens, 1978

Staebler, Gabriela, *Island of Cats – Hydra*, Edition Reuss, Glattbach, 2015

Taschen, Angelika (ed.), *Greece Style*, Taschen, Berlin, 2005

Vanderpool, Catherine, *Hydra*, Lycabettus Press, Athens, 1980

Vergas, Kostas, *Hydra*, Vergas Publications, Athens, 2001

Zemor, Sandra, *Sandra Zemor – Artist*, Editions Venezia Viva, Venice, 2014

Greek culture – general readings

Andrews, Kevin, *The Flight of Ikaros: A Journey in Greece*, Veidenfeld & Nicolson, London, 1959

du Boulay, Juliet, *Cosmos, Life, and Liturgy in a Greek Orthodox Village*, Denise Harvey, Limni Evias, Greece, 2009

Fermor, Patrick Leigh, *Mani: Travels in the Southern Peloponnese*, Murray, London, 1958

Hart, Laurie Kain, *Time, Religion, and Social Experience in Rural Greece*, Rowman & Littlefield, Lanham, Maryland, 1991

Levi, Peter, *The Hill of Kronos,* Collins, London, 1980

Megas, George, *Greek Calendar Customs*, Press and Information Department, Prime Minister's Office, Athens, 1963

Seferis, George, *Mythistorema*, Kastalia, Athens, 1935

Sherrard, Philip, *The Marble Threshing Floor: Studies in Modern Greek Poetry,* Valentine Mitchell, London, 1956

Contributors

Lindsey Callicoatt worked for many years as a stained/etched glass artisan in San Francisco and raised his sons in the northern California wine country. He retired to the Hawaiian jungle in 2010, living off the grid in an octagonal cedarwood house. He recently moved back to California and returns to Hydra whenever possible.

Penny Eyles visited Hydra for the first time in the late Sixties and came and went over the next two years, returning to live in London to work as a script supervisor on such films as *Brazil*, *Kes*, *My Beautiful Laundrette*, *Gosford Park* and *Philomena*. She occasionally lectures and leads workshops for film students.

David Fagan has published a few matters over the years, most significantly *Rhubarb!*, a creative nonfiction book about survival on the Rock. He and his wife Jennifer run the websites Hydra Ark at www.hydraark.org (to help the stray kitties of Hydra); Kamini Comet at www.davidfagan.org (a light-hearted blog about life in the Ouzo Layer) and Inside Hydra at www.hydraislandgreece.com.

Alison Leslie Gold is internationally renowned for her books – translated into dozens of languages – on the Holocaust, including two iconic Anne Frank-related works, as well as her innovative novels, most recently *Found and Lost: Mittens, Miep and Shovelfuls of Dirt*. With a home base in New York City, she has been writing in her Hydra hide-away for almost fifty years.

Helle V. Goldman has lived only on islands: Hydra (early childhood), Rhode Island (alright, not actually an island), Manhattan (New York University graduate school), Pemba (doctoral fieldwork in Tanzania), Zanzibar (job) and now Tromsø. A science editor at the Norwegian Polar Institute, Helle also translates books and publishes her research on Zanzibar's culture and wildlife.

Daniel Martin Klein lived on Hydra in 1967-68 and has been visiting the island and his friends there frequently since then. He is the author of the London *Times* bestseller, *Travels with Epicurus* and co-author of the *New York Times* bestseller *Plato and a Platypus Walk into a Bar*.

Angelika Lialios is a painter whose work includes acrylics, watercolours and etchings. She arrived on Hydra in 1972, when she met her future husband George Lialios, a Greek who lived on the island. Angelika has written and illustrated her own successful cookbook, *My Greek Cookery Book*. She still visits the island.

Kevin McGrath is a poet and Indologist. His recent publications include include *Supernature, Eroica, In the Kacch, Windward* and *Eros*. McGrath lives in Cambridge, Massachusetts, with his family.

Painter and sculptor, **Charlotte Mensforth** was married to the writer Jack Beeching. She has lived all over the world, mainly in Europe, looking, travelling, working towards exhibitions and hoping to find a few answers. Greece is where it all began. She now lives in Ibiza, a Mediterranean island which, like Hydra, has a history as a place for artists and eccentrics.

Panagiotis Rappas was born on Hydra. Having studied painting, engraving and animation in Germany, he works as an animator and director in animated film productions in Europe and USA. He is a lifelong member of the Academy of Motion Pictures Arts and Sciences.

Johanne Rosenthal is a water-colourist and sculptor of miniatures who lives in Providence, Rhode Island, with her husband and children. Inspired by the freedom of her childhood on Hydra, she home-schooled her son and daughter through high school. Johanne shares her innovative vegan recipes and musings on life, love and loss on her blog, Sunnyside Hanne, at www.sunnysidehanne.com.

Brian Sidaway studied architecture at Adelaide University and worked in television production in Sydney. Arriving in Greece in 1965, he has captained yachts sailing throughout the Mediterranean, Caribbean and South East Asia. He has resided on Hydra since 1972 and has worked on marine exploration documentaries and served as a fixer for film productions set on the island.

Painter, stone sculptor and haiku poet, **Valerie Lloyd Sidaway** took private passage to Australia from her native England as a child. She has worked in public relations for New York art galleries, voyaged extensively in South East Asia and travelled the world as a yachtswoman. She first visited Hydra in 1966-67 and has been a permanent resident since 1972.

Stamatis Vlachodimitris is a fisherman from Hermione, on the Peloponnese. As a young man he settled on Hydra, married an Hydriot and eventually played a role in the island's transformation into a destination for world travellers. More recently, Stamatis has become a novelist. His most recent book is *Έρωτας και Πόλεμος στον Αργοσαρωνικό (Love and War in the Argosaronic).*

Made in United States
Orlando, FL
12 October 2022